The Rewriting of Njáls Saga

TOPICS IN TRANSLATION

Series Editors
Susan Bassnett (*University of Warwick*)
Edwin Gentzler (*University of Massachusetts, Amherst*)
Editor for Translation in the Commercial Environment
Geoffrey Samuelsson-Brown (*Aardvark Translation Services Ltd*)

Other Books in the Series
Annotated Texts for Translation: French – English
BEVERLY ADAB
Annotated Texts for Translation: English – French
BEVERLY ADAB
'Behind Inverted Commas': Translation and Anglo-German Cultural Relations in Nineteenth Century
SUSANNE STARK
Constructing Cultures: Essays on Literary Translation
SUSAN BASSNETT and ANDRE LEFEVERE
Culture Bumps: An Empirical Approach to the Translation of Allusions
RITVA LEPPIHALME
Linguistic Auditing
NIGEL REEVES and COLIN WRIGHT
Paragraphs on Translation
PETER NEWMARK
Practical Guide for Translators
GEOFFREY SAMUELSSON-BROWN
The Coming Industry of Teletranslation
MINAKO O'HAGAN
The Pragmatics of Translation
LEO HICKEY (ed.)
Translation, Power, Subversion
ROMAN ALVAREZ and M. CARMEN-AFRICA VIDAL (eds)
Words, Words, Words. The Translator and the Language Learner
GUNILLA ANDERMAN and MARGARET ROGERS
Written in the Language of the Scottish Nation
JOHN CORBETT

Other Books of Interest
About Translation
PETER NEWMARK
Cultural Functions of Translation
C. SCHÄFFNER and H. KELLY-HOLMES (eds)
More Paragraphs on Translation
PETER NEWMARK
Translation and Quality
CHRISTINA SCHÄFFNER (ed.)
Translation and Norms
CHRISTINA SCHÄFFNER (ed.)

Please contact us for the latest book information:
Multilingual Matters, Frankfurt Lodge, Clevedon Hall,
Victoria Road, Clevedon, BS21 7HH, England
http://www.multilingual-matters.com

TOPICS IN TRANSLATION 16
Series Editors: Susan Bassnett (*University of Warwick*) and
Edwin Gentzler (*University of Massachusetts, Amherst*)

The Rewriting of Njáls Saga

Translation, Ideology and Icelandic Sagas

Jón Karl Helgason

MULTILINGUAL MATTERS LTD
Clevedon • Buffalo • Toronto • Sydney

In the memory of my parents-in-law
Karólína Eyþórsdóttir and Jón Hraundal

Library of Congress Cataloging in Publication Data

Jón Karl Helgason
The Rewriting of Njáls Saga: Translation, Ideology and Icelandic Sagas
Topics in Translation: 16
Includes bibliographic references and index
1. Njáls saga–Translations–History and criticism.
2. Njáls saga–Appreciation–Foreign countries.
I. Title. II. Series.
PT7269.N5J66 1999
839'.63-dc21 99-31270

British Library Cataloguing in Publication Data

A CIP catalogue record for this book is available from the British Library.

ISBN 1-85359-457-1 (hbk)

Multilingual Matters Ltd

UK: Frankfurt Lodge, Clevedon Hall, Victoria Road, Clevedon BS21 7HH.
USA: UTP, 2250 Military Road, Tonawanda, NY 14150, USA.
Canada: UTP, 5201 Dufferin Street, North York, Ontario M3H 5T8, Canada.
Australia: P.O. Box 586, Artarmon, NSW, Australia.

Typeset by Solidus, Bristol.
Printed and bound in Great Britain by The Cromwell Press Ltd.

Contents

List of Figures

Introduction
Towards the Erotics of Rewriting

Imagine a tourist in the real world wandering around the Danish capital of Copenhagen and wondering about the origin of the street-name *Njalsgade*. A few days later, she visits the Norwegian town of Grünerløkka and notices that the local athletic club is called *Njaal IF*. At that point, she vaguely recalls passing years before through the Canadian town of Gimli, buying groceries at the local shop of *Njalsbud*. Back at home, interested in the origin and connection of these names, she confers *The Reader's Encyclopedia*, an American publication referring her from the name of 'Njal' to that of 'Burnt Njal' and this brief entry:

> **Burnt Njal**. The hero of one of the best-known of the early Icelandic sagas, *The Story of Burnt Njal*. The plot concerns the grim blood feud between the families of two well-to-do landowners, Njal and Gunnar, who are personal friends. Hallgerda, the spiteful and selfish wife of Gunnar, is the instigator of the feud, which progresses with a regular alternation of murders between the two sides until it culminates in the burning of Njal's home and his death within. (Benét, 1965: 149–50)

Our imaginary tourist has been crossing four different paths of an extensive textual tradition spanning a period from the Middle Ages to modern times, a tradition that has reached most western languages and some others as well, disseminated into the fields of poetry and drama, and transgressed narrowly defined borders of literature. The textual fragments mentioned above are all products of a continuous process of writing and rewriting, a process involving numerous people and institutions, including some Copenhagen city officials (*Njalsgade*) and a Canadian businessman (*Njalsbud*). The origin of this tradition is uncertain and its destination unclear – this book examines a few of its paths.

This introduction, on the other hand, outlines some of the theoretical concerns and impulses that have guided my research of *Njáls saga* (or *Njála* or *Brennu-Njáls saga*, as the two alternative Icelandic titles go) in the past decade or so. By degrees, I have learned to appreciate the saga not only as a fascinating and complex medieval narrative, but as a text in motion, driven by variable contemporary interest and vivid human desires.

Translation and Rewriting

The background for this approach to *Njáls saga* lies in Translation Studies, an academic field which has become firmly established in the past two decades (cf. Bassnett, 1991: xi). Contrary to traditional discourse on translation, which examines, discusses and evaluates the translated text in view of the original text, Translation Studies recognises the translation as a product in its own right, constrained by the poetics and ideology of the receptor culture as much as the linguistic elements of the original. This change in emphasis can partially be traced back to the work of Israeli scholar Itamar Even-Zohar, with its roots in the writings of Russian Formalism. In a series of papers written from 1970 to 1977 and collected in his *Papers in Historical Poetics*, Even-Zohar laid the foundations of his polysystems theory, stressing that semiotic phenomena, such as culture, language, literature, and society, need to be studied and understood as a multiple, dynamic system. In particular, he was interested in the ways in which various semiotic systems were hierarchised within the polysystem (central vs. peripheral, canonised vs. non-canonised, primary vs. secondary) and in the struggle among the various strata. As a part of that approach, Even-Zohar (1978: 27) claimed it necessary to regard translated literature as a subsystem within the literary polysystem and to study translation as 'an activity dependent on the relations within a certain cultural system'.

Another important premise for the approach of Translation Studies is the acknowledgment that translation is only one of many forms of rewriting. Inspired by Roland Barthes' discussion of meta-language – a class of writing which 'deals not with 'the world' but with the linguistic formulation made by others' – American poet, translator and scholar James S. Holmes (1970: 91) suggested the term of meta-literature for this class of writing. Discussing verse translation and verse form, he arranged the various kinds of meta-literature in a fan-shaped half-circle according to their interpretive or poetic nature. In the middle, Holmes (1970: 93) placed translations which have the 'double purpose as meta-literature [interpretation] and as primary literature [poetry]'. Despite the central status he gave to the original

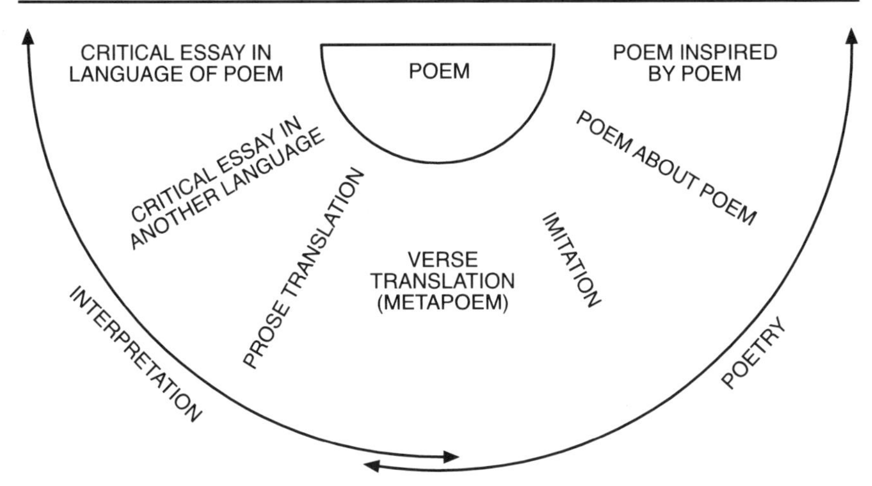

Figure 1 James Holmes' (1970: 93) fan of meta-literary forms

text, Holmes' identification of translation as being *also* a primary literature in the receptor culture pointed towards later developments in Translation Studies.

Even-Zohar and Holmes belong to a larger group of scholars working in Israel and the Low-Countries who were sharing ideas in the 1970s and networking with various other scholars and traditions in Britain, the United States and elsewhere in the 1980s (cf. Gentzler, 1993: 74–143). The research of these scholars was efficiently presented is the 1985 collection of essays *The Manipulation of Literature* where, as Susan Bassnett (1991: xii) later put it, she and the other contributors 'argued that translation, like criticism, editing and other forms of rewriting, is a manipulatory process'. Contributing to the theoretical position of the group, Belgian scholar André Lefevere (1985: 226–27) emphasised in his essay that the production of literature in a culture is influenced by a series of poetical, ideological, and power-related elements or constraints, which are active both inside and outside of the literary system:

> The first element is represented by interpreters, critics, reviewers, teachers of literature, translators. They will occasionally repress certain works of literature because these works go all too blantantly against the dominant concept of what literature should (be allowed to) be – the poetics – and of what society should (be allowed to) be – its ideology, the world view – of a certain society at a certain moment. ... The second control factor, the one which

> operates mostly outside the literary system proper, will be called 'patronage' here, and it will be understood to mean something like 'the powers (persons, institutions) which help or hinder the writing, reading, and rewriting of literature.'

In conformity with his broad view of the literary system, Lefevere also revisited Holmes' discussion of meta-literature. Instead of that term, Lefevere (1982: 4) introduced the notion of the 'rewrite' (or 'refraction'), which he defined as 'the adaptation of a work of literature to a different audience, with the intention of influencing the way in which that audience reads the work'. The concept applies to various texts such as editions, translations, literary histories, reference works, anthologies, and criticism.

In his *Translation, Rewriting, and the Manipulation of Literary Fame,* Lefevere (1992: 7) made a point of the fact that, at present, non-professional readers are 'exposed to literature more often by means of rewriting than by means of writing.' For this reason, he continued, and in view of the role rewriting has played in the evolution of literature in the past, 'the study of rewritings should not be neglected. Those engaged in that study will have to ask themselves who rewrites, why, under what circumstances, for which audience.' The present work responds to Lefevere's challenge. It is devoted to the act of rewriting, the very process which enables texts to cross cultures and endure history. Structured as a series of six case studies, the focus in each chapter is placed on the variable constraints and influences under which the Icelandic medieval text of *Njáls saga* was translated or edited and hence rewritten in Britain, the United States, Denmark, Norway, and Iceland in the period from 1861 to 1945. The first chapter, on the other hand, contains a historical summary of the saga's dissemination in the West over the past centuries and of the general reception of the Icelandic sagas in context of nationalism, racism and the wavering concept of World Literature.

A major premise of the Translation Studies approach is the view that a work of literature is not a fixed entity with intrinsic values, but rather a complex textual tradition exposed to various influences. Edwin Gentzler (1993: 196) observes: 'What becomes apparent when analyzing the evolution of one text in history, viewing its multiple forms and the processes of reintegration into different historical epochs, are not the eternal verities of the original, but the mechanisms of history which mask any sense of the original at all.' This view is appropriate when one approaches *Njáls saga*, as the original text is lost (if it ever existed). Written in the late thirteenth century, and claiming to relate historical events taking place in Iceland some 250–300 years before, the saga was based (to an uncertain extent) on an oral tradition, but it is by now only preserved in copies (or copies of copies) of the first written version. For this reason, the case of *Njáls saga* may undermine the distinction customarily made between oral traditions and written texts.

In her 'Translation in Oral Tradition as a Touchstone for Translation Theory and Practice', Maria Tymoczko (1990: 54) discusses how the study of translation in an oral tradition 'reveals that the process of refraction is a regular part of translation; . . . oral literary translations manipulate narrative frankly, radically, unabashedly'. The present case studies reveal how this process of manipulation continues in a written culture, even within the most narrowly avowed scope of deviation. The two popular Icelandic editions of *Njáls saga*, analysed in part four, are cases in point here. Published in 1944 and 1945, these are initially both intra-lingual translations of an earlier scholarly edition of the saga, but due to different sets of spelling, kinds of illustrations, and dissimilar editorial material, they are without a doubt two distinct 'performances' within the saga tradition.

In this context, it may be useful to revisit Holmes' diagram of meta-literature. As Holmes (1970: 93) suggested, many rewritten texts are themselves subject to further rewriting; verse translation of a poem, for instance, 'aspires to be a poem in its own right, about which a new fan of meta-literature can take shape'. Hence, it is inviting to think of a literary tradition in terms of a series of fans, or – borrowing an idea from Jorge Luis Borges (1983) – as a garden of forking paths. The entry in *The Reader's Encyclopedia* mentioned earlier can serve as an example for this line of thinking. The sentences quoted may have been based (on a blurb?) on a revised edition of an English translation of an Icelandic edition based on a medieval transcript of the 'original' written manuscript of *Njáls saga*. Somewhere on the way, the saga characters Gunnar and Njáll were labelled as 'two well-to-do landowners', oddly placing the saga in the vicinity of Jane Austen or even Faulkner rather than Chaucer for instance. Of course, the interpretation of this entry on these pages represents yet another step on this forking path of meta-literature.

Ideology and Desire

At the outset, scholars adapting Itamar Even-Zohar's polysystem hypothesis tended to focus mostly on poetic aspects of the translated text, but in the past two decades there has been an increasing interest within Translation Studies in the political, social and economical dimensions of the literary system. In the 1980s, André Lefevere's conception of rewriting was, for instance, inspired by ideological criticism in the tradition of Terry Eagleton and Fredric Jameson and studies of power and imperialism in the tradition of Michel Foucault and Edward W. Said. The widening range of influences incorporated by scholars in the field over the past decade is suggested by the anthology *Translation, History and Culture*, edited by Lefevere and Bassnett, containing essays on topics ranging from translation and colonialism (Sengupta, 1990), and translation and feminism (Godard, 1990), to translation and the mass media (Delabastita, 1990).

To a degree, *The Rewriting of Njáls Saga* follows the course of these studies. In terms of literary history, it also connects with recent research into the modern reception of Icelandic medieval literature in Europe and the United States (cf. Wawn, 1994). *Njáls saga* belongs to a large corpus of prose texts written in Iceland in the Middle Ages, but which was for the most part unknown outside the country until the seventeenth and the eighteenth centuries, and not generally available in editions and translations until the nineteenth and early twentieth century. Significantly, the growing general interest in this literature was influenced by the development of nationalism in Europe during this period. In some respects, the scholarly and semi-scholarly inquiry into the Icelandic Middle Ages was a part of a wider quest of people of Germanic origin to discover their racial and cultural roots. A glorious ancestry, represented by individual saga heroes, was one of the means suitable to unite a nation and even to justify its existence as a separate social entity. In this context, the Icelandic Viking became an emblem of the British coloniser (cf. Chapter 2) and a prototype for Aryans of the Third Reich (cf. Chapter 1). The language of the Vikings also served as a model for the nineteenth century development of a modern Norwegian language (cf. Chapter 5). In these cases and many others, the sagas were used as channels for contemporary ideologies, ranging from racism to ideals of national sovereignty. Even the name of the athletic club *Njaal IF* fits into this pattern, however innocently. In the club's brief history, readers were informed that even though the saga character of Njáll was not 'exactly the athletic type', his sons were indeed 'energetic, and particularly from a physical point of view' (Hopp and Jargård, 1953: n.p.). The most valiant son, named Skarphéðinn, is singled out in this context, serving as an ideal model for the modern Norwegian 'sons' of Njaal IF.

In other aspects, this study parts from the traditional approach of Translation Studies. From the outset, a major objective of polysystems theory was to develop a scientific method for the study of literature, to discover the laws governing the production of literature in society. According to Even-Zohar (1990: 3), the main task of this science 'is therefore not necessarily to interpret texts, or writers, or the matter discussed'. Similarly, Lefevere frequently contrasted his proposal for the (objective) study of rewriting with (subjective) contemporary literary criticism. In an article called 'Beyond Interpretation', Lefevere (1987: 18) expressed, for instance, his ambitious desire to 'restore to criticism at least some of the social relevance it possessed in the past'. While sharing these scholars' interest in the networks regulating the production and reception of literature, I make no claim for my study to have an objective or scientific status, 'beyond interpretation'. In every chapter of this book, writers and texts are interpreted – being just one more rewriter of the saga, my work is as constrained by the poetics and ideology of my time as any other.

Matthijs Bakker and Ton Naaijkens (1991: 200) have acknowledged this ambiguous relationship between the field of Translations Studies and its objects of study. Updating James Holmes' fan of meta-literature, they suggest that the field should be located 'as a whole in a new ring around the fan . . . : the texts of Translation Studies written 'in another language', are secondary to meta-literature'. I am attracted to their suggestion, but movement beyond that metaphorical stage is unevitable. We need to bear in mind how an enterprising Translation Studies scholar might readily construe the extensive study of rewriting as a symptom of a literary establishment which, in a desperate need for new topics, is retreating into its own reflections.

Of the various texts interpreted in this book, prefaces and introductions to individual rewrites of *Njáls saga* are the most significant. These texts foreground 'the presence of the second hand', as Sherry Simon (1990: 111) puts it. Whether produced by an editor or a translator, they are generally essential for determining who rewrites, why, under what circumstances, and for which audience. But at the same time, Simon (1990: 111) adds, the preface speaks a double language: 'Offering information, it also seeks protection from the outrages of power; advancing propitiatory disclaimers, it also propels the work towards new markets and audiences'. Dealing with that double language, I partially follow Lefevere by indentifying the rewriters' universe of discourse, but I have also gone back to Roland Barthes, one of the scholars inspiring Translation Studies in the first place. In his *Pleasure of the Text*, Barthes (1975: 17) defined the specific kind of irony required of those who analyse criticism or other meta-texts:

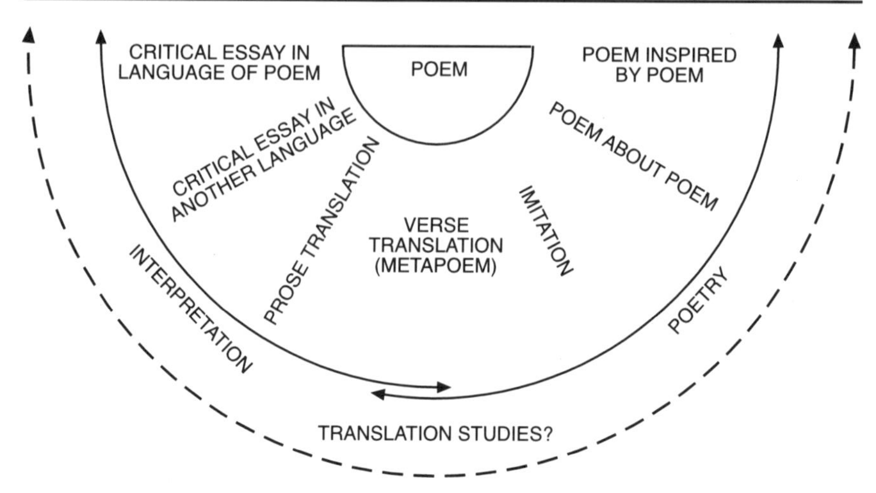

Figure 2 Matthijs Bakker's and Ton Naaijken's (1991: 201) revised fan of metaliterary forms

> since I am here a second-degree reader, I must shift my position: instead of agreeing to be the confidant of this critical pleasure – a sure way to miss it – I can make myself its voyeur: I observe clandestinely the pleasure of others, I enter perversion; the commentary then becomes in my eyes a text, a fiction, a fissured envelope.

Special attention is, for instance, paid to some of the metaphors the rewriters of *Njáls saga* have produced in their prefaces. These metaphors unveil the saga to us as sometimes resembling a valuable jewel (cf. Chapter 6), sometimes Njáll himself (cf. Chapter 2), and sometimes even an attractive but overdressed woman (cf. Chapter 3).

The reader of this book should not expect any single or final (scientific) conclusion regarding the status or the meaning of *Njáls saga* in the respective cultures. On the contrary, numerous and sometimes conflicting conclusions are being reached, depending on the perspective chosen. Some of the personal concerns and desires rewriters and patrons seem to have invested in individual editions and translations are explored. In this respect, *The Rewriting of Njáls Saga*, however preoccupied with ideology, patronage and poetics, should also illustrate that behind the mechanisms of the literary systems, we find individual human beings.

As I have come across more and more rewrites of the saga from diverse cultures and historical periods, the thought has surfaced that the act of rewriting might, in some sense, be regarded as a psychological obsession; *Njáls saga* amounting to a narrative virus. These speculations have been inspired by Peter Brooks' (1992: 36) *Reading for the Plot,* a work which the author presents as a contribution to the 'erotics of art . . . , or, more soberly, a reading of our compulsions to read'. The present study may be defined as a contribution to the erotics of rewriting. From that perspective, *Njáls saga* – with countless other textual traditions that constitute our global literatures – bears witness, in Brooks' (1992: 54) words, to the very human desire 'to be heard, recognised, understood, which, never wholly satisfied or indeed satisfiable, continues to generate the desire to tell, the effort to enunciate a significant version of the life story in order to captivate a possible listener'.

Part I

***Njáls Saga* in Motion**

Chapter 1

The Tradition of Forking Paths

A Brief History of *Njáls Saga*

In Jorge Luis Borges's (1983: 26) short story, 'The Garden of Forking Paths', the title concept applies primarily to a labyrinthine garden and a chaotic novel by the Chinese author Ts'ui Pên:

> In all fictional works, each time a man is confronted with several alternatives, he chooses one and eliminates the others; in the fiction of Ts'ui Pên, he chooses – simultaneously – all of them. He *creates*, in this way, diverse futures, diverse times which themselves also proliferate and fork.

In the present study, the image of the garden of forking paths serves as a metaphor for the traditions of rewrites generating from the 'original' version of *Njáls saga*. As suggested by James Holmes' fan, discussed in the introduction, each of the saga's rewriters has been confronted with several alternatives, ranging from writing a critical essay on the saga to composing a poem, play or a prose narrative inspired by its plot. With numerous rewriters responding to the same version, different alternatives can be chosen not only 'simultaneously', but more than once. From this perspective, *Njáls saga* exists in diverse times and contexts.

Historically, the saga's dissemination can be divided into five periods:

1280–1593: The circulation is mostly limited to manuscripts written and preserved in Iceland.

1593–1772: Manuscripts and sparse fragments of the saga reach Scandinavia and some other European countries.

1772–1875: The saga is published, first in Icelandic, but later in Latin, Danish and English translations.

1875–1954: The first critical edition of the saga is published. It is followed by various popular editions and translations into Swedish, Norwegian, German and French. Several new Danish translations are also produced. Extensive rewriting of the saga takes place in Scandinavia, Britain and Germany.

1954–1999: Following a new critical edition, new editions, translations and various other rewrites are produced in the languages mentioned above, but the saga is also introduced into numerous other languages, most significantly those of eastern Europe.

In this chapter, I will briefly outline the forking courses of *Njáls saga* in each of these periods, providing a necessary background for the individual case studies of later chapters. However, I will begin by illustrating how the original written version itself can be seen as an intersection of various older traditions and texts.

The 'Original' Text as Rewrite (-1280)

To the best of our knowledge, acquired from the earliest written texts of Icelandic literature and supported by archaeological evidence, Iceland was first settled in the ninth century, primarily by Scandinavians migrating from western Norway and the northern shores of the British Isles. These people formed a new society on the basis of laws, religion and traditions they brought with them over the ocean, and for the next centuries they would maintain active economic, political and cultural contacts with Scandinavia, especially with Norway. In 930, when the country was fully settled, a united assembly for different districts of Iceland was established, with a system of legislation and judicial courts, but there was no central authority, neither a king nor a royal court, holding the executive power. This system, generally referred to as the 'Icelandic commonwealth' (Kristjánsson, 1988: 16), lasted until 1262 when Iceland formally became subject to Norway.

Around the year 1000, under pressure from the Norwegian king, the Icelanders agreed at their assembly to give up their heathen beliefs and to accept Christianity. This event is referred to and described in several preserved early texts, including *Njáls saga*. Over the next decades, following the education of the clergy and the forming of local monasteries and schools, the influence of the church transformed the society radically. In a relatively short period, it developed from being primary an oral culture to becoming one of the centres of written vernacular literature in high medieval Europe. In the first decades of the twelfth century, the Icelanders began by translating canonised works of the church and writing down their own law, genealogies and records of Iceland's early history. In the late twelfth and the thirteenth century, the growing corpus additionally included collections of poems and heathen myths, biographies of Norwegian kings and Icelandic bishops, local history and hagiography, mythical-heroic sagas as well as romantic chivalric literature, both original and translated.

Additionally, the Icelanders composed prose narratives mostly set in Iceland, typically dealing with feuds between Icelandic families of the tenth and the eleventh centuries. That genre, commonly termed the Icelandic family sagas (*Íslendingasögur*), was influenced by the various other genres mentioned above. Hence, the family sagas contain historical data and genealogy, motives borrowed from myths, romances and hagiography, and are intertextually related both to the genre of the king sagas and each other. But as Jónas Kristjánsson (1988: 203–204) has summarised, there are as many uncertainties surrounding this particular genre as there are certitudes:

> We cannot identify the author of a single saga .... Neither do we know for sure when and where sagas were written .... We do not know what matter in them comes from oral tradition and what from the imagination of the authors. And although we assume the existence of oral traditions, we do not know what they were like: detailed or bare, immutable or variable in content, factual or fictitious, fixed or free in form?

Njáls saga is the largest of the family sagas; the text is usually divided into 159 chapters and amounts to almost 400 pages in modern paperback editions. It seems that the 'original' written version was finished around 1280, and the number of preserved vellum manuscripts and fragments – the oldest dating from 1300 – suggests that it soon became one of the most popular works of the saga corpus (cf. Sveinsson, 1954: lxxv–lxxxiv). Despite typical uncertainties about the saga's creation, the narrative is indisputably related to various literary and cultural tradition. The following three examples should give an idea of its intertextual nature:

(1) Like many other family sagas, *Njáls saga* (Ch. 1) opens with a genealogy: 'There was a man named Mörður, whose nickname was Fiddle.' Mörður, we are told, was the son of Sighvatur the Red and father of Unnur. Next, the family of Höskuldur Dalakollsson is presented:

> His mother was Þorgerður, the daughter of Þorsteinn the Red, who was the son of Ólafur the White, whose father was Ingjaldur Helgason. Ingjaldur's mother was Þóra, the daughter

> of Sigurður Snake-in-the-eye, who was the son of Ragnar Shaggy-breeches. Þorsteinn the Red's mother was Unnur the Deep-minded; she was the daughter of Ketill Flat-nose, who was the son of Björn Buna.

We are also informed that Höskuldur was a half-brother of Hrútur and the father of Hallgerður, Bárður, Þorleikur, and Ólafur. Þorleikur was the father of Bolli, and Ólafur was the father of Kjartan. To a modern reader, this list of names may seem confusing and irrelevant, but with the plot generated by the union and the conflicts of the descendants of Mörður Fiddle and Höskuldur Dalakollsson, a part of these genealogies certainly serves the narrative. Originally, the two families are united by the short-lived marriage of Hrútur (Höskuldur's brother) and Unnur (Mörður's daughter) and get in conflict following their divorce. To regain her dowry, Unnur seeks the assistance of her cousin, Gunnar Hámundarson, who in his mother's line is a great-grandson of Unnur's grandfather, Sighvatur the Red. Later, Gunnar marries Hallgerður, the daughter of Höskuldur. Their turbulent relationship determines the course of action in the subsequent chapters. Additionally, these genealogies place the saga within the tradition of earlier genealogical writings and historiography in Iceland. Mörður, Unnur, Gunnar, Höskuldur and Hallgerður are, for instance, all mentioned in the twelfth-century historical work of *Landnámabók* (*Book of Settlement*) devoted to the settlement of Iceland and its history through the first centuries. Furthermore, Höskuldur, his son Ólafur, and his grandsons Kjartan and Bolli are central characters of another (and presumably an older) family saga, that of *Laxdæla saga* (Sveinsson, 1954: xxxix–xl; 1971: 16–21).

(2) The single most famous scene of *Njáls saga* (Ch. 75) involves Gunnar Hámundarson (Unnur's cousin) and his brother Kolskeggur. The two of them have been sentenced to exile as outlaws, and they are riding to take ship when Gunnar's horse stumbles and throws him:

> He happened to be facing the hillside and the farm of Hlíðarendi, and he spoke: 'So lovely is the hillside [*Fögur er hlíðin*] that it has never before seemed to me as lovely as now, with its pale fields [*bleikir akrar*] and mown meadows; and I will ride back home, and not go anywhere at all.'

Gunnar's characterisation has been identified as being inspired by that of Hector in *Trójumanna saga*, a romantic adaptation of the

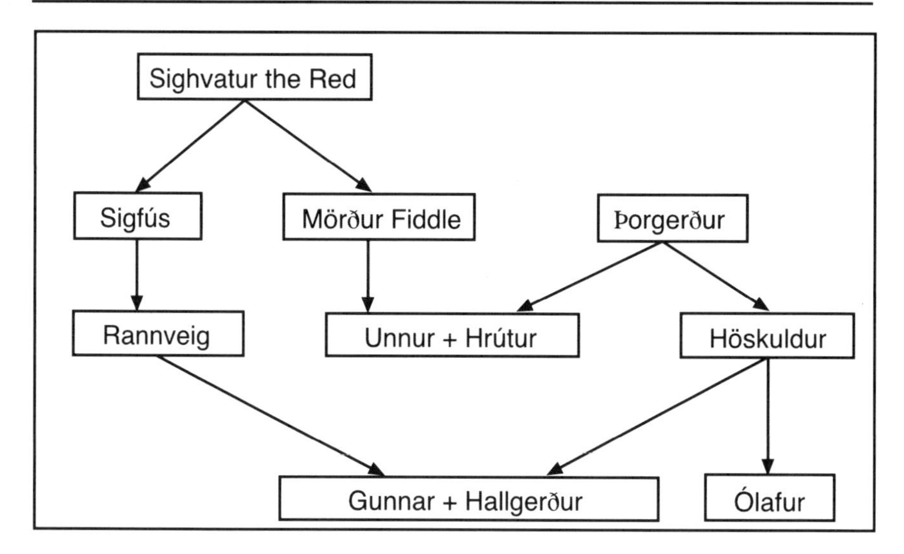

Figure 3 A genealogy of Gunnar Hámundarson and Hallgerður Höskuldsdóttir of *Njáls saga*

Troy legend, and of King Gunnar in *Þiðreks saga*, a Norwegian text based on German legends about Theodoric the Great (cf. Lönnroth, 1976: 119). Gunnar's words about the lovely hillside can, on the other hand, be compared to a speech Alexander the Great delivers in *Alexanders saga*, a Norwegian prose translation of the twelfth-century Latin poem *Alexandreis* by Gautier of Châtillon. One morning, on his expedition in Asia, the saga tells us, Alexander climbs a high mountain and looks out over the country:

> There he could see in all directions *lovely meadows* [*fagra völlu*], *pale cornfields* [*bleika akra*], large forests, blooming vinyards and strong cities. And when the king looked over all this beauty, he said to his attending officers: 'This country, which I am now looking over, shall be all mine. But Greece, which my father has left me, I shall now give up to you.' (Lönnroth, 1976: 153)

Einar Ólafur Sveinsson (1954: xxxvi) suggests that the author of *Njáls saga* was inspired by this description of Alexander 'when he created its perfect antithesis', but contrary to his Greek counterpart, Gunnar does return to his patrimony of Hlíðarendi. Soon after that, he is attacked at his home and killed by his enemies. His brother Kolskeggur, on the other hand, goes abroad as law orders and becomes a Christian guardsman at the court of Constantinopel.

(3) Another fatal point of the saga describes Njáll Þorgeirson's final hours, as he is burned alive with his family at the farm of Bergþórshvoll by a confederacy of enemies. It is specially noted that Njáll, his wife Bergþóra and their grandson Þórður lie down under an ox-hide when the flames rise inside the house. As the burning of Bergþórshvoll is referred to in several other older Icelandic texts, including *Landnámabók,* it is normally regarded as having taken place in reality (cf. Sveinsson, 1954: v–xi). But some of the circumstances of Njáll's death are more questionable. Soon afterwards, *Njáls saga* (Ch. 132) tells us, Kári Sölmundarson (Njáll's son-in-law and father of Þórður) goes with a group of men to Bergþórshvoll to search for Njáll's bones.

> ... there was a great deal of ash to clear away. At the bottom, they found the ox-hide, shriveled up from the fire. They lifted it off, and underneath lay the two of them, unburned. They all praised God for this and thought it a great miracle. Then the boy who was lying between them was taken up, and one of his fingers, which he had stuck out from under the hide, was burned off.

In particular, it is noted that Njáll's body and entire appearance is exceptionally radiant. That description follows a topos surfacing in some other saga literature but originating in Christian hagiography, where a radiant and beautiful corpse was considered to be the sign of the innocent soul of the deceased, admitted to the gates of heaven. Lars Lönnroth (1963–64: 32) proposes that the author of *Njáls saga* may have based his narrative here on *Placidus saga* (*Vita Eustachii*), a hagiographic *passio* translated into Icelandic around 1200. It tells the story of a Roman martyr who is burned to death with his wife and children inside a 'brazen ox', a sort of a large oven. Three days later, the bodies of the family are removed from the ox, and to everyone's surprise they are intact and white as snow.

Examples of this kind are countless and have been studied by many scholars in the past, who have emphasised sources ranging from written Icelandic law to Pope Gregory's *Dialogues* (cf. Lönnroth, 1976; Sveinsson, 1971: 7–40; Pálsson, 1984). These examples indicate how, by the time *Njáls saga* was written, an advanced literary system existed in Iceland, incorporating Latin and vernacular literature, original and translated works, canonised texts of the church as well as secular texts of various kinds. That system, it seems, was interrelated to the Norwegian literary system, sharing the same language, and was additionally in close contact with other European cultures. It is certainly challenging to outline its development from twelfth century on, with the aid of Itamar Even-Zohar's polysystem theory. Even-Zohar (1990: 67) himself (currently translating *Njáls saga* into Hebrew) has, for instance, referred to 'the role of French for the crystallization of Norse – Norwegian and Icelandic – literatures' in this early period, to exemplify how source literature (literary models, works for translation, etc.) may be selected for translation from another culture/ system by prestige. However, the primary focus of the rest of this chapter will be the evolution that starts with the oldest manuscript of the saga, at that chronological point many scholars consider its creation to be completed.

Dizzying Net of Oral and Written (1280-1593)

As suggested above, 'original' is a misleading concept in the case of *Njáls saga;* we can safely assume that the first written text had various written and oral sources. In fact, the narrative reflects directly on a few of these sources. Inspired by Helga Kress' (1991) analysis of the metatextual characteristics of the family sagas, I would like to begin by drawing the attention to Chapters 154 and 155 that relate how Flosi Þórðarson, Gunnar Lambason and a few other Icelanders who had participated in the burning of Njáll and his family, sail to Mainland in the Orkneys, ruled by Earl Sigurður Hlöðvisson. When some visitors at the earl's court wish to learn the circumstances surrounding the burning of Njáll, Gunnar Lambason is selected to tell the tale. He, the saga highlights, 'slanted his whole account and lied about many details'. Gunnar is unaware that Njáll's son-in-law, Kári Sölmundarson, is present at the scene, but after listening to Gunnar's narrative, Kári reveals himself and utters a 'skaldic' verse stressing that he and his allies have indeed been avenging Njáll and his family. By way of verification, Kári then 'struck Gunnar Lambason on the neck; the head came off so fast that it flew onto the table in front of the king and the earls.' Later, after Kári has escaped and Gunnar's corpse been carried out, Flosi Þórðarson renders his version of the burning: 'He spoke well of everybody, and his account was trusted.'

In this scene, *Njáls saga* is picturing the early stages of its own creation. Within the space of a few paragraphs, no less than three characters deliver their interpretation of the burning. Each version is different from the other, depending on the narrators' motives and the circumstances of their performances. Gunnar's version can be characterised as being fictional ('lied about many details'), Flosi's version as historical ('his account was trusted'), while Kári's action can be seen as a criticism of the fictional version (communicated with the aid of poetry and a sword). The reader is made to believe that Flosi's version is similar to that of the written saga, but the passage implies nonetheless how other oral versions of the narrative might have been circulating in the Middle Ages, some perhaps in the unorthodox tradition of Gunnar Lambason. In any case, the saga tradition seems to be already growing and dispersing within a few pages after the events in question have been disclosed. In this respect, *Njáls saga* proves to be its own meta-text.

'Skaldic' verses (*dróttkvæði*), like the one Kári utters, are found in great many of the saga narratives, but the term refers to a genre of poetry distinguished by its complex metaphorical diction (cf. Kristjánsson, 1988: 83–88). In general, scholars distinguish between two roles of these verses in the sagas: *evidence verses* that are supposed to support the historicity of the prose, and *narrative verses*, that usually act as direct speech of a character (cf. Einarsson, 1974; O'Donoghue, 1991: v). The origin of individual verses in both of these categories has been debated for reasons that can be exemplified through two different verses from Chapters 77 and 78 in *Njáls saga*.

Soon after Gunnar Hámundarson's death, his son Högni and Skarphéðinn, son of Njáll, stand outside Gunnar's mound. 'It appeared to them that the mound was open, and that Gunnar had turned around to look at the moon' (Ch. 78). He is cheerful and recites a verse suggesting that he had decided to stay at his farm, instead of accepting the sentence of outlawry, because he did not want to yield to his enemies. His verse, like the one Kári utters in Chapter 155, is a typical *narrative verse*, and in view of its supernatural frame, someone might gather that the writer of the saga must have composed it. But then it is puzzling how Gunnar's poetic explanation differs from what he said to his brother at the point of his fatal return ('So lovely is the hillside' etc.; Ch. 75). Accordingly, Einar Ólafur Sveinsson (1954: xxxvi–xxxvii) infers that the verse must be older than the written saga; 'the author did not have the heart to leave it out, even though it contradicted his narrative'.

By contrast, we find an apparent *evidence verse* in Chapter 77, just following the description of Gunnar's slaying. Interrupting the flow of the narrative, the verse is ascribed to Þorkell Elfaraskáld, a poet of the thirteenth century whose identity is unknown apart from this reference. According to his testimony, Gunnar was daring as he defended himself, wounding sixteen and killing two. Predating the oldest manuscripts of *Njáls saga*, this verse may have served as a verification of the foregoing prose account of the hero's defence. It suggests that medieval Icelanders found Gunnar's death remarkable and his skill in arms a desirable quality, years before the written version of the saga existed.

The reference to Þorkell Elfaraskáld is found in the three oldest preserved manuscripts of the saga – *Kálfalækjarbók*, *Reykjabók* and *Gráskinna*, all dated around 1300 (cf. Sveinsson, 1953: 6–8) – and it has been accepted as a genuine part of the 'original' text. But in *Kálfalækjarbók*, it is accompanied by another skaldic verse, ascribed to Þormóður Ólafsson, possibly a man of the thirteenth century (cf. Sveinsson, 1933: 31–32). He attests that nobody from heathen times had more fame than Gunnar and that he had deserved his praise, killing two men and inflicting huge wounds on sixteen others (Sveinsson, 1954: 477–78). This verse is rarely published in later editions or translations, but its existence in one of the earliest manuscripts reveals how clouded the distinction between the 'genuine' text of the saga and the saga tradition really is. It seems impossible to determine whether Þormóður Ólafsson composed his verse under the influence of the written version or some of its (oral?) sources. For the present purposes, it does not really matter; the example is presented here merely to emphasise how the early manuscripts already incorporate and anticipate the complex rewriting of *Njáls saga*.

The difference between *Kálfalækjarbók* and the other early manuscripts typifies the initial forking of the written saga tradition. These manuscripts have been studied by scholars of traditional philology, a field set out to determine how manuscripts are internally related. The problem with the Icelandic family sagas, as most ancient and medieval texts, is that an unknown number of manuscripts may be lost. For this reason philologists, in their attempt to reconstruct a textual-pedigree, frequently suppose lost links in the chain of copying. Einar Ólafur Sveinsson's (1953) research of the manuscript tradition of *Njáls saga* is generally accepted as the most reliable study. Sveinsson imagines that two different manuscripts were copied from the original text sometime between 1280 and 1300. He labels these two manuscripts as *X and *V and supposes that parts of *Kálfalækjarbók* and *Reykjabók* were copied directly from *X while he regards other parts as being sub-sub copies of *X. On the other hand, he characterises *Gráskinna* primarily as a sub-sub copy of *V. None of these manuscripts is complete; in printed editions, they are either made to complement each

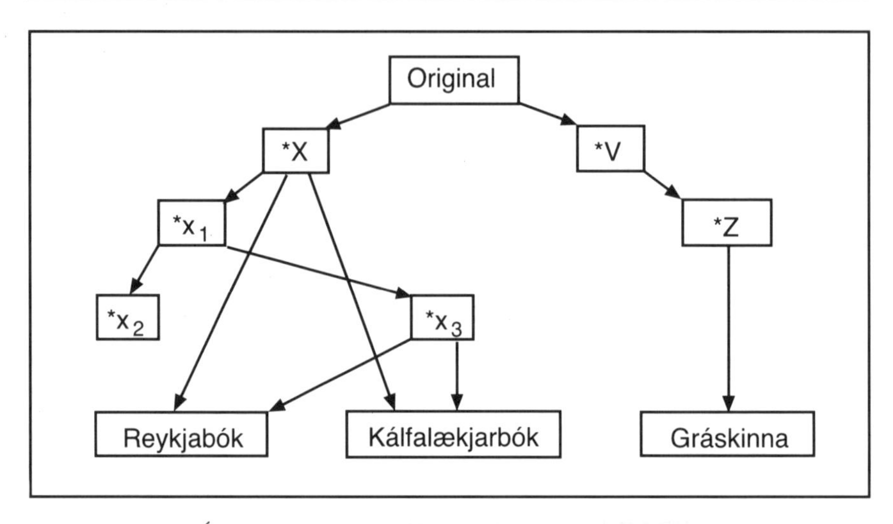

Figure 4 Einar Ólafur Sveinsson's (1953) 'genealogy' of the early manuscripts of *Njáls saga*

other or their missing portions are filled with material from younger manuscripts. Already at this stage, Ts'ui Pên's vision of 'an infinite series of times, in a growing, dizzying net of divergent, convergent and parallel times' (Borges, 1983: 28) seems to fit the labyrinth of the saga tradition.

Over the first three hundred years, *Njáls saga* primarily circulated within Iceland, in transcripts and orally. In addition to the three manuscripts already mentioned, eight other vellum manuscripts and fragments are preserved from the fourteenth century and nine are considered to be from the fifteenth and the sixteenth centuries (an uncertain number of manuscripts is lost). There is only scarce contemporary documentation of how these texts were utilised between 1300 and 1600, but as Hermann Pálsson has convincingly illustrated, we may suppose that semi-public readings of family sagas and various other non-secular literature, were a favourite pastime on Icelandic farms in this period. Supporting his case, Pálsson (1962: 35) quotes a passage from an account Reverent (and later Bishop) Oddur Einarsson wrote in Latin in 1590, describing the hospitality of Icelandic farmers: 'The concern even farmers have for their guests is so great that they do not neglect anything which they think might be of entertainment. Sometimes they seize the storybooks of the home and read, for several hours in a clear voice, sagas of various people and other ancient texts of interest.' This tradition of reading, which continued up to the present century, reveals how the typical Icelandic audience of *Njáls saga* perceived the narrative initially in an oral form. And just as individual scribes rewrote the manuscripts they were transcribing – adding and omitting words, sentences, verses and even passages – so can one imagine each reading (or performance) of a particular manuscript to be different from the other.

Regarding the manuscript tradition, it is interesting how some of the scribes felt the urge to curse the enemies of such men as Gunnar Hámundarson and Njáll Þorgeirsson. For example, in a fifteenth-century manuscript notable for its inserted expressions, the scribe refers to the killers of Gunnar Hámundarson as 'bastards' and to Mörður Valgarðsson, who plots the death of Gunnar and may be seen as partially responsible for the burning of Bergþórshvoll, as an 'infamous moron' (Sveinsson, 1953: 18–19). Comments of this sort, alien to the detached style of the saga, can be regarded as a belated literary revenge for the death of individual saga characters, but they testify more generally to the tendency of the Icelandic audience to think about the saga-plot in terms of heroes and villains (cf. Helgason, 1998: 20–29).

From this first period of the saga's reception, a few poems referring to the saga are preserved, most notably those belonging to the genre of hero-poems (*kappakvæði*), in which a number of male characters from diverse sagas and romances are glorified, one verse generally devoted to each hero (cf. Johannessen, 1958: 12–18). A hero-poem by Bergsteinn Þorvaldsson, dating from the second half of the sixteenth century, may serve as an example. Here, two characters from *Njáls saga* – Kári Sölmundarson and Skarphéðinn Njálsson – are briefly portrayed, along with Roland and about twenty other heroes known to the Icelandic public at the time, either through prose narratives or the versified narratives of *rímur*. Kári is specifically praised for avenging those who died in the burning of Bergþórshvoll; 'on behalf of his burned best kinfolk / he sent farmers to hell' (Þorkelsson, 1886: 373).

It is also possible that two preserved ballads that focus on the circumstances of Gunnar Hámundarson's death were already circulating in the sixteenth century. One is in Faeroes (Hammershaimbs, 1855: 51–52), suggesting the *Njáls saga* tradition found a path to that neighbouring island of Iceland relatively early, but the other one is in Icelandic (Ólason, 1979: 278–79). The native term for such ballads (*sagnadans*) means literally dance-song; these were generally sung or recited to accompany a group dance, with the participants holding hands in a circle (cf. Kristjánsson, 1988: 370–77). Since both the ballads in question are primarily composed as a dialogue between Gunnar and his wife Hallgerður Höskuldsdóttir, with a refrain in the third person, it seems likely that the men and the women dancers (or just one dancer of each sex) took turns in singing the dialogue, with the whole group uniting in the refrain. We may imagine ten or twenty young people thus dancing the night away, continuing the tradition of *Njáls saga* within a semiotic field on the uncertain boundaries of poetry and drama.

A Glorious National Past (1593-1772)

The second period of *Njáls saga's* dissemination is characterised by the fact that the saga corpus was being brought to the attention of readers outside of Iceland, most significantly Scandinavian antiquarians (cf. Andersson, 1964: 1–21; Benediktsson, 1981). Icelander Arngrímur Jónsson was an important initiator of this development, composing several books on Icelandic history in Latin for the enlightenment of misinformed European readers. Jónsson's patron was his cousin, Bishop Guðbrandur Þorláksson, one of the pioneers of Icelandic printing, especially remembered for publishing (and partially translating) the first Icelandic edition of the Holy Bible in 1584. Agitated by several inaccurate, unflattering descriptions of Iceland published in Europe in the sixteenth century, Bishop Þorláksson prompted Jónsson to write his earliest work, *Brevis commentarivs de Islandia* (*A short account of Iceland,* 1593). It was followed by three other works relating to the history of Iceland, most significantly *Crymogæa, sive rerum Islandicarvm libri III* (*Crymogæa, or the history of Iceland in three books,* 1609).

Eager to portray the cultivation of his nation in past and present, Jónsson frequently refers to characters and incidents from the genre of the family sagas. In *Brevis,* for instance, he rewrites *Njáls saga's* characterisation of peacemaker Njáll Þorgeirsson, highlighting the saga's description of his final hour:

> [When Njáll] saw death approaching, he said: No one can escape destiny, meaning: this is according to God's will. But I put all my hope and faith in Christ, and trust that even though our base bodies will suffer the same fate as all mortal flesh and will be devoured by the enemy's flames, God will not let us (here he is referring to him and his wife) burn in the eternal fire. With these words on his lips he died in the fire in the year of 1010, with his wife and son . . .; his words would be befitting to any of God's children and gave him uppermost comfort in his bitter death-struggle. (Ionam, 1593: 53)

It is not known for certain which version of the saga Jónsson was citing, but in the preserved manuscripts, Njáll's final words are not given in the first person. We are only told that Njáll and his wife Bergþóra 'crossed themselves and the boy and turned their souls over to God's hand' (Ch. 129). But Jónsson's rendering of these lines certainly fits the ideological purpose of his broader discussion, as he is trying to illustrate how 'advanced' the Christian faith in Iceland was just a few years after the acceptance of Christianity. In *Crymogæa*, Jónsson's use of the saga literature is even more substantial, with the genealogy and deeds of individual saga characters substituting descriptions of royal lineage and international warfare in histories of other nations (cf. Benediktsson, 1957: 31–81).

These works and the interest they aroused should be seen as a part of the national historiography sweeping northern Europe in the wake of Italian humanism. Indeed, Jónsson characterised the age of the saga characters as the most glorious time of Icelandic society, providing his countrymen with a past comparable to the past of other European nations. But ironically, the Danish and Swedish antiquarians who familiarised themselves with the saga corpus under Jónsson's influence were primarily interested in it as a source of their own national histories. Two works ascribed to Snorri Sturluson (1179–1241) were of uttermost importance to them in that context: *Heimskringla*, a comprehensive collection of king's sagas, and *Snorra-Edda*, a handbook of poetics incorporating summaries of the pan-Scandinavian heathen myths. In Sweden, high priority was also placed on the publication and translation of some mythical-heroic sagas set in that country but, as Theodore M. Andersson (1964: 11) points out, the whole enterprise was politically motivated:

> Moreso than in Denmark, the rise of antiquarian interest in Sweden was the corollary of a political development. The rediscovery of ancient Sweden coincided with the rise of contemporary Sweden as a European power. ... Her newly awakened national consciousness was a factor in the search for a glorious past, a past which the Icelandic sagas promised to illuminate.

Since the antiquarians generally had limited knowledge of the ancient Icelandic/Scandinavian language in this period, a number of Icelandic interpreters were employed in Denmark and Sweden, to where numerous Icelandic codices were being gathered.

Primarily set in Iceland, *Njáls saga* proved to be of marginal interest to the non-Icelandic historians. Still, most of its preserved vellum manuscripts ended up in libraries in Denmark and Sweden in the seventeenth and the eighteenth centuries, where some of them were copied, translated or paraphrased. Symbolic of this phase of rewriting are the three paper manuscripts presently preserved at the Swedish Royal Library in Stockholm (cf. Þorkelsson, 1889: 759–60). *Isl. håndskr. 9 fol. chart* is a rather accurate copy of an earlier version, presumably the fifteenth century vellum manuscript of *Oddabók* (*AM 466 4to*). The copying was done in Iceland in 1684 by Jón Vigfússon, who states that he began his job on July 1 and finished it by October 7. *Isl. håndskr. 93 fol. chart* is a manuscript of a Swedish translation of the saga, done by Þorvaldur Grímsson Brockmann, an Icelander working in Sweden around the middle of the eighteenth century. To an unusual degree, this text reveals the subtle mechanisms of rewriting in progress, as the first part of the translation (Ch. 1–75) has been revised and written in a more readable hand by Karl Hagelberg, a native of Sweden. Finally we have *Isl. håndskr. 96 fol. chart*, which is a seventeenth-century plot-summary of *Njáls saga* and some other sagas in Swedish, presumably done by antiquarian J.F. Peringskjöld. None of these rewrites has of yet been published.

For more general circulation, the narrative of *Njáls saga* was primarily available to non-Icelanders in this period through extracts in Latin works such as *Antiqvitatum Danicarum* and *Orcades sive rerum Orcadensium historiae*, both published at the end of the seventeenth century. The former was written by the royal Danish antiquarian Thomas Bartholin and contains citations from various sagas and ancient mythical poetry concerning laconic and defiant comments on death. From *Njáls saga*, Bartholin quotes and translates, for instance, the description of deceased Gunnar Hámundarson's singing in his mound (Bartholini, 1689: 279–81). The latter work, devoted to the history of the Orkneys, was written by Icelander Þormóður Torfason, who, for a part of his life, held the post of the royal Norwegian historian. He paraphrased various old Icelandic sources in his *Orcades*, including chapters of *Njáls saga* set in the British Isles (cf. Torfæus, 1866: 27–38). However fragmented, the saga was hence slowly being assimilated into the Latin discourse of European historiography.

And from there, new paths would fork. For instance, both of the fragments mentioned above were subject to further rewriting by two English poets of the eighteenth century. In 1761 Thomas Gray composed his 'Fatal Sisters', based on a skaldic verse which forms a part of chapters from *Njáls saga* employed both by Bartholin and Torfason (cf. Nordby, 1901: 3–8). Some thirty years later, Richard Hole published 'The Tomb of Gunnar' on the basis of Bartholin's account of Gunnar

Hámundarson's mound. Introduced as an imitation of a passage 'from an old Gothic romance', Hole's (1789: 937) poem opens:

> 'What mean those aweful sounds that rise
> From the tomb where Gunnar lies?'
> Exclaim the shepherd in affright;
> As by the moon's uncertain light,
> Athwart the solitary plain,
> He homeward drive his fleecy train.

In the corresponding description of *Njáls saga* (Ch. 78), a shepherd and a housemaid drive cattle past the mound: 'Gunnar seemed to them to be in high spirits and reciting verses in the mound.' They went home and told Gunnar's mother Rannveig about this. It is this experience that motivates Skarphéðinn Njálsson and Högni, the son of Gunnar, to examine to mound for themselves: 'The moon was shining brightly, though occasionally dimmed by clouds.' What a perfect inspiration for an English poet writing in the tradition of the graveyard school. Here, the discovery of Iceland's medieval literature was coinciding with pre-romantic reaction against French classicism; textual fragments from Icelandic sagas and heathen myths complementing the Arthurian romances and Ossian (cf. Omberg, 1976).

Back in Iceland, with the majority of the vellum manuscripts being exported, numerous new copies of the saga were produced in this period. In addition to four vellum manuscripts and fragments, fifteen paper manuscript are preserved from the seventeenth century. Thirteen more paper manuscripts are dated from 1700 to 1770 (cf. Þorkelsson, 1889: 774–75). A few of these manuscripts are enriched by contemporary poetry, generally verses (sometimes composed by the scribe in question) containing remarks on the personality of individual saga characters. Similar to the traditional hero-poems (*kappakvæði*), the poets frequently glorify the masculine saga heroes, but sometimes they also express their disapproval of certain characters, most notably Hallgerður Höskuldsdóttir, the controversial wife of Gunnar Hámundarson. In a verse, preserved in the seventeenth-century manuscript *Kallske samling 612 4to*, Gunnar is for instance said to have loved 'a damned woman' and she is held responsible for his death (Þorkelsson, 1889: 749).

Some other Icelandic poems from this period similarly curse Hallgerður, making a special reference to the passage in *Njáls saga* (Ch. 77) describing Gunnar's final hours. When attacked, he is alone at home with Hallgerður and his mother; his skill with the bow enables him temporarily to halt the band of enemies, but when his bowstring has been cut and he himself is wounded, Gunnar turns to wife:

'Give me two locks of your hair, and you and my mother twist them into a bowstring for me.'

'Does anything depend on that?' she said.

'My life depends on it,' he said, 'for they'll never be able to get at me as long as I can use my bow.'

'Then I'll remind you,' she said, 'of the slap on my face, and I don't care whether you hold out for a long or a short time.'

'Everyone has some mark of distinction,' said Gunnar, 'and I won't ask you again.'

Initially, the poetry preoccupied with this scene and the turbulent marriage of Gunnar and Hallgerður may be regarded as a separate network of paths within the *Njáls saga* tradition. Until the present century, these poems primarily verified the supreme status of the hero/husband. In the early eighteenth century, Reverend Brynjólfur Halldórsson was the remarkable exception, making attempts to defend Hallgerður on the grounds of Christian compassion (cf. Johannessen, 1958: 19–25; Helgason, 1998: 51–75).

Strands of Nationalism and Imperialism (1772-1875)

It is finally in the third period of *Njáls saga*'s dissemination that the complete narrative becomes available in print, the earliest publication being Ólafur Ólafsson's 1772 edition, printed in Copenhagen (Olavius, 1772). The text was primarily based on the manuscript of *Reykjabók* and served as the 'original' version of saga for about one hundred years. It was the direct or indirect source of several editions, both of parts of the saga used for language teaching in Scandinavia (Müller, 1837; Friðriksson, 1846; Svensson, 1867) and the saga as a whole (Olavius, 1844), as well as influential translations into Latin (Johnsonius, 1809), Danish (Rahbek, 1819–21; Petersen, 1839–44), and English (Dasent, 1861).

In the nineteenth century, the Icelandic family sagas in general were being discovered and recognised throughout Western Europe, not only as sources of supplementary references to, say a Swedish or Irish past, or descriptions of sublime heathen practices, but also as literature with its own merits, truthfully illustrating a developed medieval society in Iceland. This emphasis on Icelandic history is clearly disclosed by the collective title of N.M. Petersen's (1839–1844) saga translations in Danish, *Historiske fortællinger om islændernes færd hjemme og ude* (*Historical Accounts of the Icelanders' travels, home and abroad*), and the subtitle of George Webbe Dasent's (1861) English translation of *Njáls saga; Life in Iceland at the End of the Tenth Century.* Both Petersen's and Dasent's translations of *Njáls saga* were energetically reproduced in their home countries and beyond. Hence it is possible to follow the path from Petersen's 'original' text, via Guðbrandur Vigfússon's revised edition (Petersen, 1862–68), to the Danish paraphrase of the saga by H. H. Lefolii (1863), which later was faithfully translated into German by J. Claussen (1878). Petersen's collection of saga translations was also reissued into the present century; a modern edition of his *Njáls saga* translation was published just a few years ago (Petersen, 1994). The fifth edition of *Historiske fortællinger,* released during World War II (Petersen, 1942–43), will be discussed in Chapter 4 in context of the German occupation of Denmark and influential ideas about the cultural and political unity of Scandinavia.

The paths forking from Dasent's translation are quite as extensive as those originating in Petersen's work. *The Story of Burnt Njal* was the only complete English translation of the saga for almost a century, surviving in numerous editions into the present age. It generated a range of rewritings, from children's books (Clay, 1907), to drama (Bottomley, 1909), to lyric poetry (Oswald, 1882; Green, 1890). This English translation seems also to have been the source of the monumental epic poem *Gunnar von Hlidarendi* by the Russian poet Helene von Engelhardt-Pabst (1909), published in two volumes of around 300 pages each. The Victorian context of Dasent's translation is the topic of Chapter 2, while *Heroes of Iceland,* Allen French's (1905) American abridgement of Dasent, will be analysed in Chapter 3.

As for the continuous dilution of the saga narrative, Herbert Malim's *Njal and Gunnar* – in which Dasent's translation was specifically 'Retold for Boys' – is somewhat symbolic. It was published in 1917 in the series 'English Literature for Secondary Schools'. Following the general editorial agenda, Malim (1917: 122–23) prepared a list of 'Subjects for Essays' at the back of the volume. Here, the students were asked to rewrite parts from the saga, such as 'The burning of Bergthorsknoll', in prose or even verse. They were also asked to write an essay on questions such as: 'Does civilisation make men less cruel?' In this way, the boys who read *Njal and Gunnar* in school in the last years of World War I – whether in England, India, Canada, or elsewhere – extended, even through to a limited audience, the written textual tradition of the saga into their own generation.

The greater ideological framework of the saga's dissemination in the nineteenth century is a complex one and can only be addressed in this chapter through some broad generalisations. In a study of the Greek heritage in Victorian Britain, Frank M. Turner (1981: 8) states:

'Writing about Greece was in part a way for Victorians to write about themselves.' To a great degree, the same can be said about the general reception of Icelandic medieval literature in Europe from the early 1800s up to World War II. Even as a few nations were starting to identify this corpus in its full scope, the fundamental question remained: How does this literature relate to 'us', to what degree is it a part of 'our' heritage and culture? The answers varied depending on who was asking and when, but usually they involved a reference to cultural and/or racial kinship. This approach to the 'text' of ancient Iceland can be referred to as Teutonism, forming the flip side of Orientalism as defined by Edward W. Said (1979: 7): 'the idea of European identity as a superior one in comparison with all the non-European peoples and cultures.' The Icelandic 'viking' was made to represent the (lowest?) common nominator of either the Scandinavian, Germanic or Teutonic race.

In this context, the 'Saga Island' was often seen as a parallel to ancient Greece, the sanctioned cradle of Western civilisation. *Tales of the Teutonic Lands* can serve here as an indicator. In the preface to this British collection, George W. Cox (1872: vii–viii) stated:

> No one probably will be disposed to question the importance of determining the degree of credibility to be attached to the burning of Ilion and the burning of the house of the Icelandic Njal, if the differences between the two be capable of measurement.

In addition to a paraphrase of parts of *Njáls saga*, the book contained rewrites of several other Icelandic sagas and mythical poetry, along with 'the Nibelung Story', 'Walter of Aquitaine' and 'the Story of Hugdietrich and Hildeburg'. In his introduction, Cox (1872: 29) analysed these narratives with the methods of comparative mythology – in his view *Njáls saga*, despite some mythical details, 'may be simply an over-coloured narrative of events which may really have occurred' – but he also frequently referred to a more extensive discussion of the subject in his monumental *Mythology of the Aryan Nations*.

Within the broad field of Teutonism, as relating to Iceland, one finds numerous prominent personages of late eighteenth- and nineteenth-century European culture, ranging from Johann Gottfried Herder, the brothers Grimm and Richard Wagner in Germany (cf. See, 1970), N.F.S. Gruntvig, Henrik Ibsen, and August Strindberg in Scandinavia (cf. Mjöberg, 1967–68), to Walter Scott, Richard F. Burton and William Morris in Britain (cf. Wawn, 1992a). Even in Russia, material from heathen Scandinavian myths and Icelandic sagas was regarded as a part of a 'pan-Northern' culture, attracting authors such as Alexander

Pushkin and Alexander K. Tolstoi (cf. Bergmann, 1995). But while the Icelandic medieval culture was sometimes characterised by these and other writers as an alternative to classical culture and learning, the underdeveloped Danish colony of ninteenth-century Iceland was also subject to the traditional views of Western cultural 'imperialism'. Its ancient history, its natural wonders, and its 'naive, half-primitive people' made it a perfect place for pilgrimages, a place to be mapped, measured and wondered at (cf. Aho, 1993).

Finally, like other semiotic fields, Teutonism was not without its internal ambiguities – the notion of 'us' Europeans has never been a concerted one. Chapter 5, which looks at Karl L. Sommerfelt's translation of *Njáls saga* published in Norway in 1871, addresses some of these contradictions as apparent in the saga's reception. On the one hand, this translation can be seen as a product of the general endeavour of eighteenth- and nineteenth-century Norwegians to develop a national language and literary system distinct from Danish and Danish literature (Norway split ties with Denmark in 1814). On the other hand, it evinces how many Norwegians regarded the corpus of Icelandic medieval literature as being initially at the centre of Norwegian national literature. Indeed, Iceland had been settled from Norway, and a few of the greatest sagas deal primarily with early Norwegian history and kings. Some Norwegians even thought that when Norway separated from Denmark, Iceland should have been redefined as a Norwegian territory. In this context, the Icelandic sagas were caught up between the strands of nationalism and imperialism; they could most certainly be used in various ways to define cultural and political borders. In 1888, rewritten scenes from *Njáls saga* and various other family sagas were published in the Norwegian collection *Vore Fædres Liv* (*The Life of Our Fathers*), a title that editor Nordahl Rolfsen (1888: n.p.) admitted in his preface was not 'strictly correct; but in a deeper sense, the men here described were indeed our fathers'.

But it would be inaccurate to state that the rewriting of *Njáls saga* in this period was solely motivated by self-serving politics. Another influential literary notion of the nineteenth century was embodied by Goethe's conception of *Weltliteratur*, 'the ideal of the unification of all literatures into one great synthesis, where each nation would play its part in a universal concert' (Wellek and Warren, 1977: 48). This was the context of *Njáls saga's* earliest appearance in American letters, a plot summary published in the first issue of the journal *The American Eclectic*. As stated by Absalom Peters (1841: 2), one of the two editors, the journal's fundamental principle was to advance the idea 'of a *Literature of the World*':

> We should learn to admire the true, the good and the noble in whatever country or costume they appear. These qualities bestow honor and dignity on the person or the nation that has them, but they receive nothing in return from their possessor. They should be valued wholly on their own account; and, as we admire, we should embrace, and cherish, and represent them.

The summary of *Njáls saga* in the journal was accompanied by another summary of *Gunnlaugs saga*. Both of these were translated by Elihu Burritt from Peter Erasmus Müller's (1817: 51–62) *Sagabibliothek*, a Danish collection containing extensive presentations of the major sagas. Burritt's (1841: 101) purpose was to give 'a somewhat general *coup d'œil* of ancient Icelandic life and customs', and he trusted that, through a few pages of Njáll's history, his reader would discover a variety of incidents and actors which 'still develope to the life many of the strongest lineaments of human character'. Nonetheless (and more narcissistically), he chose to conclude his introduction to Icelandic literature with a summary from those sagas relating to the first Icelandic settlers of Greenland and their adventures along the American coast.

Turning back to the Icelandic tradition of *Njáls saga* in this period, it is hard to determine if and how it was different from that of earlier times; but the documentation we have is fuller. Most fundamentally, the Icelandic saga literature, now circulating in printed editions, continued to be read aloud into the present century at the so-called *kvöldvaka*, the traditional nightly gathering at Icelandic farms. According to people remembering this custom, the night's reading was followed by sometimes heated discussions between family members about attributes of individual characters, their moral strengths and psychological weaknesses (cf. Helgason, 1998: 30–41). The influence carried on into the world of the children. Many, particularly the men, recalled games of role-playing in which saga heroes were imitated. In a letter to Holger Kjær, a Danish scholar gathering information about the *kvöldvaka* in the 1920s, a man born in northern Iceland described this tradition: 'One played Gunnar from Hlíðarendi, another one Grettir, the third one Skarphéðinn. Each had his own "sword", initially a broken shaft of a rake, and to win, you needed to break the "sword" of your enemy' (Kjær-Collection: 24/199). In this local context, the saga was continuously re-entering an oral folk tradition, perhaps not dissimilar to that preceding the saga's earliest written version (interestingly, *Njáls saga* (Ch. 8) contains a scene of two small boys and a girl mimicking certain events that have just taken place within the narrative).

But there are also signs of a new and more politically motivated use of the saga by the Icelanders in this period. Influenced by the philosophy of Herder and general political developments in Europe, Icelandic students and intellectuals in Copenhagen developed the idea that their country also deserved independence; in fact, it was seen as a prerequisite for the nation to experience again the 'golden age' described in the saga literature. A key figure of this conception was poet Jónas Hallgrímsson, who found the inspiration for his 1838 poem 'Gunnarshólmi' in the chapter of *Njáls saga* describing Gunnar Hámundarson's speech about the 'lovely hillside'. Already explored in a poem by the Reverend Gunnar Pálsson in the middle of the eighteenth century, the scene reveals the hero's strong affection for nature and his home (Johannessen, 1958: 25–35), but with Hallgrímsson's poem, Gunnar's decision to stay in Iceland, despite the risk, was interpreted for the first time as an optimum symbol of Icelandic patriotism. The poet rephrased Gunnar's speech from the saga, stressing his romantic, yet somewhat practical sense of beauty:

> 'Never before has Iceland seemed so fair,
> the fields so white, the roses in such glory,
> such crowds of sheep and cattle everywhere!
> Here will I live, here die – in youth, or hoary
> hapless old age – as God decrees. Good-bye,
> brother and friend.' Thus Gunnar's gallant story.
>
> For Gunnar felt it nobler far to die
> than flee and leave his native shores behind him,
> even though foes, inflamed with hate and sly,
> were forging links of death in which to bind him.
> His story still can make the heart beat high (Hallgrímsson, 1997)

By the middle of the twentieth century, Gunnar's 'return' had so fully been accepted by the Icelanders as a patriotic gesture that the scene – and thereby the saga which contained it – was becoming a national emblem, encompassing the entire Icelandic character. Matthías Johannessen (1958: 167) sums up the case in his study of the poetic tradition of *Njáls saga*: 'If you mention *Njáls saga*, everybody knows what you mean. And "lovely is the hillside" has only one meaning: the deepest and the truest patriotism you can imagine.'

From Racism to Aestetics (1875-1954)

Even though the interval between 1772 and 1954 is presented here as two different periods in the history of *Njáls saga*, the borderline between them is clouded. Many of the saga rewrites and themes surfacing in the former period continue to be predominant in the second. Primarily, this division is determined by the publication of two scholarly editions of the saga replacing Ólafsson's 1772 edition as the practical 'original' text.

The published versions of *Njáls saga* mentioned so far are primarily descendant texts of *Reykjabók*, but with the first critical edition of the saga, published in Denmark by Icelanders Konráð Gíslason and Eiríkur Jónsson (1875–89), the initial forks of the manuscript tradition again begin to intersect internally. Even though Gíslason uses *Reykjabók* as a basis, accounting for variations in footnotes, he selectes readings from other manuscripts, 'whenever it suits his taste' (Sveinsson, 1954: clix). The same formula was applied by Icelander Finnur Jónsson (1908), who prepared the second scholarly edition for a saga-series published in Germany early this century. While the philological methods in question aimed at reconstructing the lost original written version, these editions were in effect further removed from such a hypothetical source than the manuscripts in question.

Both these editions served as the source for various rewrites. The text prepared by Gíslason and Jónsson (1875) was printed separately without the variants and notes for those who were mainly interested in reading the story, and it later became the source of popular Icelandic editions (i.e. Ásmundarson, 1894; Thorsson, 1991), Danish school readers with selections chosen to illustrate the ancient Scandinavian language (Hoff and Hoffory, 1877; Levy, 1893), as well as translations into Swedish (Bååth, 1879), French (Dareste, 1896) and Norwegian (Aasmundstad, 1896). A French paraphrase also belongs to this branching path (Gourdault, 1885), as does a growing corpus of Icelandic poetry inspired by the saga (cf. Johannessen, 1958: 95–163). Jónsson's 1908 edition seems similarly to have been the source text of German (Heusler, 1914), Norwegian (Paasche, 1922; Lie, 1941), Danish (Holstein and Jensen, 1931), Swedish (Alving, 1935–45) and English (Bayerschmidt and Hollander, 1955) translations, several new Icelandic editions (Jónsson, 1942; Finnbogason, 1944; Laxness, 1945), as well as abridged Czech (Zeyer, 1919) and Danish (Larsen, 1946) versions. But once again, we can easily get lost within this textual labyrinth. In the cases just mentioned, it is conceivable that the rewriters consulted both of the scholarly editions and even made independent decisions by apprehending the manuscript variations supplied in footnotes.

The German path of the saga's dissemination in this period is particularly extensive, taking the principles of Teutonism to the extreme. Aspects from Icelandic medieval literature, in particular the texts relating to the ancient heathen mythology and the Nibelungen-myth, played a significant part in late eighteenth- and nineteenth-century German letters and culture, with Richard Wagner's 1876 *Der Ring der Nibelungen* as the principal example (cf. See, 1970; 1994). However, it was not until the present century that the Icelandic family sagas and the king sagas became generally known to the German public through translations and various rewrites (cf. Zernack, 1994). Marking the beginning of this period was Arthur Bonus' 1907–1909 *Isländerbuch*, a collection of extracts from the sagas (including *Njáls saga*). In his introduction, Bonus (1907–9: 1:ix) stressed that Iceland's ancient literature could provide German readers with clear insights into their own historical past. In fact, as representatives of the genuine German, the old Icelandic saga heroes should, in Bonus' view, strengthen for contemporary Germans the sense 'of the real spirit of our race, which still forms a part of our existence'. Among the qualities of the Germanic nature Bonus celebrated in this context were greatness and determination, the will to power and being true to one's word. *Isländerbuch* was reprinted several times over the next three decades and selected parts from it were reissued for children. Probably Bonus' version also inspired Nobel Prize novelist Paul Heyse's (1912: 103–12) 'Gunnar', a poem focusing on the events leading to Gunnar Hámundarson's death.

Additionally Bonus influenced his friend, publisher Eugen Diederichs, who in the period between 1911 and 1930 released the monumental Thule-series, a comprehensive collection of translations of mythical poetry *Snorra Edda*, the family sagas, along with king sagas, bishop sagas and mythical sagas. The fourth volume of the series contained Andreas Heusler's translation of *Njáls saga*, *Die Geschichte vom weisen Njal*, 'the zenith' of the corpus of sagas, as Heusler (1914: 1) suggested in his introduction. Reprinted in 1922, this text became a source for some abridged versions, including *Njal der Seher. Eine isländische Heldensaga*, in which the text was specifically rewritten for boys (Weber, 1930), as well as the chapter 'Hallgerdur und Bergthora' in the collection *Urmutter Unn. Geschichten um altnordische Frauen*, where the implied audience were young German girls (Kath, 1936).

The views of men like Bonus, Diederichs and Heusler on Icelandic medieval literature were affected by the nineteenth-century discourse of German Romantic nationalism, Nietzschean ideas about 'Herren-Moral', and mysticism in tradition of Søren Kirkegaard and Henri Bergson, to name only a few influences (cf. Bollason, 1990: 55–62; Bjarnason, 1995–96: 11–73; Schier, 1996). Comparable views had already been attached to the sagas in other cultures, but, intertwined with political and ideological developments in Germany between the two World Wars, 'die isländische Sagenwelt' became a significant thread in official Nazi ideology of the 1930s. Of a particular interest are a number of articles and works devoted to the pedagogical uses of the sagas. Titles such as 'Alt-Island als Bildungsgut im neuen Deutschland' (Old-Iceland as a Cultural Source in New Germany) and *Sagadichtung und Rassenkunde* (*Sagas and Racial Knowledge*) give an idea of the spirit in much of that writing (cf. Zernack, 1994: 394–97). In *Die altnordische Bauernsaga in der deutschen Erziehung* (*The Old Nordic Farmer-sagas in the German Edification*), Heinrich Lohrmann defined the Germanic ideals, as presented by the Icelandic sagas, as a foundation of the National Socialist Weltanschauung. The saga characters, he spelled out, were known to love their native soil. They were filled with a fighting spirit and ready to sacrifice their lives for their clan. Furthermore, Lohrmann (1938: 19–38) defended their exposure of infants on eugenic grounds and took heroes such as Gunnar Hámundarson and Skarphéðinn Njálsson as examples of this exceptional race (cf. Bollason, 1990: 89–100). In particular, Gunnar's characterisation in *Njáls saga* (Ch. 19) harmonised with Lohrmann's racial views, but Gunnar is said to have been

> big and strong and an excellent fighter .... He was handsome and fair of skin and had a straight nose, turned up its tip. He was blue-eyed and keen-eyed and ruddy-cheeked. ... He was very courteous, firm in all ways, generous and even tempered, a true friend but a discriminating friend.

Some of the women in the saga were also seen as optimum models for the future mother and wives in the Third Reich: chaste, faithful, and determined (cf. Bollason, 1990: 108–11). Lohrmann (1938: 57) made a special reference to Bergþóra who says in *Njáls saga* (Ch. 129) she will rather perish with her husband in the fire of Bergþórshvoll than outlive him: 'I was young when I was given to Njáll, and I promised him that we should both share the same fate.'

It is interesting to compare the German discourse to some of the prevalent ideas Icelanders had about the role of their ancient literature for their nation and culture during World War II. In a period of only four years, three separate popular editions of the saga were published in Reykjavík. One was editied by Guðni Jónsson (1942) as volume ten of the *Íslendinga sögur* series; it was reprinted twice in the following five years. Another edition by Magnús Finnbogason (1944) was published under the aegis of the Icelandic parliament. The third one was edited by Halldór Laxness (1945), one of Iceland's leading novelists (he received the Nobel Price for literature in 1955). Although in many respects different from each other, all of these editions can be seen as related to Iceland's acquiring independence from Denmark in 1944. The words of Jónsson (1942: 1:xxv), in the preface to his series, are symbolic:

> This is a reading edition, meeting in that respect the needs of both the learned and the lay-man. It is to be a kind of a morning-gift to the Icelanders at the day-break of the restored republic and it is designed to pass the nation's saga knowledge on to future generations. In the first years of independence, it is supposed to help Iceland's youth to know its true nature, itself, and its role in the community of nations.

Just like the German boys and girls, Icelandic youth was expected to read the saga to know its own nature and calling. The fundamental difference was that Icelanders in general had more moderate and considerably less aggressive views about their role in the community of nations than the leaders of Nazi Germany had about the international role of the Third Reich.

A closer analysis of Finnbogason's and Laxness' editions in Chapters 6 and 7 will, on the other hand, reveal how they represented two competing views towards the saga and general political developments in Iceland. Partially, the issue was whether *Njáls saga* should be defined as history or fiction, as an ancient relic, or as a modern work of art. In that respect, these two editions may be contextualised within an ongoing debate about the origin and the nature of the Icelandic family sagas in general, a debate that can be traced to earliest scholarly treatments of these texts in the seventeenth century (cf. Anderson, 1964). As already mentioned, the prevailing assumption for centuries was that *Njáls saga* was essentially historical, based on a reliable oral tradition. Exceptional early sceptics, like the Icelandic manuscript collector Árni Magnússon (1663–1730), still measured the text on the scale of historicity, but in his view, most of the family sagas were historically unreliable, written too long after the events which they described were supposed to have taken place. Specifically (and untraditionally for an Icelander), Magnússon chastised the saga authors for elevating the Icelanders and their merits, 'just as if they were superior to all other nations. The author of *Njáls saga* has especially been impudent in this respect' (Þorkelsson, 1889: 786).

In the late eighteenth and nineteenth century, there was a slow but growing awareness of the saga's stylistic and literary merits. As demonstrated in Lars Lönnroth's (1976: 3) thorough treatment of the early critics of *Njáls saga*, Danish historian and novelist P.A. Suhm was a pioneer in this respect, but as early as 1781, he regarded the saga 'as one well-structured narrative, controlled by one artistic mind, that of "the unknown author".' This view was reiterated in Peter Erasmus Müller's *Sagabibliothek* in 1817, by the Danish poet Carsten Hauch in 1855 (Lönnroth, 1976: 4–6) and by the Swedish antiquarian Hans Olof Hildebrand in 1867, naming only a few. A reader of Dasent's 1861 English translation, Hildebrand retold a number of passages from *Njáls saga* in his *Lifvet på Island under sagotiden* (*Life in Iceland in the Saga Age*), stressing the 'mastery' which the saga author had 'of the language and the characterisation' – the saga was by no means a dry history chronology, Hildebrand (1867: 149) revelled, but truly 'a work of art'.

In the last decades of the nineteenth century, the issue of the saga's origin was being taken up by scholars such as Guðbrandur Vigfússon, an Icelander working in Britain, and Konrad von Maurer, a German expert in legal history. In Lönnroth's (1976: 7) view, these men can be said 'to have started a new and a more scientific era in the history of *Njála* scholarship'; Vigfússon with his study of the saga's dating and his theory about the author and his sources and Maurer by applying German *Quellenkritik* to the study of sagas. Partially following contemporary trends in scholarly research of the Homeric epics, Vigfússon (1878) and several of Maurer's students (Brenner, 1878; Lehmann and Carolsfeld, 1883) argued that the saga was to a great degree based on various written sources, not only genealogical lists and law manuals, but also shorter sagas or episodes. This theory is thoroughly represented in Karl Lehmann's and Hans Schnorr von Carolsfeld's study of *Njáls saga's* legal sources: 'The end result of their investigation was that the present *Njála* came about through the combination of (a) a lost *Gunnars saga*, (b) a lost *Njáls saga*, (c) written laws, (d) a lost saga about the conversion (*Kristni þáttr*), (e) a lost *Brjáns saga*, and (f) lost genealogical sources' (Lönnroth, 1976: 9).

These scholarly theories are not an isolated network of paths within the *Njáls saga* tradition, as they variously influenced saga rewritings of other kinds. The case of poet Albert Ulrich Bååth, the first Swedish translator of the saga, is of particular interest. In addition to his 1879 translation, he dealt with the composition of *Njáls saga* in his 1885 dissertation, further elaborating the ideas of the 'Homeric analysts'. In Bååth's (1885: 138–46) view, the saga had been composed by a thirteenth-century saga author out of thirteen episodes or short stories, themselves lost but belonging to preserved genre of the so-called *þættir*. Bååth initiated this theory in the introduction to his translation, and he rearranged certain chapters and chapter divisions in the narrative accordingly. One of the episodes he demarcated was the episode of Höskuldur Þráinsson, the foster-son of Njáll, who is killed by his foster-brothers on little or no accounts. In the complete saga narrative, Höskuldur's story is divided into two parts by the episode dealing with the conversion of Iceland, but in Bååth's (1879: vii) translation the five chapters devoted to the conversion were united into one chapter and moved in front of the chapters treating the episode of Höskuldur. In this way, the translation was designed both to reinforce the translator's ideas about the original episodes of the text and structuraly to 'improve' the preserved version of the saga. Echoing his countryman Hildebrand, Bååth (1885: v–vi) was of the opinion that *Njáls saga* most significantly was an aesthetic piece of writing, its historical threads mainly serving as 'a background for the author's own train of thought'.

In Iceland, one the other hand, belief in the factual historicity of the family sagas continued to prevail for a while. One of its signs was the extensive archaeological research carried out in the late nineteenth and the early twentieth century on the basis of individual sagas (cf. Friðriksson, 1994). Particularly prominent was the approach of Sigurður Vigfússon to several of the *Njáls saga* sites, undertaken under the authority of The Icelandic Archaeological Society. This work resulted in the publication of a number of articles on the issue and even in a scientific investigation of white mysterious chemicals that were found at the site of Bergþórshvoll. With reference to *Njáls saga's* (Ch. 129) testimony of the burning, in which the women of Bergþórshvoll try to put out the fire with whey, these white chemicals were believed to be 'remains of Bergþóra's "skyr" [whey], or, in other words, preserved remains of milk products that had been prepared at Bergþórshvoll in the year in which Njáll and his sons were burnt according to the saga' (Storch, 1887: 3). The chemicals were not unambiguously identified, but in a published report by the Danish chemist Vilhelm Storch (1887: 22) it was admitted that they might be remains of a milk-product of some sort, most probably 'cheese, which has been prepared from sour milk'. The purpose of this investigation, like most of the archaeological research inspired by *Njáls saga*, was to verify the narrative's testimony 'scientifically'.

There were indeed some voices of scepticism in Iceland by that time, but it is interesting that those who questioned individual points of *Njáls saga* seemed to believe, nonetheless, that the true account of Gunnar, Njáll and other saga characters could still be conjectured 'behind' the preserved narrative. In 1839, poet Sigurður Breiðfjörð published a poem in defence of Hallgerður Höskuldsdóttir, but as already noticed, Hallgerður was generally being held to be responsible for her husband's death, since she refuses him strands of her hair for a bow-string at his fatal hour. Breiðfjörð (1839: 15), however, doubted that one could make bow-strings from human hair and suggested that some malicious person had fabricated the scene to belittle Hallgerður.

Even more remarkable examples of this search for the 'genuine' account of *Njáls saga* were the dreams of Hermann Jónasson, introduced to the Icelandic public in February of 1912 and published a few months later. Jónasson opened his lecture by relating various prophetic dreams he had dreamed from an early age, dreams that enabled him to locate lost sheep and save himself and fellow travellers from danger. Having established his credibility as an oracle, he then described how Ketill Sigfússon from Mörk, one of the characters of *Njáls saga,* visited him in a dream in 1893 to rectify the narrative of the saga. Early in their conversation, Ketill said he knew that Jónasson doubted the reliability of specific scenes in *Njáls saga.* Ketill confirmed some of that mistrust, but in other instances, he said, the preserved text was historically truthful. His main concern was to disclose how the story of Höskuldur Þráinsson Hvítanesgoði – originally a separate saga according to the dream (here we may sense an intertextual relation to the writings of Bååth) – was falsified in the preserved version. At this point, Jónasson noted, the dream became a mixture of Ketill's voice, recounting *Höskuldar saga Hvítanesgoða* word for word, and a vision of the events described. When the telling was done, six hours or thirty pages later, Ketill asked Jónasson (1912: 80) to publish this original version; 'otherwise some people will continue to believe in a fabrication, while others will dispute the saga as a whole because they sense that some of its points must be faulted' (cf. Helgason, 1998: 80–92).

In the following decades, the question of the sagas' veracity became a matter of a heated debate in Iceland. Illustrative are the words of Björn M. Ólsen (1937–39: 43), the first professor of Icelandic studies at the University of Iceland, who claimed in the nineteen-twenties that some of his countrymen found 'it almost blasphemous to question the historical value of our sagas. They feel that the sagas are denigrated if something in them can be doubted.' As will be shown in chapter 6, that sentiment had not changed much two decades later when the Icelandic parliament imposed restrictions on the publication and rewriting of medieval Icelandic literature. Ólsen himself, however, was of a different mentality. Influenced by the German saga translator Andreas Heusler, he was a pioneer of Icelandic literary scholars who approached the sagas particularly from an aesthetic viewpoint. These scholars, who are frequently referred to as the Icelandic School in saga studies, will be relevant to the discussion of Halldór Laxness' edition of the saga in Chapter 7. Einar Ólafur Sveinsson's extensive and lasting research on *Njáls saga* is of the utmost importance in that context, but the publication of his 1954 edition of the saga marks the beginning of the most recent period in the saga's dissemination.

New Horizons (1954-)

When Sveinsson published his critical edition of *Brennu-Njáls saga* in the Icelandic saga series of Íslenzk fornrit (Ancient Icelandic Texts), he had already established himself as the leading authority in the field. In addition to numerous articles addressing topics ranging from the mysterious identity of the saga author (Sveinsson, 1937) to the resemblance between Hallgerður Höskuldsdóttir and Clytemnestra (Sveinsson, 1956: 91–114), he had published three books on *Njáls saga*, one dealing with its sources and composition (Sveinsson, 1933), another discussing its aesthetic qualities (Sveinsson, 1943), and the third devoted to the manuscript tradition (Sveinsson, 1953). The motor behind all this work was Sveinsson's conviction that the saga was indeed a literary masterpiece, created by one man at a particular place and moment.

For more than forty years now Sveinsson's 1954 edition has, for all practical purposes, served as the 'original' text of *Njáls saga*. Based on his study of the manuscript tradition, it takes readings from its various branches but follows most closely the early fourteenth-century manuscript of *Möðruvallabók*. Certified by Sveinsson's scholarly authority, this edition has given rise to a new generation of popular editions in Iceland (Böðvarsson, 1968–69; Helgason and Ólason, 1973; Finnbogason, 1977; Sæmundsson 1986) and a multitude of translations, most notably into languages in which *Njáls saga* had not been translated before. These include Russian (Steblin-Kamenskogo, 1956), Rumanian (Comsa, 1963), Czech (Heger, 1965), Hungarian (Istvan, 1965), Faeroese (Niclasen, 1966), Serbo-Croatian (Majstorovica, 1967), Polish (Zaluska-Strömberg, 1968), Slovenian (Anko, 1970), Georgian (Jabasvilma, 1977), Japanese (Taniguchi, 1979), Spanish (Bernárdez, 1986), and Finnish (Tuuri, 1996). Here, we may also note two French translations published within a span of two years (Stefánsdóttir and Chinotti, 1975; Boyer, 1976). The general reception of *Njáls saga* in this last period deserves a separate study and language capacities I do not have. What now follows are a few impressions of the saga tradition in Britain in this period.

Einar Ólafur Sveinsson's extensive influence on the rewriting of the saga can be detected in the English translation by Magnus Magnusson and Hermann Pálsson, originally published in the Penguin Classics Series in 1960 and running through numerous printings to the present day. Both translators are of Icelandic origin but they have lived most of their adult life in Britain. According to the Penguin edition, Magnus Magnusson 'is a well-known Scottish television personality', and Hermann Pálsson 'studied Icelandic at the University of Iceland and Celtic at University College, Dublin' (Pálsson and Magnusson, 1960: 1). The translators dedicate their work to Sveinsson, explaining in their 'Note on the Translation' that the English text is based on his edition.

> In this splendid edition, Professor Einar Ólafur Sveinsson of the University of Iceland has provided a text as nearly definitive as we can ever expect, the fruit of a life-long study of the saga and its manuscripts. Every student of *Njal's Saga* is indebted to him for his inspired researches; to us in particular they have proved quite invaluable in dealing with the numerous problems of interpretation which abound in a work of such complexity and subtlety. (Pálsson and Magnusson, 1960: 33)

Sveinsson's inspiration can be further noted in Magnusson's introduction, in observations such as: *Njáls saga's* 'author is one of the world's great story-tellers, and the saga he wrote is one of the finest achievements of medieval literature' (Pálsson and Magnusson, 1960: 31).

The Penguin translation has been the source of some interesting adaptations, including *The Burning of Njal*, a children's version written by Henry Treece (1964), and *The Tree of Strife*, David Wade's (1989) dramatisation for radio, originally produced by the BBC and later adapted by the German National Broadcasting. It is worth noting how Treece's introduction to *The Burning of Njal* contradicts the emphasis on Teutonism prevalent in the nineteenth- and early twentieth-century reception of *Njáls saga*. Similar to some of the earlier rewriters, Treece (1964: 9) defines the medieval Icelanders in terms of their racial heritage, but his characterisation does not exactly compliment the saga heroes:

> The men and women who were quite suddenly drawn or flung northward towards this island near the Arctic Circle after AD 867 were, in all essentials, various remnants of the same Nordic or Aryan stock which had tormented Italy, Spain and North Africa

> for half a millennium. In truth, there was nothing to distinguish them racially from the Gauls who sacked Rome in 390 BC, the Goths who did the same in AD 410 or the Celts of Vercingetorix who pushed Julius Caesar so close to defeat in 52 BC. Iceland, indeed, was the last migration-place of the northern folk: it was their final refuge, against whose volcanic rifts and rocks, mountains and rivers, this fair-skinned people who had set forth as Steppeland cattlemen before the time of Homer, worked off their furious energies against one another and no longer against great Mediterranean empires.

The ancient Icelanders were, in short, the last living branch of the Aryan race of troublemakers who had fought great empires throughout history. The two World Wars are not mentioned in this context, but some of Treece's (1946: 1–12) other writings imply that the twentieth-century military record of Germany applied in his view the most recent example of the 'furious energies' of the Nordic or Aryan stock. Through its portrayal of 'the constant bickering among farming families' and 'the almost casual manslaughters in ambush' (Treece, 1964: 10), *The Burning of Njal* was designed to teach juvenile readers a lesson about the dire consequences of violence.

However, here is also a rub: At the end of his introduction Treece (1964: 10–11) claims *Njáls saga*, 'with its threatening dreams and its sudden screaming ambushes and crackling flames', to be as familiar to his young readers 'as a grim fairy-tale, half-heard in early childhood; it is about the lives and deaths of people very much like our own ancestors'. In the following chapter, we will consider how this view of the saga, as a myth about British racial and cultural origin, was at the heart of its initial English translation, George Webbe Dasent's *The Story of Burnt Njal*.

Part II

Njáls Saga **in English**

Chapter 2
The Victorian Tour
Tourism and Teutonism

In *Orientalism*, Edward Said (1979: 67) adresses the narcistic tendency generally inherent in people's reception of other cultures:

> It is perfectly natural for the human mind to resist the assault on it of untreated strangeness; therefore, cultures have always been inclined to impose complete transformations on other cultures, receiving these other cultures not as they are but as, for the benefit of the receiver, they ought to be.

Said's observation may serve as a motif in the present discussion of George Webbe Dasent's *The Story of Burnt Njal*. Published in 1861, this monumental work marked a new period of British interest in Icelandic medieval literature. It was the first complete saga translation into English and was soon followed by numerous other publications devoted to Icelandic issues (cf. Wawn, 1992a). In many respects, it supplied British (and even American) Victorians with the model to transform early Icelandic culture for their own benefit. Most interestingly, *Njáls saga* – in its 'English garb' (Dasent, 1861: 1:vi) – was neither presented nor perceived as belonging essentially to 'other' culture; the saga's success was based on the conception that Icelandic medieval history was, in its very nature, like parts of early and even contemporary British history. Uncovering that conception, we will first consider how the translation was intertextually related to nineteenth-century British travelogues. Later we will see how it also reflects the Victorians' concern with the cultural and racial origins of the British Empire.

Touring Njal's Country

Similar to many later saga editions and translations, *The Story of Burnt Njal* rendered geography an important subtext to *Njáls saga*. Imitating aspects of the contemporary genre of travel literature, this expensive two-volume publication featured one plan of 'Thingvalla or

Thingfield', and another of 'Almannagiá and Althing', one general map of Iceland, another map of the south-western part of Iceland, and finally a map of 'the North-West of Europe, illustrating the settlement of the Northmen in the Tenth Century' (Dasent, 1861: 1:xxx). Furthermore, Dasent (1861: 1:i) opened his two-hundred page introduction with a detailed chapter on Iceland's 'Physical Features', writing from the perspective of a traveler who was 'nearing the island after the usual passage'. Later, describing parliamentary procedures in medieval Iceland, he also informed his readers about the route a contemporary traveler would take from Reykjavík to the 'Thingfield': 'after riding for hours over barren and rugged tracts of moss-grown lava, [the traveler] suddenly reins up his galloway on the very brink of the upper lip of the Great Rift and gazes upon the sunk field, stretching miles before him' (Dasent, 1861: 1:cxxxvi–cxxxviii). Comments of this sort reveal to us how the reader of *The Story of Burnt Njal* was not merely encountering a medieval narrative. In a certain sense the reader was taking an exotic tour or even a pilgrimage to 'the very edge of the Arctic Circle' (Dasent, 1861: 1:i).

Dasent's reference to the 'usual passage' ties his translation to the growing interest of the Victorians in Iceland as a place to visit. Ever since Joseph Banks' expedition in 1772, there had been a steadily growing stream of travelers setting out to explore this land of volcanoes, geysers and sagas (cf. Ponzi, 1986; Wawn, 1987). Originally, it was mainly professional explorers and scientists who went on these expeditions, but by 1861, Iceland had become a regular tourist attraction. That change was made possible by the scheduled trips of steamboats from Britain to Iceland, starting in 1856 (Aho, 1993: 206). In her review of Dasent's translation, Hannah Lawrence (1861: 323) firmly associated the publication of *Njáls saga* in Britain with this trend and the related genre of travel literature:

> Truly Iceland, that region of perpetual frost and fire, that 'ultima Thule' of the habitable globe, is attracting no little attention just now. We have had of late yacht voyages to Iceland and rambles in Iceland, and ladies' visits to Iceland, besides Commander Forbes's elaborate work on its volcanoes and geysers, for the information and amusement of stay-at-home travellers; while advertisements of pleasant little parties to visit the 'lions' of Iceland meet us in the weekly literary periodicals, and letters appear in the *Times*, pointing out the best routes, and giving most useful warnings as to guides, and most needful information on all subjects relating to the commissariat department.

Lawrence's review echoed the tone of some earlier British travel accounts, portraying 'ultima Thule' as a sublime destination – the perfect Romantic place. As exemplified in chapter 1, that conception coincided with the discovery of Iceland's medieval literature in eighteenth-century Britain and its consequent influence on Romantic poets and novelists, ranging from Thomas Gray to Walter Scott (Phelps, 1893: 137–170; Nordby, 1901: 3–22; Lieder, 1920).

Dasent's discovery of medieval Icelandic literature had a slightly different origin. In 1840, at the age of twenty-three, he had been 'posted to Stockholm, where he was employed for four years as secretary to the British envoy. It was during these years that his interest in early northern literature awakened' (Turville-Petre, 1957: ix). During this period, he learned Icelandic and produced his first Icelandic translation, *The Prose or Younger Edda* by Snorri Sturluson (1842). Before leaving Sweden, Dasent also translated from the Swedish *Anvisning till Isländskan eller Nordiska Fornspråket* (*A Grammar of the Icelandic or Old Norse Tongue*) by Erasmus Rask (1843), a pioneering work in the field of Scandinavian linguistics.

Despite his Scandinavian residence, Dasent's 'Northern' interest developed fully in accordance with British contemporary interests. *The Prose or Younger Edda*, a prime source for the study of Scandinavian mythology, is dedicated to Thomas Carlyle and evidently inspired by Carlyle's *On Heroes, Hero-Worship and the Heroic in History*. Originally presented in 1840 as a series of lectures, Carlyle focused in the opening chapter on 'The Hero as Divinity. Odin. Paganism: Scandinavian Mythology'. Dasent's translation linked the Victorians more directly with the mythology which Carlyle (1840: 14) had characterised as 'the creed of our fathers', and with the character of Óðinn, whom Carlyle (1840: 26) had fancied 'to be the Type Norseman; the finest Teuton whom that race had yet produced'.

In the preface to Rask's (1843: iii) grammar, Dasent claimed that his purpose was to 'excite attention toward a language and literature, of vast importance to the English student, but hitherto little understood or valued in England'. For almost a century, the British reputation of Icelandic literature had primarily been made by sublime rewritings such as Richard Hole's (1789: 937) 'The Tomb of Gunnar', discussed in Chapter 1. In Dasent's opinion, the premise for a different emphasis was the systematic study of the ancient Icelandic language. Such a study, he explained, was also a necessary background to the academic study of English:

In my opinion a man who could teach English with comfort to

> himself and profit to his hearers – a man in short who will earnestly do his dayswork and make a job of it – should have a thorough knowledge of Anglo Saxon, and Anglo Norman, of our Old, Middle, and New English, beside a considerable proficiency in the Old Norse, and early German tongues. There are men in England capable of doing this, but as yet they are few and far between. (Rask, 1843: vi)

Evidently, Dasent was preparing himself for that demanding task. He opened his preface to Rask's (1843: iii) grammar by explaining that the translation had been undertaken to further his 'own studies in Old Norse', and he concluded by calling for a position of Professor of English to be established at the University of Oxford.

Upon his return to England in 1845, Dasent was appointed to a different field, becoming an assistant editor of *The Times* (Turville-Petre, 1957: ix). Over the next sixteen years, he continued nontheless to work on his translation of *Njáls saga* (a project he had started in Sweden). He also became involved with the editing of the monumental Cleasby and Vigfússon *Icelandic-English Dictionary*, in 1859 he published a successful translation of fairy-tales from the Norwegian collection of Asbjørnsen and Moe, and two years later, *The Story of Burnt Njal* was finally released (Wawn, 1991). At that time, in the spring of 1861, Dasent had not yet found the opportunity to travel to Iceland by the 'usual passage' (he visited the country the following summer; Umbra, 1863; cf. Wawn, 1992b; Aho, 1993). Consequently, his geographical description in the introduction and the maps of the country owed their existence to earlier travelers and travel accounts. In his preface, Dasent (1861: 1:xix) acknowledged his debt as he explained that the plans of 'Thingfield' were 'chiefly from a sketch kindly furnished by Captain Forbes' while Mr. Metcalfe 'furnished some valuable topographical information'. He also refered approvingly to Forbes' book, *Iceland; Its Volcanoes, Geysers, and Glaciers*, which had been published in 1860.

But just as the reading of Dasent's translation involved a tour of Iceland for the British arm-chair traveler, so could touring Iceland involve a close reading of the saga. A few months after the publication of *The Story of Burnt Njal*, Frederick Metcalfe – the man who had supplied Dasent with 'valuable topographical information' – released an account of his travels under the title *The Oxonian in Iceland*. In one of the chapters of this handsome volume, Metcalfe (1861: 358) detailed his 1860 visit to Rangárvallasýsla, 'the country made famous by the most interesting of all the Icelandic sagas – the story of Burnt Niál'.

For a number of pages, he wove together descriptions of landscape and scenes from the saga. The reader followed Metcalfe (1861: 358–62) and his Icelandic travel companion to the site of Knafahólar, 'the scene of an exploit of Gunnar's'; together they pause at 'Ostre Rángá' where the 'notable fight between Gunnar's black horse and Starkardr's red one took place'; and at length, they reach 'Hlidarende, once the abode of that noble fellow Gunnar'. Repeatedly, past and present were intermingled in the account, as when Metcalfe's (1861: 369) companion noted on the way to Bergþórshvoll that they were following the very route 'that Flossi and his hundred incendiaries rode that terrible night from their rendezvous under the Thrihyrningr to attack poor old Niál'.

In a footnote, Metcalfe (1861: 365) emphasised that Dasent's 'admirable version' of the saga had appeared *after* his stay in Iceland. In that respect, *The Oxonian in Iceland* confirms that the Victorian tour to Iceland could include a topographical reading of *Njáls saga* prior to 1861. But most certainly, Dasent's work was essential in popularising such journeys. For the famous explorer Richard Burton, who visited 'Ultima Thule' in 1872, *The Story of Burnt Njal* was one of the three most important readings for a study of Iceland: 'It has sent one, it will send many an English tourist to gaze upon the Lithe-end', Burton (1875: 1:252) asserted.

And there were other English travelers visiting Iceland in 1872 under Dasent's decisive influence. One was a young painter, S.E. Waller, who published his illustrated journal, *Six Weeks in the Saddle*, two years later. In his introduction, Waller (1874: 1) wrote that 'Burnt Njal' 'was at the bottom of it'; he had read Dasent's translation 'and was wild to visit the scene of such a tremendous tragedy'. Evidently, the experience of the arm-chair traveler had not been satisfactory. Waller was compelled to go by himself, not to see Iceland, we should note, but to re-read the saga in the original, i.e. in the Icelandic landscape. Characteristic of Waller's (1874: 75–76) experience was a visit to 'the far-famed Bergthorshvoll', where he could observe 'with much interest the little hollow where the burners hid their horses, and the small bog or quick moss called Kári-tiorn, where Kári extinguished his burning clothes'. In such details, Dasent's translation harmonised with the realities of Rangárvellir.

Metcalfe, Burton, and Waller are only three of the numerous Victorians who traveled through the setting of *Njáls saga* and other Icelandic sagas in the last decades of the nineteenth century. These travelers included William Morris, who had been on his first 'pilgrimage' to the country in 1871, accompanied by his co-translator of

Icelandic sagas, Eiríkur Magnússon, and a long time college-friend, Charlie Faulkner. They stayed at Bergþórshvoll on July 20, and on the following day 'the bonder' at Hlíðarendi showed them 'the traditional places about the stead' (Morris, 1966: 44). Illustrative of the development of this tourism is Charles G. Warnford Lock's (1879: 317) *The Home of the Eddas,* in which a trip to 'Njal's Country' was included in a twelve day 'sketch route' with '*Þingvellir, Geysir, Gullfoss, Hekla* [. . .] *Eyrarbakki* and *Krisuvik*' as the other destinations . Echoing Waller, Lock (1879: 319) recommended his readers to 'examine the site of *Bergþórshvoll*' and 'the little peat moss called *Káratjörn*', and he also added some practical information: 'The accommodation in the existing hovels is poor, and they must not be depended on for a stay.'

While Lock's book mainly served the tourists who trekked Rangárvallasýsla, most of these accounts also permitted the realisation of the saga in the mind of the arm-chair traveler. That purpose is particularly explicit in *Six Weeks in the Saddle.* Describing the advance to Hlíðarendi, Waller (1874: 112) noted that his desire was to realise for himself 'the circumstances of the last dreadful scene' in Gunnar's life, but at the same time, he was 'very anxious to make a correct sketch of the place and was determined to spare no pains to accomplish it'. Waller printed the sketch with fourteen others in his journal, enabling his readers to picture certain scenes from the saga without ever leaving their Victorian parlors. The epitome of such graphic saga 'translations' in the late nineteenth century was undoubtedly the publication of *A Pilgrimage to the Saga-Steads of Iceland* by W.G. Collingwood and Jón Stefánsson. This 'picture book' was chiefly designed to supply 'the background of scenery' for several major Icelandic family sagas. As this was scenery, the authors noted, 'which the ancient dramatic style takes for granted,' the idea was to help 'the modern reader, out of Iceland' to '*stage* these dramas, to *visualise* the action and events' (Collingwood and Stefánsson, 1899: v; cf. Wawn, 1992a: 223). The book contained a special chapter on the south part of Iceland – 'Country of Burnt Njal' – in which the observer could, for example, see Gunnar's home and cairn at Hlíðarendi and join him and his brothers before the fight at Knafahólar (Collingwood and Stefánsson, 1899: 20–32).

Past and Present

Maintaining that George Webbe Dasent's English translation of *Njáls saga* involved a sublimated trip to Iceland only reveals a small part of its agenda. As implied by the sub-title of his two volumes, *Life in Iceland at the End of the Tenth Century,* the reader was invited to visit not only an exotic geographical area but the distant past. As an author, Dasent was preoccupied with this second realm. The six-page opening section of his introduction, devoted to Iceland's physical features, was followed by almost two hundred more pages dealing with the country's settlement, the religion and superstitions of the Icelanders, the social principles in Icelandic medieval society, the civil power of the priests, provincial organisation, public life and parliamentary procedures, and daily life in Njáll's time. Additionally, Dasent published an appendix of more than sixty pages at the end of the second volume, containing articles on the Vikings, the Norwegian queen Gunnhildur, and on money and currency in the tenth century. No less important than the saga narrative, this appendix, the full eighty-page index, and the aforementioned introduction, all served to make Dasent's work more than a translation of *Njáls saga*; initially it was a comprehensive introduction to the history of medieval Iceland.

As far as the testimony of *Njáls saga* was concerned, Dasent explained in his preface that the Icelandic sagas could be divided into three sub-genres: mythical sagas, histories of kings, and family sagas. Of these, Dasent (1861: 1:v) found the family sagas most trustworthy, as they were 'told by men who lived on the very spot, and told with a minuteness and exactness, as to time and place, that will bear the strictest examination'. *Njáls saga*, he continued, not only belonged to that reliable group of sagas related to Iceland; this 'tragic story,' Dasent (1861: 1:vi) alleged in strikingly Romantic diction, 'bears away the palm for truthfulness and beauty'.

Backing up his belief in the historicity of the narrative, Dasent (1861: 1:vii) explained how every event recorded in the saga had been talked about as a matter of history as soon as it occurred; then, when the whole story had unfolded, 'it was handed down from father to son, as truthfully and faithfully as could ever be the case with any public or notorious matter in local history'. That oral tradition had, in Dasent's opinion, preserved the saga for one hundred years before it was written down, but other sagas, songs and annals also backed up its testimony. Regarding the 'wild superstition' which was 'intermingled' with this history, Dasent (1861: 1:vii–viii) claimed such material would 'startle no reader of the smallest judgement'; the saga's description of ghosts, dreams, warnings and tokens was, on the contrary, 'one great proof of its truthfulness', reflecting 'popular belief in the age to which it belonged'. Dasent (1861: 1:vii) noted in this context that all ages, 'our own not excepted, have their superstitions'. Still, he felt compelled to explain some wonders of the saga in terms of the scientific superstitions of his own age. The strange sound coming from Gunnar's halberd before great events, Dasent (1861: 1:viii) conjectured, probably meant that its shaft had been 'of some hard ringing wood unknown in the north. It was a foreign weapon, and if the shaft were of lance wood, the sounds it gave out when brandished or shaken would be accounted for at once without a miracle.'

As a translator, Dasent situated himself at the end of this paternal line of Icelanders who had originally preserved the saga in oral tradition. Dasent (1861: 1:xx) compared his toil to the duty of a foster-father, in old times, 'to rear and cherish the child which he had taken from the arms of its natural parents, his superiors in rank'. In his case, these natural parents were Icelandic scholars, men such as Grímur Thomsen and Guðbrandur Vigfússon who, in Dasent's words (1861: 1:xviii), had preserved the knowledge of 'the life, law, and customs of the early Icelanders' – the historical subtext of the saga – and were able to pass it on to the next generation (cf. Wawn, 1991).

Although Dasent (1861: 1:xviii; 1:xvi) realised that much still remained to be done in the investigation of Iceland's early history, 'even by Icelanders themselves', and furthermore expressed his humble despair that some of his own shortcomings 'should mar the noble features of the masterpiece which it has been his care to copy', the theme of his preface was that *The Story of Burnt Njal* maintained the essence or, more specifically, the tradition of the historical past which had produced the saga in the first place. In that spirit, Dasent (1861: 1:xix) refered to the Icelandic artist Sigurður Guðmundsson, whose elaborate plan of 'the old Icelandic Hall' adorned the publication, as being 'a living proof that the skill of hand which adorned the Hall at Hjarðarholt in the tenth century [ref. to *Laxdæla saga*], still exists in Iceland at the present day'. Furthermore, Dasent (1861: 1:xx) expressed the hope that the saga would, in the English translation,

> go forth and fight the battle of life for itself, and win fresh fame for those who gave it birth. It will be reward enough for him who has first clothed it in an English dress if his foster-child adds another leaf to that evergreen wreath of glory which crowns the brows of Iceland's ancient worthies.

According to this metaphor, the English publication was to be compared with the medieval Icelander, whom Dasent (1861: 1:clxxi–clxxiv) described in his introduction as having belonged to 'the courts and body-guards of kings and earls', never failing 'to prove his right to an honourable seat on one of the benches in the hall'. Stories of such men, he claimed, proved 'that the Icelanders were looked upon as the first and foremost of the Scandinavian race'. His spirited foster-child, the British translation of *Njáls saga,* was designed to confirm that consensus at Victorian 'courts', to prove its right to an honorable place on the Victorian bookshelf.

Dasent's reviewers unanimously praised his efforts. Robert Lowe (1861: 218) attested that the translator was

> well qualified for the undertaking by a complete and accurate knowledge of the subject and by the possession of a pure vein of English undefiled, which enables him to transfuse into our own language much of the racy vigour and quaint homeliness of the original.

Richard John King (1874: 150) characterised Dasent's introduction and appendices, along with his sketch of the 'Northmen in Iceland' published in the volume *Oxford Essays* in 1858, as being 'beyond all doubt the most valuable aids to a real knowledge of the ancient North which the English reader has hitherto received'. Alexander Nicolson (1861: 305) stated that the editor could 'congratulate himself on the comely dress in which he sends forth this strong foster-child of his to the world'. Hannah Lawrence (1861: 330) developed the discourse even further, writing that the translation had been 'indeed a labour of love to Dr. Dasent, who tells us he commenced it as far back as the year 1843'. Lawrence (1861: 330) added that, in view of the perfect construction of the work, its lifelike portraits and its simple beautiful style, it was

> not surprising that the reader of the nineteenth century should linger over its pages with an interest well nigh as absorbing as the Icelander of the eleventh century felt when the events were new, and he heard it told near the cairn of the well-remembered Gunnar, or beside the still recent ruins of wise Njal's homestead.

As far as Lawrence was concerned, the saga tradition was perfectly maintained in the English translation.

Addressing the proposed historicity of the saga, Nicolson (1861: 296) claimed that although the narrative was, 'of course, to some extent indebted to the invention of the narrator', it was 'substantially an authentic piece of biographical history'. Lowe (1861: 229) was a little more skeptical, as he found that the supernatural stories were 'unfortunately' not merely ornaments but 'closely interwoven with the structure of the story itself'. Still, Lowe (1861: 228) stated that there was 'no reason to reject the main incidents of the story'. Accordingly, he spent a considerable space in his review on a summary of Dasent's writings on the historical background of the narrative, presenting it as a necessary aid for the understanding of his outline of *The Story of Burnt Njal*. Lawrence's review was similarly structured as a short introduction to Iceland's medieval history, followed by a synopsis of the plot of the saga. King was also preoccupied with the historical aspects of *Njáls saga*, using the writings of Dasent and the testimony of his translation as sources for a detailed discussion of 'The Change of Faith in Iceland', as indicated by his title.

In the opening of his review, Lowe (1861: 217) wrote that the British tourists, 'who, year by year, lay before us their descriptions of the steam-clouded valleys, lava-covered plains and mud volcanoes of Iceland, seem scarcely aware that the land of their pilgrimage ever had a history'. Dasent's work was instrumental in changing that state of ignorance. Those who toured 'Njal's Country' were not only realising scenes from the saga; most fundamentally, they wanted to encounter or uncover the distant historical past which it characterised. But as indicated by Charles G. Warnford Lock's comment on the 'poor hovels' at Bergþórshvoll, the responses of English tourists were mixed. Nineteenth-century Iceland did not always meet the expectations that the sagas may have raised within their British admirers. The contrast of past and present was acutely sensed by William Morris, who visited Hlíðarendi and other saga sites in 1871 (cf. Aho, 1982). Morris (1898: 122) expressed his feelings and undoubtedly the feelings of many others in the poem 'Gunnar's Howe Above the House at Lithend', reflecting, on 'this gray minster of lands, / Whose floor is the tomb of time past, / and whose walls by the toil of dead hands / Show pictures amidst of the ruin / of deeds that have overpast death'. Similarily, S.E. Waller described how he met an old man at Hlíðarendi, who read to him a part of the saga and showed him Gunnar's grave. 'How strange it all seemed,' Waller (1874: 115) contemplated: 'The stern reality of the story, the romantic incidents connected with the place, the splendid qualities and chivalrous courage of the man. An what remained? An old-world legend and this heap of battered stones.'

There were, nonetheless, a few ways of rescuing the glorious historical past at the Icelandic scene, and even of becoming an active participant in the plot of *Njáls saga*. Hence, Waller (1874: 76) also commented on some digging that had taken place at Bergþórshvoll, noting that everything unearthed 'was immediately bought up by the roving Englishmen who make pilgrimages to this most interesting spot'. The same image was also developed in an introductory article on the sagas by Andrew Lang (1891: 151), who reported that the remnants of the black sand and the whey which Bergþóra and her maids 'cast on the flames, when water failed them' during the burning, had been found 'when an English traveler dug up some of the ground last year'. As a less reliable piece of information, he added that it was also said that 'an American gentleman found a gold ring in the house of Njal'. These semi-archaeologists at Bergþórshvoll can be seen as acting out the scene from *Njáls saga* (Ch. 132) which takes place soon after the burning of Berþórshvoll. The fugitive Kári and his ally, Hjalti Skeggjason, come to the site of the burning to dig out Njáll and his family from under a large heap of ashes. Miraculously, the bodies of Njáll, his wife Bergþóra, and their grandson are found intact under an ox-hide, and after examining the corpses Hjalti comments: 'The body of Bergþóra looks as it was likely she would look, and still fair; but Njall's body and visage seem to me so bright that I have never seen any dead man's body so bright as this.'

Other examples could be quoted, but I have focused on accounts of the tomb of Gunnar and the site of Bergþórshvoll since these places supply us with an illuminating image of the Victorian interest in *Njáls saga* as a point of destination. In reference to Morris' poem, quoted above, we might say that many British saga travelers were driven to Iceland by an urge to enter the 'tomb of time past'. As Susan Bassnett (1993: 106) has highlighted, Morris himself 'is an example of what can be termed the 'idealistic traveller', the utopian socialist aesthete who had already created an Iceland of the imagination that he went in homage to visit'. His ultimate destination were the hinterlands of history, not yet polluted by the ugliness of modern life (cf. Faulkner, 1980: x). From this perspective, the British Victorian appetite for Iceland was a part of a widespread interest – shared by the Romantics, the Pre-Raphaelites, and others – in the Middle Ages as an alternative to the industrialised nineteenth century.

The travelers' identification with Hjalti and Kári at the site of the burning appears to have been already projected in *The Story of Burnt Njal*. In the preface, Dasent (1861: 1:xviii) thanked the publishers for having 'spared no expense or pains to lay Njal before the world in a beautiful and becoming shape'. Dasent (1861: 1:xix) also expressed his gratitude to everyone else who had enabled him 'to send Njal out into the world with a smiling face'. This habit of referring to the translation as 'Njal' himself might, of course, be taken as a humorous figure of speech, but it can also be read as an echo of Hjalti's description of Njáll's radiant corpse. In this context, we may want to uncover a new level in Dasent's (1861: 1:xx) discussion of foster-fathering, in which he claimed that he had taken the text of the saga 'from the house of

Icelandic scholars' and 'reared and fostered' it for so many years 'under an English roof'. Bergþórshvoll, Dasent implied, was only the first of many structures from which the body of 'Burnt Njal' had been recovered.

Burnt Njal and the British Empire

Apart from its concern with British tourism in the nineteenth century, *The Story of Burnt Njal* can be placed within the tradition of nineteenth-century British literature on Iceland. The comments of people like Burton and King have given reason to assume that Dasent's work soon became a canonised text within that tradition. But while such an accomplishment must have pleased the translator, his objective was clearly more ambitious. Arguing for the authenticity of *Njáls saga*, Dasent (1861: 1:vii) claimed in his preface: 'Much passes for history in other lands on far slighter grounds, and many a story in Thucydides or Tacitus or even in Clarendon or Hume is believed on evidence not one-tenth part so trustworthy as that which supports the narratives' of the sagas. While his overt message was that one could just as well distrust some well-known historians as the evidence of *Njáls saga*, Dasent was indirectly claiming a place for his work (translation and commentary) on the Victorian bookshelf, next to canonised histories of Western civilisation. Collectively, the four historians mentioned had written the histories of Ancient Greece (Thucydides), the Roman Empire, and the Ancient Germans (Tacitus), as well as the history of Great Britain from Caesar's time to the Civil Wars (David Hume and Edward Hyde Clarendon). To this impressive table, Dasent wanted to add his own name and the history of medieval Iceland.

It is difficult to discuss Dasent's ambitions without over-simplifying a complex historical discourse. We may start our inquiry by noting how the British rewriters of the saga associated its characters and their morals with the heroes of Ancient Greece. Initiating this tradition, Dasent (1861: 1:clxxv–clxxvi) characterised the Icelanders as combining 'in a wonderful degree, the dash, and daring, and genius of the Athenian, with the deliberate valour and mother wit of the Spartan mind'. In the same spirit, Dasent (1861: 1:cxcix) called Flosi Skeggjason 'an Icelandic Ulysses'. His point, it seems, was that *The Story of Burnt Njal* contained superb models of behavior, fully comparable to the ones provided by Ancient Greek literature. Some of Dasent's reviewers were even more enthusiastic over this issue. Alexander Nicolson (1861: 297–301) compared Skarphéðinn to 'the Homeric Achæan', even to 'Achilles himself', he also refered to Hallgerður as 'the Helen of this

Northern prose epic', and characterised one of the battles in the saga as 'a most Homeric scene of cutting and thrusting'. Robert Lowe was no less pointed in his discussion. Gunnar, Lowe (1861: 224–25) wrote, goes on a viking expedition 'with as little notion of any evil in such calling as the Pylian Nestor himself, when he asks Telemachus whether he is a pirate'; later, when Gunnar returns to Hlíðarendi, instead of going abroad as an outlaw, he is 'Ulysses rejecting the offer of Calypso'. Such a comparison between the works of Homer and *Njáls saga* became a topos in the writings of the Victorians, coinciding with a much wider definition of medieval Iceland as the northern equivalent to Ancient Greece. The Icelanders, in this context, were typically conceived of as superb representatives of the Vikings, who, in Andrew Lang's (1891: 142) words, 'lived like Odysseus, the hero of Homer, and were equally skilled in the arts of war and peace'.

André Lefevere (1992: 77) has observed that a successful construction of an image of a literary work in a foreign literary system often depends on the rewriters' ability to find an appropriate 'slot' in the system's poetics; as a ploy for cultural acceptance, they tend to rewrite the alien text 'in terms of a system their potential audience [is] able to understand'. The prestige enjoyed by ancient Greek literature applied Victorian saga rewriters with suitable models for such an analogy. For centuries, the study of Latin and Greek had been the basis of European educational tradition; Greece being defined as the cradle of Western civilisation (cf. Clarke, 1959; Jenkyns, 1980). According to Frank M. Turner's (1981: 1) study of the Greek heritage in Britain, this sense was so firmly established in the early nineteenth-century, that a list of 'poets, critics, philosophers, historians and scholars concerned at one time or another with the Greeks reads like an index of the major contributors to the intellectual life of the age'.

But the Homeric analogy only reveals one side of Dasent's historical contextualisation of *Njáls saga* within British Victorian culture. Ideas regarding the racial origins of the British people also deserve special attention. In the Middle Ages, the discourse in that field had been influenced by various accounts relating how the Trojans had founded Britain in antiquity. While the historical credibility of such a myth was undermined in the sixteenth and the seventeenth century, its essence survived through the nineteenth-century discipline of comparative philology. With linguists associating Sanskrit, Persian, Greek, Latin, Celtic, Teutonic, Slavic and other languages under the term 'Aryan', it was surely possible for British intellectuals to see themselves – linguistically at least – related to the heroes of Homer. More importantly, however, this new science of language instigated the alternate racial myth of a Teutonic or an Anglo-Saxon origin of the Englishmen. Ideas of that kind had been developing in Britain even since the sixteenth century, but according to Hugh A. MacDougall (1982: 2) it had four postulates in its most developed form:

(1) Germanic peoples, on account of their unmixed origins and universal civilising mission, are inherently superior to all others, both in individual character and in their institutions.
(2) The English are, in the main, of Germanic origin, and their history begins with the landing of Hengist and Horsa at Ebbsfield, Kent, in 449.
(3) The qualities which render English political and religious institutions the freest in the world are an inheritance from Germanic forefathers.
(4) The English, better than any other Germanic people, represent the traditional genius of their ancestors and thereby carry a special burden of leadership in the world community.

To a substantial degree, this theory was adopted from German fifteenth- and sixteenth-century humanists who, in return, had founded their argument of German racial superiority on Tacitus' *Germania,* in which the purity and virtues of the Germanic races were contrasted with the degeneration of the Roman Empire. In early sixteenth-century English paraphrases, scholars like Richard Verstegen set out to demonstrate how the German nation was 'the Tree from which English men, as a most stately and flourishing branch, are issued and sprung forth' (MacDougall, 1982: 47).

One primary question which the English advocates of these racial ideas had to confront concerned the influence of the Norman conquest of Britain in 1066 and the Danish conquest that preceded it. Had not the Normans and the Scandinavians changed the Saxon (German) character of England? In his 1605 *Restitution of Decayed Intelligence,* Verstegen had addressed the issue by claiming, on the one hand, that the Normans and the Danes had been few in respect to the English and, on the other hand, that the Normans and the Danes were initially Vikings of a German descent (MacDougall, 1982: 48). In the following decades, this argument was echoed by numerous historians and laymen, and by the mid-eighteenth century, the distinguished Germanic origin of the English people had become an accepted fact. Cultivated by scholarly work in comparative linguistics, the political theories of Montesquieu and Hume and the historiography of Kant and then made manifest in Britain's imperial success, the power of the 'Teutomania' on the Victorians was so significant that one of its contemporary critics, Luke Owen Pike, affirmed in 1866 that there were

> probably few educated Englishmen living who have not, from their infancy, been taught that the English nation is a nation of almost pure Teutonic blood, that its political constitution, its social customs, its internal prosperity, the success of its arms and the number of its colonies have all followed necessarily upon the arrival, in three vessels, of certain German warriors under the command of Hengist and Horsa. (MacDougall, 1982: 91)

This summary must suffice as a background to the racial aspects of Dasent's translation. While the Ancient Classics were conceived of as a significant thread in Victorian culture, being a part of a nineteenth-century 'Western' canon of World Literature, Dasent presented *Njáls saga* as having immediate relevance to the history of Britain and the racial affinity of its folk. In a significantly Hegelian–Darwinian spirit, Dasent (1861: 1:ix–x) saw history as a continuous 'march of civilisation and progress'; following Verstegen, he dealt with the Danes and the Normans in British history by assuming them to be descended from a common Germanic root, and he celebrated their influence on the Saxons, 'who were losing their old dash and daring and settling down into a sluggish sensual race'. Like many other conquerors, Dasent (1861: 1:clxxxiv) suggested, they had infused 'a new life into the community' and left it 'with the best particles of their nature'. In this context, the Icelandic saga heroes were made to represent those 'best particles' which the English had inherited from the Vikings and the Normans. After describing everyday life in Medieval Iceland and the reputation of the Icelanders abroad, Dasent (1861: 1:clxxvi–clxxx) asserted, for instance, that they had been regarded as the first and foremost of the Scandinavian race:

> They were man by man, unit by unit, what their kinsmen in Normandy became afterwards as a nation, – bold as lions, but wary as foxes, tough as the ash, but pliant as the bow; no feat was too daring for their courage to attempt, and no race in any time, whether ancient or modern, has ever shown greater aptness in suiting themselves, at the shortest notice, to the peculiar circumstances of every case.

The description of this 'fittest' of races continues, but the quotation should indicate how Dasent's rhetoric, notwithstanding his 'old Njal', was designed to refresh the good influence of the Vikings on the Victorians.

Some of Dasent's reviewers heartily shared his historical/ethnological view of the saga. Hannah Lawrence (1861: 333) contended that 'the gallant Northman was no unworthy representative of that race to whom we ourselves owe so much'. With even greater enthusiasm, Alexander Nicolson (1861: 295) traced in the character and the deeds of Britain's worthies – contemporary men of courage, displaying 'fearlessness against odds', 'trustiness', 'invincible endurance', and brotherhood – 'the same staff of manhood, the same features of a race born to rule land and sea by force of valour joined to wisdom, as found nine centuries ago in the vales of Rangriver and on the banks of the Markfleet'. That conviction, with its striking imperialistic implications, inspired him to enter into a lengthy discussion of the Saxon, the Celtic and the Norse/Danish streams of British blood. Even though Nicolson (1861: 295) was aware that such analysis was 'apt to run into nonsense', he stressed that the Vikings had planted the 'seed' of the Victorians' 'highest intelligence and power', most significantly 'the regal force', which was the foundation of the British Empire: 'It has sent our explorers to cut their way to new worlds, or die; our bold adventurers to build up states and civil order in the primeval wilds; our great captains to carry the old 'meteor-flag' triumphant through the smoke of a thousand battles.'

Captain Speedy

In this chapter, some possible motivations for the Victorian tour of 'Njal's Country' have been offered. It has been suggested that readers of *The Story of Burnt Njal* may have used the work to 'sail' to Iceland without ever leaving their living-rooms, spending less time, effort and money than the regular traveler. At the same time, the saga translation might have generated an increasing 'expenditure'. If not ending up literally as a tourist in Iceland, the reader of, let us say, Hannah Lawrence's review was perhaps tempted to continue the quest, first by reading Dasent's translation, and later by buying further travel accounts or picture-books enabling him or her to visualise the Icelandic setting. The rewriting of *Njáls saga*, from this perspective, formed a part of a complex commercial enterprise.

As Henry Holland observed in his 1861 review of Captain Forbes' book on Iceland, the tour to this land of hot springs, volcanoes and sagas somewhat mirrored Victorian travel in Greece. Athens, Marathon and Corinth were simply replaced by Geysir, Hekla and Þingvellir (cf. Aho, 1993: 207). Similarly, the interest in the Icelandic past was in many ways comparable to the British conception of

Ancient Greek culture. What made the Nordic 'Vikings' of *Njáls saga* surpass even the heroes of Homer as a suitable source of inspiration was their assumed cultural and racial ties with the British people. In this context, we may recall the excavation at Bergþórshvoll and see it as an image of the Victorian quest for racial and cultural roots. Through the tradition of *Njáls saga,* the British Empire was commemorating and reviving 'those who gave it birth'. Hannah Lawrence (1861: 349) suggested that the saga could be read as an illustration 'of the state of society among us during the earlier portion of the Middle Ages'. Specifically, Lawrence (1861: 337) said that the chapter of the saga dealing with Gunnar's voyages (Ch. 30) read 'wonderfully like one in the history of our early voyagers. The same delight in danger, the same reckless bravery, the same uprightness and generosity.' Alexander Nicolson similarly interpreted Skarphéðinn Njálsson's reaction to the expected death of his family in the burning of Bergþórshvoll in terms of British history. After quoting Skarphéðinn's words – 'it befits us surely more than other men to bear us well, and it is only what is looked for from us' – Nicolson (1861: 303) asked his readers: 'Doesn't that remind one of another Njalson and his 'England expects'?' Skarphéðinn, in this context, became the true ancestor of Captain Nelson.

The publication and the reception of *The Story of Burnt Njal* in nineteenth-century Britain reveals how myths of the past are used as a validation of contemporary ideology. Illuminating, if somewhat humorous, are the final words of Andrew Lang's (1891: 151–52) essay, 'The Sagas', in which he speculated on how the fame of the old Icelandic heroes had widened year by year:

> For the story of Njal and Gunnar and Skarphedin was told by Captain Speedy to the guards of Theodore, King of Abyssinia. They liked it well; and with queer altered names and changes of the tale, that Saga will be told in Abyssinia and thence carried all through Africa where white men have never wandered. So wide, so long-enduring a renown could be given by a nameless Sagaman.

The recitation of *Njáls saga,* Lang exhibits, was inseparable from the European ('Aryan') colonist quest. As Edward W. Said (1979: 12) has detailed, that quest was not 'a mere political subject matter' but rather 'a *distribution* of geopolitical awareness into aesthetic, scholarly, economic, sociological, historical and philological contexts'. If the 'white man', our Captain Speedy, was (despite his name) not able to colonise all of Africa soon enough, his cultural heritage was, at least, going to colonise the African mind. In *Heroes of Iceland,* Allen French's

(1905) rewriting of Dasent's translation, which is the topic of Chapter 3, similar and related ideological concerns are at stake. These, however, are inseparable from French's interest in adapting the Victorian translation towards the reading conventions of his American audience.

Chapter 3

'American' Heroes

Abridgement and Immigration

Late in his life, writer Allen French (1951: 133) recalled how a 'curious chance' had once taken him into the Old Corner Bookstore. There, from a pile of second-hand books, he picked up a volume

> with the curious title of *The Story of Burnt Njal.* The first two pages were enough to fascinate me with a glimpse of life in Iceland a thousand years ago. I bought the book for twenty-five cents, recast it as *Heroes of Iceland,* and after much reading of other sagas, wrote what I suppose is my best Icelandic book, *The Story of Rolf and the Viking's Bow.*

A native of Massachusetts, French had started his writing career by producing several juvenile novels. These included *Sir Marraok: A Tale of the Days of King Arthur* (1902) and *The Colonials* (1902), which deals with the siege of Boston in 1775–1776. This interest in the Middle Ages and history may account for French's positive response to George Webbe Dasent's *The Story of Burnt Njal.* As detailed in Chapter 2, it was originally published in an expensive two-volume edition in Edinburgh in 1861. In 1900, the work was reissued in Britain and the U.S. in a new single-volume edition, with Dasent's extensive preface, introduction and appendices condensed, but the translation itself was left intact. French continued this process of adaptation in his *Heroes of Iceland* (1905) by rewriting Dasent's (already abridged) preface and introduction, partially restructuring the narrative, and making it considerably shorter than the source text. A few years later French also released *Grettir the Strong* (1908), an abridgement of William Morris' and Eiríkur Magnússon's translation of another eminent family saga.

French's work with the sagas can be approached from several different angles. In Chapter 1, it was noted how he belonged to a diverse group of mostly Scandinavian, German and British writers and artists who, in the nineteenth and the early twentieth century, discovered Icelandic medieval literature as a source of inspiration. Richard Wagner's *Der Ring der Niebelungen* in Germany, Henrik Ibsen's historical plays in Norway, Rider Haggard's *Eric the Bright-eyed*, and William Morris's *The Lovers of Gudrun* in Britain; these are only a few titles in a massive but now somewhat obsolete corpus, frequently reflecting the ideological concerns of the authors. But from a different and a poetical perspective, *Heroes of Iceland* can also be studied as a case of abridgement, being one of innumerable simplified versions of the so-called World Literature.

Njáls Saga as a Great Epic

In a preface to *The Story Rolf and the Viking's Bow*, Allen French (1904: vii) lamented that the reading of 'translations of the Icelandic sagas', which had appeared in Victorian Britain, had 'so completely gone out of style that their names are rarely mentioned in schools or even colleges. What boy feels his blood stir at the mention of Grettir?' His saga rewritings were intended to respond to that turn of taste and to bring the sagas back into style. In the case of *The Story of Rolf*, a novel inspired by *Orkneyinga Sǫga* and some other early Icelandic narratives, French (cf. 1905: 299) followed the style of his earlier juvenile works, which had been consciously written for 'boys'. The implied readership of *Heroes of Iceland* was not so precisely defined, but it was distinctly different from Dasent's Victorian audience.

French's pursuit as a rewriter can be marked in the title of his work. *Heroes of Iceland* carries a sense quite different from Dasent's title, postulating a narrative of heroic deeds in opposition to the tragic, even horrific idea of 'Burnt Njal'. The significance of this difference was further spelled out in French's (1905: viii) preface, in which he presented *Njáls saga* not only as the greatest of the Icelandic sagas, but as a story 'which is to be compared, in interest and beauty, with the great epics of the earlier races'. The qualifications of these great epics were spelled out by French (1905: viii): 'Each of them tells of the distant past of some race or nation and so expresses the heroic period of the youth of the world. And while, from age to age, the world renewed its youth through the uprising of some new race, one of these great stories would rise into life.' This line of universal renewal and heroic narratives, French (1905: viii–ix) added, ran unbroken in history from ancient Greece, which produced the *Iliad* and the *Odyssey*, through the Roman *Aeneid*, the German *Niebelungenlied*, the French narratives of Charlemagne and Roland, and the Arthurian Romances: 'Each of these nations made an imperishable book concerning its own national heroes.' French's objective was 'to add to these great stories yet another', to place the heroes of Iceland next to the heroes of Greece, Rome, Germany, France and Britain.

By choosing the title *Heroes of Iceland*, French obviously wanted to equate a relatively unknown Icelandic text with works or traditions which his audience knew and accepted. Such a process of poetic codification is important for the various forms of rewriting (cf. Lefevere, 1992: 27), but it proved a little tricky in the case of *Njáls saga*. French (1905: ix–x) realised at least that a careful reasoning was needed to convince his readership that *Njáls saga* was comparable to canonised texts such as the *Iliad* and the stories of King Arthur. He began his appeal by listing seven primary characteristics of the great epics. These were:

(1) majesty of theme,
(2) heroic grandeur in the personages,
(3) a portrayal of what is highest in human nature,
(4) a great catastrophe,
(5) poetic justice,
(6) unity of conception and action, and
(7) beauty of power and expression.

French doubted that any book would meet all these qualifications but he warranted that, on the whole, *Njáls saga* would pass the test of a great epic.

At the outset, he explained that, while history had acquired a mythical dimension in the other great stories, *Njáls saga* was basically an accurate account of Iceland's early heroes. Written relatively shortly after the events which it describes took place, French (1905: xiii–xiv) claimed, it was mostly deprived of the 'romantic and delightful' elements of traditional epics. This did not mean that the saga was deprived of (1) majesty of theme, only that it depended 'for its interest upon truly human men and women, and upon very natural conditions'. With regard to (2) heroic grandeur in the personages, French (1905: xiv) was able to point out more compelling analogues: 'Gunnar is an Achilles who depends upon himself'; 'Njal is a Nestor who neither prattles nor boasts'; and with them, 'there are other noble figures, man for man equal with the heroes of the Trojan war, whether in personal courage or greatness of soul – Skarphedinn, Kari, even Flosi himself'. Furthermore, French (1905: xv) suggested that the saga displayed (3) what was highest (and lowest) in human nature, 'whether it be pride, affection, love, hate, revenge, spite, avarice, friendship, ambition'. He was also proud to proclaim that the saga was tragic, supplying in the burning of Njáll's farm, in the second part of the saga, (4) the grand catastrophe 'which the definition requires' (French, 1905: xv).

As far as the remaining three categories were concerned, the argument became more ambiguous. Addressing (5) poetic justice, French (1905: xvi) emphasised, for instance, that the idea of justice and the growth of law were predominant in the saga and correctly pointed out that 'we see the atonement of foes' at the end of the book. However, he conveniently refrained from mentioning that the villainous character of Mörður Valgarðsson never gets just retribution. Furthermore, French (1905: xv–xvi) claimed that even though the plot of the saga was doubly centred around (a) the life of Gunnar Hámundarson and (b) the fortunes of Njáll Þorgeirsson's family, (6) unity of action was preserved,

> for while the numerous characters and incidents give constantly shifting interest, the main lines of the narrative are skilfully maintained, and the story as a whole is so complete that, stripped of the genealogies which earlier ages demanded, the action of the book is continuous and of great interest.

It is interesting to compare this statement – especially the reference to the 'stripping of the genealogies' – to another paragraph in French's (1905: xxxvi) introduction where he announced his agenda as a rewriter:

> Clearness of meaning and continuity of narrative have been the sole aims. Only so much of genealogy has been retained as is of direct interest. Irrelevant episodes . . . , as well as many minor incidents, have been omitted; many of the verses (mostly regarded as spurious) have been cut out; and little beside the main narrative has been retained. Most of the accounts of trials, and much of the legal phrasing in the great suit for the Burning, have also been omitted.

Clearly, the problem with Dasent's translation of *Njáls saga* was that it did not have the required unity of action. In this respect, French's abridgement was initially designed to make the saga correspond better to the other great epics. [They, of course, were also circulating in various rewritten forms (cf. Lefevere, 1992: 87–98)].

Finally, referring to (7) the text's power and expression, French (1905: xvii) felt compelled to admit that the saga's language was rather plain, lacking 'the poetic passages of Homer, or the beauty of such scenes as that in the Morte Darthur, where Palamides [sic] accounts to Tristram for his conduct toward Isoud'. Defensively, French (1905: xx) stressed, however, that the style never offended 'good taste' and explained that, in contrast to the poetic dignity of the other epics, the saga was dramatic, 'like a play of the modern kind, in which the speeches are brief and pithy and the stage directions few. Yet, its force is undeniable.'

To sum up, the preface to *Heroes of Iceland* prepared those who had never read an Icelandic saga for that experience. It formatted their expectations ('this is a great epic') and gave warnings about the points where the saga departed from the traditional poetic code (more dramatic, less poetic, historical rather than mythical). More importantly, in an attempt to integrate the saga into an accepted literary canon, French's abridgement tailored the saga in accordance with his definition of a great epic.

Sigmundur's Head

In order to exemplify Allen French's agenda as a rewriter, let us compare Chapter 45 of *The Story of Burnt Njal*, entitled 'The Slaying of Sigmund and Skiolld', to the analogous text of *Heroes of Iceland*. Through this comparison, we will see how French's claim about the saga's style, its dramatic qualities, and its assumed unity of action are reinforced through his abridgement. For those not familiar with *Njáls saga*, it should be noted that Chapter 45 is the last of eleven consecutive chapters devoted to disputes between Hallgerður Höskuldsdóttir, the wife of Gunnar Hámundarson, and Bergþóra Skarphéðinsdóttir, the wife of Njáll Þorgeirsson. After being offended by Bergþóra, Hallgerður sends Kolur, one of her farm-hands, to kill Svartur, one of Bergþóra's farm-hands. Gunnar pays Njáll a fine for the atonement of Svartur's death, but Bergþóra is not satisfied until another of her farm-hands has killed Kolur in revenge. Despite their husbands' protest, the two women continue the feud, finally resulting in the death of Gunnar's kinsman Sigmundur Lambason and Sigmundur's partner, Skjöldur, who are killed by Njáll's sons.

In *Heroes of Iceland*, the slaying of Sigmundur and Skjöldur completes a chapter titled 'The Friendship of Gunnar and Njal', which covers the disputes of Hallgerður and Bergþóra and the repeated reconciliation between their husbands. Such condensation of chapters is characteristic of French's rewriting; Dasent's translation, contains 158 chapters while *Heroes of Iceland* has only 25. Chapter 45 in *The Story of Burnt Njal* starts with the following paragraph:

> *Now they, Njal's sons,* fare up to Fleetlithe, and were that night under the Lithe, and when the day began to break, they *came near to Lithend.* That same morning, both Sigmund and Skiolld rose up and meant to go to the stud-horses; they had bits with them and caught the horses that were in the 'town' and rode away on them. They found the stud-horses between two brooks. Skarphedinn caught sight of them for *Sigmund was in bright clothing. Skarphedinn said, 'See you now the red elf yonder, lads?'* They looked that way and said they saw him.
>
> Skarphedinn spoke again: 'Thou, Hauskuld, shalt have nothing to do with it, for thou wilt often be sent about alone without due heed; but *I mean Sigmund for myself;* methinks that is like a man; *but* Grim and Helgi, they *shall try to slay Skiolld.'* (Dasent, 1861: 1:141–42; my emphasis)

French's (1905: 37–38) description is significantly shorter but, as emphasised in the text above, most of his text comes directly from Dasent:

> Now they, Njal's sons, slept that night in the open, and at morning came near to Lithend. There they saw Sigmund and Skiolld among the horses; Sigmund had on bright clothing, and Skarphedinn said: 'See you now the red elf yonder, lads? I mean him for myself, but you two shall try to slay Skiolld.'

By comparing the two paragraphs, we notice how *The Story of Burnt Njal's* elaborate narrative presumably creates more anticipation for the readers than the straight-forward account of *Heroes of Iceland;* the deleted details of Sigmundur's and Skjöldur's encounter with the horses are symptomatic of the 'minor incidents' which French omits in order to maintain 'clearness of meaning and continuity of narrative'.

In the consequent description of the fight between the two parties, French adheres to Dasent's text more closely, only leaving out certain items relating to Sigmundur's attire. The focal point of the narrative remains Skarphéðinn's killing of Sigmundur, which French preserves almost without making any changes (variations from Dasent are shown in square brackets):

> Skarphedinn cleft the shoulder-blade right through, and at the same time pulled the axe towards him. Sigmund fell down on both knees, but sprang up again at once.
>
> 'Thou hast bowed [lilted] low to me already,' says Skarphedinn, 'but still thou shalt fall [up]on thy mother's bosom ere we two part.'

'Ill is that then,' says Sigmund.

Skarphedinn gave him a blow on his helm, and after that gave [dealt] Sigmund his death-blow.

Grim cut off Skiolld's foot at the ankle-joint, but Helgi thrust him through with his spear, and Skiolld [he] got his death there and then. (French, 1905: 38–39; Dasent, 1861: 1:143)

We may recall, in this context, that French compared the saga in his preface to 'a play of the modern kind, in which the speeches are brief and pithy and the stage directions few'. This statement could be used to characterise *The Story of Burnt Njal*, but it applies even better to *Heroes of Iceland*, in which certain dramatic scenes (i.e. the killing of Sigmundur and Skjöldur) are singled out.

As far as the language is concerned, French made one very interesting change in the paragraph quoted above, replacing the term 'lilted' in Skarphéðinn's speech with the word 'bowed'. It needs to be recalled here that Dasent himself had been eager to demonstrate that the Vikings and the British Victorians were of the same cultural and racial origin. This eagerness was clearly revealed in the preface to his translation of Erasmus Rask's (1843: vii) *A Grammar of the Icelandic Old Norse Tongue*, in which the study of Old Norse was presented 'as an accessory help for the English student, . . . not only in tracing the rise of words and idioms, but still more in clearing up many dark points in our early history'. This inclination encouraged Dasent to find English expressions for his translation of *Njáls saga* that were etymologically, or at least phonologically, related to the original expressions. With 'lilted' he was translating the Icelandic verb 'lúta', appearing in the context of the saga in the past tense 'laustu' (Olavius, 1844: 104). Although French had no objections to certain English archaisms like 'ere' and 'shalt', he seems to have suspected that 'lilted' would unsettle his American readers. Other similar examples can be found throughout his version.

Before leaving the corpses of Sigmundur and Skjöldur, we should notice the sentence that concludes this scene in *Heroes of Iceland*: 'Skarphedinn sent the news to Hallgerda.' With these six words, French (1905: 39) summarised a page-long account in Dasent (1861: 144–45), in which Skarphéðinn hands the head of Sigmundur to a shepherd, who happens to be nearby, and asks him to give the head to his mistress, Hallgerður. When Njáll's sons have left him, the shepherd casts the head down on the ground, but nonetheless goes to Hlíðarendi to tell Hallgerður about the killings. She is disappointed when she learns that the shepherd has left Sigmundur's head behind:

'I would have brought it to Gunnar, and then he would have avenged his kinsman or have to bear every man's blame', says Hallgerður.

Like the shepherd, French leaves Sigmundur's head behind when he presents the killing of Sigmundur and Skjöldur to his American audience. We can only guess his reasons. From one perspective, it is possible to see this account as being one of the 'irrelevant episodes' which, in French's view, encumber the course of the action. On the other hand, he must have recognised the dramatic qualities of this scene and its importance in demonstrating how the disputes of Bergþóra and Hallgerður threaten to ruin the friendship of Gunnar and Njáll. Perhaps French had something more in common with the shepherd, who told Hallgerður that he dared not bring the head, 'for I knew not how thou wouldst like that' (Dasent, 1861: 144). French, we may assume, complied in this case with the pledge in his preface, in which he guaranteed that the style of the saga never offended 'good taste'.

But French was not only preoccupied with literary genres and the canon. As implied by his treatment of Sigmundur's head, he was also very concerned with the reading conventions of his prospective audience. Such concerns are generally the primary motive of abridgement and need to be viewed in reference to some ideas of why and how we read.

'Stripping' a Saga

In *The Pleasure of the Text*, Roland Barthes (1975: 10–11) suggests that 'we do not read everything with the same intensity of reading'; we establish our own rhythm, 'unconcerned with the *integrity* of the text':

> Our very avidity for knowledge impels us to skim or to skip certain passages (anticipated as 'boring') in order to get more quickly to the warmer parts of the anecdote (which are always its articulations: whatever furthers the solution of the riddle, the revelation of fate): we boldly skip (no one is watching) descriptions, explanations, analyses, conversations.

It is tempting to characterise *Heroes of Iceland* as such a performed or documented reading. French skips 'boring' passages from *The Story of Burnt Njal* and retains 'the warmer' parts. It was on this ground, French (1905: xxxvii) asserted in his introduction: 'the present edition contains everything of real interest, in a story without halt, or repetition, or irrelevancy.'

In his habitual playful manner, Barthes (1975: 11) compares the pleasure of reading to the pleasure of the corporeal striptease, proposing that, when we skim or skip certain passages of a narrative, 'we resemble a spectator in a nightclub who climbs onto the stage and speeds up the dancer's striptease, tearing off her clothing'. Most certainly, French did envision himself as a rewriter in that situation. However, it is worth noting that French (1905: xv) not only used the term *strip* for the act of abridgement ('stripped of the genealogies'), but also promoted his version of the saga as an 'attractive' text, hardly to be resisted. That latter sense was already conveyed in the first paragraph of the preface, in which French (1905: vii) asserted that the book contained 'a story of such interest and beauty that, after an existence of more than forty years in its English dress, it is here presented in an abridged form with full confidence in both its charm and its value'.

Clearly, the 'dress' metaphor just quoted is highly formulaic. Theo Hermans (1985: 114) has, for instances, traced some of its variants in a study of the renaissance discourse on translation where translating was often portrayed 'as exchanging the sumptuous garb of the original for a rough and homespun garment'. The underlying idea, Hermans (1985: 120) points out, is 'the view of language in which form and substance, words and meaning ... can be separated'. It is possible that, by referring to the saga's English dress, French was deliberately echoing a comment in the preface to *The Story of Burnt Njal*, 'which we', as Dasent (1861: vi) put it, 'lay before our readers in an English garb'. But while Dasent's other metaphors suggested that his readers would symbolically recover the intact corpse of 'old Njal' (the meaning/substance of the saga) from beneath a great heap of ashes at the site of the burning, French promoted the saga more as a charming woman, originally introduced to an English-speaking audience in Dasent's Victorian attire. 'Unfortunately,' French (1905: xxxv) specified, 'the special Icelandic genius for genealogy has so overlaid the story with what the modern reader considers non-essentials that, in the original translation, the thread of the narrative is easily lost'. For this reason, he felt compelled to simplify the saga, deprive it beforehand of all non-essentials, making 'the thread of the narrative' more distinguishable.

But what hopes did he expect to arouse in the readers of *Heroes of Iceland*? First of all, French (1905: xxi) warranted, it 'tells a good story':

> The tale stirs the blood, it shows us people who are of perpetual interest and who become our intimates – friends in whose company we easily forget ourselves. The claim has not been idly made

> that 'some of the best fighting in literature is to be found between its covers.' Once we have tasted the flavor of the story, it tempts us on to the end: it lingers with us afterward, and we return to it periodically. It is individual, attractive, stirring.

Judging from this paragraph, the American rewriter knew how to excite his (male) audience. The reading, French proposed, was to be an enjoyable physical experience – the story stirs the blood, the reader tastes its flavour, its lingers with him afterward. Between its covers, he will acquire intimate friends in whose company he will forget himself. Last, but not least, this seductive narrative will tempt the reader to read to the very end (contrary to the 'overlaid' *Story of Burnt Njal*); and he will return to it periodically.

Irrespective of its sexist implications, Barthes' (1975: 12) analysis of reading which 'goes straight to the articulation of the anecdote', characterises French's agenda as a rewriter. The implied reader of *Heroes of Iceland* reads for the plot: a good story is 'without halt, or repetition, or irrelevancy'; a good reading is a pleasurable and fulfilling experience. But there does exist a different system of reading, says Barthes (1975: 12), a reading that 'skips nothing; it weighs, it sticks to the text, ... grasps at every point in the text the asyndeton which cuts the various languages'. Similarly, French acknowledged that it can be fascinating to read an unabridged version of *Njáls saga,* to skip nothing, not even the genealogies. The difference is that, while Barthes' (1975: 14) second system of reading is suited to the modern text – a narrative 'that discomforts (perhaps to the point of a certain boredom), unsettles the reader's historical, cultural, psychological assumptions' – French's (1905: xxxv) second system was suited to *Njáls saga* as an ancient text:

> It must be admitted that the genealogies are of great historic value, and that the instinct for their preservation is a true one. There is really a curious fascination in the subject: the present writer found himself constructing genealogical tables, very carefully comparing all the authorities at his disposal and wishing that Dasent, with his so much greater facilities, had done the same earlier.

In both cases, the reader has to be active in producing meaning. However, while French's close reading aims at reconstructing the historical sense of the text, Barthes' close reading aims at a state of loss, even confusion. French's alternative is historical knowledge, Barthes' a state of textual bliss.

French (1905: xxxvi) concluded his discussion of the genealogies by stating that the differences between Iceland's medieval audience and Dasent's modern readers had 'prevented the popularity of the saga'. In his estimation, there were not many readers interested in the saga as a historical document (and, in this pre-Barthean period, even fewer interested in it as a source of textual bliss). While *The Story of Burnt Njal* was most probably going to unsettle the reading habits of the general American readership, or, in any case, not provide it with the textual pleasure it was used to, *Heroes of Iceland* would do the job.

Heroes of the United States

Before we part with Roland Barthes, it should be noted that his ambiguous comparison of the pleasure of corporeal striptease and narrative suspense initially serves the purpose of characterising the intellectual and psychological energy invested in the act of reading. In both instances, Barthes (1975: 10) argues, we are dealing with 'an Oedipal pleasure (to denude, to know, to learn the origin and the end), if it is true that every narrative (every unveiling of the truth) is a staging of the (absent, hidden, or hypostatised) father'. In his study, *Reading for the Plot,* Peter Brooks (1992: 111) makes a corresponding claim, suggesting that it may be revealing to analyse narrative desire in view of Sigmund Freud's discussion of the compulsion of repetition, our psychological desire to remember and re-enact earlier (often traumatic) experience, to 'replay time, so that it may not be lost'. This desire takes many forms, but within the great tradition of the nineteenth-century novel (from Turgenev's *Fathers and Sons,* to Shelley's *Frankenstein,* from Dickens's *Great Expectations* to Stendhal's *The Red and the Black*), 'paternity is a dominant issue' (Brooks, 1992: 63).

The British Victorian concern with *Njáls saga,* discussed in Chapter 2, coincides with this preoccupation of many nineteenth-century novelists and their followers (e.g. Joyce, Mann, Faulkner) with paternity. By encountering 'old Njal' in Dasent's English garb, the Victorian reader was supposed to unearth the mystery of his biological and cultural origins, to identify in Icelandic Vikings 'the regal force' characteristic of the British Empire. Even as Allen French claimed that the plot of the saga was overlaid with historical data, he followed Dasent in this respect by defining *Njáls saga* as a narrative (however attractive and tempting) about paternity. *Heroes of Iceland,* French (1905: xxi) argued,

> shows us our part-ancestor, the Norseman, as he was in his

> natural surroundings. We see his command of the sea, his habits on the land, his religion, both the old and the new, and his customs and laws. Because he was what he was, we are today, in part, what we are: for he represents, with slight differences, all the old nations of Teutonic stock, and in this picture of him, the modern Scandinavian, Englishman, German and native-born American can see the strength of the root from which they spring.

There are several levels to be observed in this paragraph, but, as a starting point, we may recall French's discussion of the great epics, in which some new race would express 'the heroic period of the youth of the world'. The emphasis on the ancestry of the 'native' American suggests that *Heroes of Iceland* might – 'with slight differences' – serve as a great epic for the United States. The Americans extended the chronological and geographical line of the earlier great epics, they were the 'race' that had most recently 'renewed the world's youth'. The problem was that it lacked both a truly heroic past and an epic literature.

French himself was descended from English stock. His ancestor, John French, came to America from England in 1636 and settled in Braintree, Massachusetts (cf. National Cyclopaedia, 1967). His work with Arthurian narratives and the colonial period mentioned earlier may be seen as an attempt to supply American youth with an epic literature. However, given the diversity of the population, the Icelandic sagas were even more suitable for this purpose. Moreover, as French (1905: xxxviii) mentioned in his introduction, the Icelanders (i.e. Eiríkur the Red, Leifur Eiríksson and others) 'discovered Greenland and America'. Symbolically, the heroes of Iceland were thus American heroes.

As much as French may have been inspired directly by Dasent's analysis of the Viking influence on the Victorians, his ideas about the origins of the Americans most certainly had independent intellectual sources. In the second half of the nineteenth century, American historiography had been inspired by widespread German and British ideas about historical evolution and the so-called 'Teutonic hypothesis', which suggested that American institutions were of Teutonic origin. Edward N. Saveth (1965: 18) has highlighted how the writings of Edward Augustus Freeman were influential in this respect, but in his 1873 *Comparative Politics* Freeman postulated an original prehistoric homeland of the Aryan peoples:

> The dispersal of the Aryans from this early cradle of civilization led to institutional recapitulation wherever they or their descend-

> ants settled in Greece, Rome, Germany, England and, finally, in America. The Teutons, chronologically the last of the Aryan peoples and like their predecessors, the Greeks and the Romans, destined to be rulers and teachers of the world, were recipients of the finest fruits of the racial heritage.

The Teutonic hypothesis was variously developed by American historians and used in equal proportion to explain the Germanic origins of the American legal system and the defensive wall around the New England town.

In the preface and the introduction to *Heroes of Iceland*, we are able to distinguish echoes of such ideas. French (1905: xl) explained, for instance, that a wall usually enclosed the Icelandic medieval farm, 'making a yard of the exact use and convenience of the Yankee barnyard'. French (1905: xxxiii) also spent considerable energy on explaining the Icelandic system of government, calling the Icelandic Fifth Court (a Court of Appeals) 'a necessity in all highly developed civilizations'. In more general terms, however, French (1905: xxii) stressed that the saga would teach the reader the ideals or the virtues of the Norseman, but these included 'honesty, hospitality, friendship, the habit of work, love of family, respect for women, and above all, courage, whether moral fearlessness or personal bravery'. The duty of revenge was, according to French (1905: xxii), the only virtue of the Norseman which the Americans had outgrown; in fact *Njáls saga* suggested that this barbaric ideal was in medieval times already 'weakening before the combined forces of Christianity and law'.

French (1905: xxiii) concluded this analysis by summing up the moral value of the narrative: 'The lessons thus to be drawn from its pages, in the gentler as well as in the sterner virtues, and in the belief in the value of manliness and the ultimate triumph of right, are such as no generation and no nation can afford to pass by.' According to this conception, the young American nation should read *Heroes of Iceland*, not merely for pleasure or even for the celebration of a racial and cultural heritage. In its depiction of the Norseman, the narrative presented a stern morality, offering an appropriate father-figure for any generation in any civilised country.

Old and New Immigration

When Allen French compared the literary qualities of *Njáls saga* to those of the great epics, his argument was more or less defensive. Summing up the qualities of the saga in his preface, French (1905: xx) wrote: 'If, then, with such characteristics the Story of Burnt Njal cannot be classed among the great tales, its many admirers may at least claim that the margin of difference is very narrow.' As we have seen, French attempted to narrow this 'margin of difference' with his abridgement, but we should also note that his reference to the saga's 'many admirers' contradicted his preface to *The Story of Rolf*, in which he complained that the reading of sagas had 'completely gone out of style'. Evidently, he made alternate claims depending on their utility. He was not sufficiently convinced of his power to insert the Icelandic saga into the epic canon, so he envisioned a group of stimulated readers, backing up his views.

In addressing the moral value of *Njáls saga*, however, French (1905: xxii–xxiii) became more confident and aggressive, making an important distinction between the northern and southern epics, between the Teutons on the one hand, and the Greeks and the Romans on the other:

> Courage is the great virtue of the men of our race, – not the courage of the Greek, to whom tears and flight are no disgrace, but the steadfastness in every stress of men dependent on themselves. This is the great point of superiority of all the northern epics over the southern, for the men of the Iliad, Odyssey, and Æneid fall far short of the heroic standard of the Teutonic races.

This statement echoed another statement found in the introduction to *The Story of Rolf*, in which French (1904: ix) claimed that the Icelandic sagas on the whole revealed 'the characteristics of our branch of the Aryan race, especially the personal courage which is so superior to that of the Greek and Latin races'.

While this comparison between the northern and southern epics partially served the purpose of advancing the status of the sagas within the American literary system, it needs also to be noted that French was writing during a period when immigration to the United States was undergoing significant change. According to George M. Stephenson (1926: 9), before 1883 about 95% of the immigrants came from England, Ireland, Scotland, Wales, Belgium, Germany, France, Denmark, the Netherlands, Norway and Sweden. This group was customarily referred to as the 'old immigration'. By 1907, a drastic change had occurred. Fully 81% of the immigrants embarked from Austria-Hungary, Bulgaria, Greece, Italy, Montenegro, Poland, Rumania, Russia, Serbia, Spain, Syria and Turkey. This group was designated as the 'new immigration'. There was a strong sentiment against the new immigration, partially because of its magnitude, but also because of its ethnicity. This prejudice motivated various reports on education, productivity, family structure, criminal records and even mental defects of immigrants of various nationalities. Such reports ultimately resulted in the literacy test legislation in 1917 and the Quota Acts of the 1920s, which were effectively designed to restrain the new immigration into the United States. The issue was, as one of the Boston leaders of the Immigration Restriction League put it, whether the country wanted 'to be peopled by British, German and Scandinavian stock, historically free, energetic, progressive, or by Slav, Latin and Asiatic races, historically down-trodden, atavistic and stagnant' (LaGumina and Cavaioli, 1974: 318).

It should not surprise us to find traces of this discourse in Allen French's preface and introduction to *Heroes of Iceland*. In the six years prior to the publication of the book, he had seen the annual number of immigrants to Massachusetts more than double, climbing from 31,754 to 72,151. During this time, the yearly number of immigrants from Italy rose from 4015 to 12,758, and the yearly number of Greek immigrants rose from 427 to 2108 (cf. Massachusetts Commission on Immigration, 1914). French's reference to the Norseman as 'our part-ancestor' clearly reveals that these southern people – who 'fall far short of the heroic standard of the Teutonic races' – were not a part of his potential audience. In fact, *Heroes of Iceland* may have been seen as an optimum medium to unite the various nationalities of the old immigration.

In addition to being an inventory of literary characteristics, the poetic code of rewriting contains, in André Lefevere's (1985: 229) words, 'a concept of what the role of literature is, or should be, in society at large'. Allen French (1905: ix) implies such a concept when he writes that a great epic should display 'what is highest in human nature', i.e. 'valour, faith, tenderness, devotion to creed and country'. According to his definition, the role of the great epics was to ennoble the reader and to sanction the dominant ideology in society. In the case of *Heroes of Iceland*, which was reprinted in 1914 and again in 1925, this was the ideology of the old immigrants who were uneasy with the apparent changes in the 'racial' texture of their society. All other Americans, both the new immigrants and the truly native people of North America, did not fit into French's definition of the American society. Suitably, these people had been abridged (or stripped) from that definition.

Part III

Njáls Saga **in Danish**

Chapter 4
On Danish Borders
Rewriting and Censorship

In the fall of 1943, a classical nineteenth-century Danish translation of *Njáls saga* was reissued in Copenhagen. It formed the third and final volume of a collection of Icelandic sagas translated by the Danish scholar N.M. Petersen. These translations were originally published in four volumes between 1839 and 1844 (cf. Jørgensen, 1995: 191–206) and had been reissued three times before the publishing house Det tredje Standpunkts forlag (The Third Viewpoint's Publishing House) released its collection under the title *Islændingenes færd hjemme og ude* (*The Travels of the Icelanders, at Home and Abroad*; Petersen, 1942–43). The complex publication history of Petersen's translations is a worthy topic, but the fourth edition of his work is particularly interesting, as it allows us to look at the issues of sagas and race, prevalent in Chapters 2 and 3, from a new perspective. Similar to *The Story of Burnt Njal* and *Heroes of Iceland*, *Islændingenes færd* was presented to its twentieth-century Danish reader as a part of their national heritage. That heritage, on the other hand, was specifically defined by Det tredje Standpunkts forlag as a Scandinavian heritage, contradicting alternative myths of a common Aryan, Teutonic or Germanic culture. Accordingly, this edition will be approached in the present chapter, not as a collection of medieval Icelandic literature, not even as a product of a nineteenth-century translator, but rather as a reflection of the sensitive political situation in German-occupied Denmark in times of Nazi-censorship.

Publishing and Politics

In recent years, growing scholarly attention has been directed towards the role and status of translation in societies of censorship. Referring to fascist Italy, André Lefevere (1995: 145) outlines, for instance, how the fascist censorship contributed to the creation of a translation industry; for many 'ideologically suspect' writers, translation became not only an economic necessity and a creative opportunity, but also a 'a form of political activity'. Lefevere (1995: 147) also refers to the former USSR, where some leading poets, silenced by the regime in power, 'exercised their poetic talents through the art of translation, which enabled them to borrow the voices of foreign poets'. In both these countries, the issue for the censor was not merely (and sometimes not primarily) the literary work in question or the translated text *per se*, but the ideological packaging. One of the works Lefevere (1995: 145–46) discusses is *Americana*, Elio Vittorini's anthology of North American short stories and novellas translated by established Italian writers such as Alberto Moravia and Cesare Pavese. In 1941, the Italian ministry of popular culture (Minculpop) seized the first edition on the grounds of Vittorini's provocative editorial commentary. A year later, the collection was submitted again to the censor for ideological vetting, now with a more diplomatic introduction by Emilio Checchi. Vittorini's 'political' commentary had been deleted altogether, but the translations had remained the same. This time Minculpop saw no need to oppose to the publication of *Americana*.

The case of *Islændingenes færd* in Denmark is, in many respect, similar to that of the Italian *Americana*. As discussed in Chapter 1, the Icelandic family sagas were partially incorporated into the cultural and racial ideology of Nazi Germany. Hence, there was little chance that the German censor, operating through the Danish Ministry of Foreign Affairs, would regard the reissuing of canonised Danish saga translations as a treat in itself. But the ideological context, produced through new introduction, commentary and commercials, was a different matter, in particular as the publishing house in question had already been apprehended for exploring the subversive powers of rewriting. We shall begin by reviewing the publisher's political agenda.

Det tredje Standpunkts forlag shared its identity with the cultural journal *Det tredje Standpunkt* (*The Third Viewpoint*). Both of these ventures were closely related to the Danish political party Dansk Samling (Danish Forum), which was founded by the writer Arne Sørensen in 1936, somewhat on the basis of a cultural philosophy he had developed in his popular work *Det moderne Menneske* (*The Modern Individual*). Sørensen published the book himself in 1936; it was the first title to appear under the imprint of Det tredje Standpunkts forlag. An outspoken critic of Marxist and Fascist theories and societies, Sørensen also expressed concerns about the conditions of Danish politics during the years before the war. In his view, democracy in Denmark was bound hand and foot by a rigid party system, bureaucracy, and an increasing centralisation of power. The mission of Dansk Samling at this juncture was to lead a popular democratic revival, fight unemployment and respond to a general ideological confusion. Challenging the emphasis that Marxists and Fascists laid on the conception of class and race, Sørensen's main interest was in the 'individual human being' ('Menneske'), individual freedom and well-being. While calling for radical political changes (it was not always clear what these should involve), Sørensen was conservative in matters of culture and religion. In these areas, he was inspired by the Danish folk-high-school movement, which had originated in the nineteenth-century ideas of Reverend N.F.S. Grundtvig and his ideal of a Denmark, founded on traditional folk-culture and Christian doctrines (cf. Halvorsen, 1982–83). It was in this context, Sørensen defined Dansk Samling's viewpoint as the third alternative ('det tredje standpunkt'), in opposition both to the right and to the left wings of the political spectrum, but his perhaps impossible objective was to increase both the freedom of the people and the power of the state (Jensen, 1981: 62–71).

Sørensen started the journal *Det tredje Standpunkt* in 1937 in order to further the course of Dansk Samling. In the following years, several of his other books were published by Det tredje Standpunkts forlag. Apart from *Det moderne Menneske*, these were financially unsuccessful. The publishing house incurred debt, and the parliamentary election in 1939 did not return any seats to the party. Ironically, the momentum Arne Sørensen had been waiting for was not created until after the German troops occupied Denmark on April 9, 1940. While the parliamentary parties all agreed to cooperate with the German war council, sustaining some Danish rule over internal affairs, Dansk Samling took a definite stand against the occupation but saw it at the same time as an effective cause for the advancement of the overdue popular democratic revival. In Sørensen's own words, Dansk Samling had only been a small, ineffective party until that point; now it was destined to become 'the motto of the people' (Halvorsen, 1982–83: 2:7). In the months that followed, Arne Sørensen toured Denmark, promoting the policy of Dansk Samling on various occasions. He made important contacts with people who shared his views, and in the fall of 1940, he resurrected *Det tredje Standpunkt*, bringing forth in the first issue some of the most vocal and influential adversaries of the German occupation. These included writer Kaj Munk and historian Vilhelm la Cour. This time the Danish readership was receptive. The circulation of *Det tredje Standpunkt* soon reached approximately 5000 copies, which was more than that enjoyed by any other journal in Denmark during the war.

Of particular importance for the present discussion was Arne

Sørensen's alliance with Vilhelm la Cour. Although politically conservative, La Cour had been bitterly disappointed with the policy of cooperation which the Danish politicians conducted under the German occupation. In this field, he and Sørensen had a common objective: 'to encourage people's understanding of the forced necessity for resistance – not just in view of Denmark's position at the end the war, but first and foremost in view of our national self-respect' (La Cour, 1959: 9). This was by no means an easy objective to obtain. The German censor limited the communication of such messages. Additionally, the thought of taking direct action against the German forces did not have a particular appeal to the Danish people in the early stages of the war. Under these circumstances, various forms of public speaking were the ideal means to avoid censorship and to get the audience directly involved. To that category belonged such phenomena as 'Byens højskole' ('The Rural Seminar') advertised in the fall of 1940 on the back-page of *Det tredje Standpunkt* (4, no. 1). 'Denmark' was the theme of this two semester-long workshop, but among the lecturers were Vilhelm la Cour, dealing on 'the principle of nationality', and Arne Sørensen, speaking on the history of Danish literature and art.

In 1941, Sørensen published a number of pamphlets with individual articles by La Cour, which served their common goal. These reached a wide audience, being partially distributed to selected subscribers of the journal. One of these publications, *Ord til os i dag – noter til øjeblikket* (*Words for Us Today – Notes on the Moment*), also caught the attention of the censor. In it, La Cour had written about a speech which the German poet Fichte delivered when Germany was occupied by Napoleon in the 1807–1808, describing how a nation should behave when it was invaded by foreigners. Despite La Cour's defense, based on the premise that Fichte was indeed highly regarded in contemporary Germany, he and Sørensen were sentenced to several months imprisonment (cf. La Cour, 1945; Rosen, 1969). In May of 1941, the censor also warned *Det tredje Standpunkt* for developing 'obvious Anti-German tendencies' (Halvorsen, 1982–83: 2:19). This warning was backed up with reference to an article by Kaj Munk, who had described small afflicted birds (the Danish nation) that were waiting for the victory of the westerly wind (the Allied Forces). Sørensen, the journal's editor, was reluctant to give in to such a warning, but *Det tredje Standpunkt* was too important for the course of Dansk Samling, both economically and ideologically, to be sacrificed. Sørensen adopted the policy of printing illegal ideas in other vehicles, such as the party's newsletter, *Nyt fra Dansk Samling* (*News from Danish Forum*), and later in various underground publications (Halvorsen, 1982–83: 2:21).

The success of *Det tredje Standpunkt* encouraged Sørensen to try his hand again as a commercial publisher. Here, he was able to benefit from his experience with the journal. The cover of the 1941 March edition of *Det tredje Standpunkt* (4, no. 5) was decorated with a photograph of a harmonious family reading a book. Underneath, the text went: 'They are reading *Det tredje Standpunkt's* edition of Saxo.' On the inside of the cover the readers of the journal found more detailed information. The plan was to publish quality editions of 'some of our finest old works' and to get the price down by collecting subscribers in advance. The first volume was Saxo Grammaticus' *Danmarks krønike* (*The Chronicle of Denmark*), originally written in Latin around 1200, but issued to the subscribers in N.F.S. Grundtvig's classic Danish translation from the early nineteenth century. It was also announced that La Cour would write the introduction to this edition.

The Saxo edition turned out to be a great success. The first 2000 volumes sold out and another printing of 2000 went through the press (Halvorsen, 1982–83: 2:24). During the publication process, Sørensen had been forced by the censor to delete a few sentences from La Cour's introduction, such as 'under our present state of humiliation' (Halvorsen, 1982–83: 2:25). Sørensen was, nonetheless, delighted with the reception of Saxo, expressing in one of *Det tredje Standpunkt's* (5, no. 1) advertisements the hope that the book would become 'a new inspiration' for its subscribers. At the same time, Sørensen announced the next publication in the series: *Islændingenes færd hjemme og ude.*

Sagas and Danish Resistance

Evidently, *Islændingenes færd* served the publishing agenda of Det tredje Standpunkts forlag and Dansk Samling in various ways. From an economic perspective alone, this was literature which did not demand the payment of any royalties. A second edition of Petersen's translations, revised by Guðbrandur Vigfússon, had been published in the 1860s (Petersen, 1862–68) and a third edition, revised by Verner Dahlerup and Finnur Jónsson, with the verses redone by Olaf Hansen, was released at the turn of the century (Petersen, 1901). As this third edition had been reissued by the Gyldendal publishing house in 1923–26, and was probably protected by copyright of Gyldendal or the editors, Arne Sørensen intelligently based his publications on Vigfússon's edition. Other costs could also be kept to a minimum. *Islændingenes færd* was advertised free of charge in *Det tredje Standpunkt*, and much of the work at the publishing house was done by volunteers, but already by 1937, Dansk Samling had organised groups of young people who participated in various 'nationally productive' projects, such as archaeological excavation. The extent of this work grew under the German occupation and served in the long run the purpose of forming resistance groups (Halvorsen, 1982–83: 2:28). There is no information available about the circulation of *Islændingenes færd*, but the fact that the third volume (the one containing *Njáls saga*) was released in 1943, a year later than the first two volumes, suggests that the publication had proved to be economically a prosperous affair.

Apparently, the funds of the journal, the publishing business, and Dansk Samling were interconnected. We know, for instance, that profits from the production of postcards with patriotic themes (verses celebrating Danish nationality and photographs of Danish landscape) paid for trips of party members around Denmark. The official purpose of these trips was to keep contact with other branches of Dansk Samling, but as things developed, they served as a cover-up for various illegal activities. In 1942, Arne Sørensen and his associates came in contact with British Special Operation Executives (SOE), who encouraged organised resistance in the countries occupied by Germany. In the course of time, members of Dansk Samling received weapons from Britain and participated in some 'special operations'. These were some of the first signs of an aggressive Danish resistance under the German occupation (Halvorsen 1982–83: 2:28; Politiken, 1979: 342–43).

Concurrently, Dansk Samling had expanded its lawful activities. Det tredje Standpunkts forlag was allied with the publishing house Samleren (The Collector) in 1942, which published a respected cultural magazine with the same name. Sørensen became one of two new editors of *Samleren*, and in a few months, its circulation grew tenfold. The new company opened a bookstore, Nordisk boghandel (Nordic bookstore) in Copenhagen, which distributed both books under the imprint of Det tredje Standpunkts forlag/Samleren as well as various illegal publications sponsored by Sørensen and others. Early in 1943, Dansk Samling also participated in the Danish elections. This time, the party got three representatives elected, one of them being Arne Sørensen. Some of these activities supported the others financially, and we can assume with some certainty that *Islændingenes færd* was one of the monetary sources rather than a debit in this complex economy of publishing, politics and resistance. However, by the time the third and final volume of Petersen's saga translations was released, Sørensen had gone underground, resigning (officially at least) both as the editor of the two journals and as the director of the publishing business (Halvorsen, 1982–83: 2:44). That may explain why *Islændingenes færd* was not promoted with the same energy that the Saxo edition had been. The last documentation I have come across regarding this 'special operation' is an advertisement appearing inside the back cover of the 1943 December issue of *Det Tredje Standpunkt* (7, no. 2), in which the complete collection of N.M. Petersen's translations is presented as an ideal Christmas present for the whole family.

Apart from being designed as a profit-making phenomenon, Petersen's translations were made to suit Dansk Samling's ideological policy. We have already noted that the backbone of that policy was to inspire Danish patriotism and to sharpen the nation's sensibility for 'danskhed' ('Danishness'). Contrary to the problems they had with the idea of active resistance, the Danes were receptive to this patriotic message from the very beginning of the war. Symbolic were the Danish 'alsangstævner', gatherings of thousands of people who sang national songs together. Another influential organisation in this nationalistic awakening was the association Dansk Ungdomssamvirke (Danish Youth League), which aimed at minimising the influence of German and Nazi ideology on Danish youngsters (Wendt, 1978: 96–104).

The production of patriotic postcards and the planning of workshops featuring themes such as 'Denmark' were only two of the many ways in which Dansk Samling advocated 'danskhed'. A number of covers for *Det tredje Standpunkt* served the same purpose, as did some of its articles. Typical of the tone and techniques was an article by Steen Steensen Blicher, originally written in 1839, but presented in the journal in 1940. The opening paragraph of Blicher's (1940: 49) article gives an idea of the text that follows: ' "Dannemænd!" [Good men, and true!] – Yes! I still have the right to address you with that honorable name. We still have our Denmark – but does Denmark also have its men?'

In many respects, the Saxo edition was the epitome of this advancement of 'danskhed' in the circle of Dansk Samling. It brought together Danish medieval history and the founder of the Danish folk-high-school movement, N.F.S. Grundtvig, who was more influential than any other individual in shaping Danish national identity in the nineteenth and the early twentieth centuries (cf. Lundgreen-Nielsen, 1992). This double strength of the volume was underlined by Vilhelm la Cour in the introduction, who frequently expanded on Grundtvig's ideas to communicate his own. Many of the terms in the introduction which did not pass through the censor were actually direct quotations from Grundtvig, one of them even being a reference to the German Anti-Christ (Halvorsen, 1982–83: 2:25). Despite the revisions, Arne

Sørensen could still thank La Cour for writing an introduction which explained why Grundtvig 'in a state of emergency, much like ours' took on the task of translating the ancient history of Denmark (Saxo, 1941: 5). This state of emergency, La Cour explained in his introduction, involved the state's financial crisis after the Napoleonic wars, the shattering of the Danish fleet by Britain and the end of Norway's confederation with Denmark. Napoleon's return to power in France in February of 1815, after the brief exile in Elba, had made the prospects for a peaceful Europe all the worse. In April of that year, Grundtvig had written the article 'Europe, France, and Napoleon', reacting not only to the 'iron sceptre of an aggressor' but to the cultural tyranny which resulted in a persecution of the Christian religion (Saxo, 1941: 10). Needless to say, La Cour himself was here reflecting on the iron sceptre and the persecution of the German aggressor in his contemporary Denmark. His initial purpose was to call on the Danes to fight for 'true freedom and independence' (Saxo, 1941: 31).

Although *Islændingenes færd* was not a piece of Danish history in the same sense as Saxo's history was, it was presented in much the same way to the Danish readership. The connection between the two editions was firmly established in the first paragraph of Bjarni M. Gíslason's preface to Petersen's volume. There, Gíslason refered to the opening of the introduction to Saxo, in which La Cour had asked why Danish youth had almost ceased to read Saxo's work. When introducing *Islændingenes færd,* Gíslason (1942a: 5) added, 'one is on the contrary tempted to write: Why do the Icelanders *still* read the sagas about their ancestors' lives of heroism/fighting?' Answering this rhetorical question, he explained that, while for Icelandic adults, the sagas raised the issue of how life's many 'misfortunes shall be cured or reconciled', Icelandic children still modeled their games on the sagas' heroic characterisations. One reason for this devotion was that the Icelanders found something of their original vigor and belief in the sagas. And Gíslason (1942a: 5–6) continued : 'Here, Fate has also played a significant part. Years of severe hardship have caused one to seek this vital popular force in order to keep alive the faith in freedom and to strengthen the spirit and energy one needs to endure reality and carry its burdens.' He further developed this theme of freedom, suggesting that the sagas demonstrated how the freedom of medieval Icelanders was defined by their responsibility for the people of their own kin. According to Gíslason (1942a: 7), this freedom could not be won through 'negotiation', but in the working of 'a liberating Power', which made all visions of the future grand and glorious; what counted was not to live as long as possible, but to live in accordance with 'the ideal of freedom', even if that demanded one's life.

As with many Danish texts written under the threat of the German censorship, there are several levels to Gíslason's argument. Literally, he was communicating accepted views when he characterised the medieval clannish society in Iceland and discussed the influence of the sagas on modern Icelanders. On the other hand, his opening reference to La Cour suggested that the sagas *could* have the same good influence on the Danish nation as they had had on the Icelanders. Gíslason's description of a nation which had suffered 'years of severe hardship' and was dealing with the issue of how life's many 'misfortunes shall be cured or reconciled' certainly fitted the Danes during World War II. One of the complex reasons leading to an intensified Danish opposition to the German occupation in the years of 1941 and 1942 was of an economic nature; inflation was high and unemployment rose to 24% (Halvorsen, 1982–83: 2:14). Indeed, this was also a nation which needed to 'keep alive the faith in freedom and to strengthen the spirit and energy one needs to endure reality and carry its burdens'. On this level of interpretation, Gíslason's discussion of the medieval concept of freedom followed the policy of Dansk Samling. Writing that the Icelanders of the past had not been able to acquire their freedom through negotiation, he was indirectly challenging the Danish government, which hoped that the co-operation with the Germans would spare Danish lives. Freedom, in Gíslason's definition, was an ideal worth dying for.

When the first volume of *Islændingenes færd* was released, *Det tredje Standpunkt* also published an article by Gíslason about the Icelandic sagas, which clearly served the purpose of introducing N.M. Petersen's translations to prospective subscribers (quotations from this article were used in advertisements for the publication in the journal). After a few general remarks on Iceland's literary production in the Middle Ages, Gíslason summarised the plot of some of the texts in *Islændingenes færd*. Thematically, his approach to the topic here was more or less identical with that of his preface. The sagas, Gíslason (1942b: 170) claimed, were great literary achievements that could still 'inspire the great thinkers and inflame boyish eyes with will and courage'. With regard to the sagas' good influence on Danish patriotism, Gíslason's (1942b: 168) summary of *Njáls saga* – 'the major work of all the Family Sagas' – is worth quoting at some length:

> Preceding the narrative of Njall and his sons, is the description of the hero Gunnar of Hlíðarendi who lives at the far end of the hillside. The meadow is fertile. Further out is the ocean, breathing

> unbroken waves towards the coast. The Markár-river pulses through the wide plain, under the moonlight, looking like a broad stripe of melted gold. The seasons continue their yearly circle and the hillside is blooming. Each winter is followed by a spring. One loves the land. Here the tasks come from the inside, defiant, determined. Here the fields are pale and the meadows mown. Here, one has such a strong affection for the land that one does not want to leave, even after having been exiled. One chooses to stay at home and fight one's enemies, even though it means risking one's life.

Inspired by Gunnar of Hlíðarendi's renowned speech at the point of return (Ch. 75), Gíslason rewrote here the saga's description of Rangárvellir much along the Romantic lines of Jónas Hallgrímsson's poem 'Gunnarshólmi', discussed in Chapter 1. But while mountains and glaciers frame the setting in Hallgrímsson's poem, Gíslason characterised the stage of *Njáls saga* as one of a harmonious agricultural 'plain' ('Sletteland'). Hence, he enabled his Danish readers to identify the gentle waves, the fertile meadow, and the yellow fields, which Gunnar had such a strong affection for, with their native Denmark, deprived both of mountains and glaciers. In the course of the saga, he stressed, this harmony is challenged, not dissimilar, we may note, to the way in which the war and the German occupation was affecting Denmark. Gíslason's use of the impersonal pronoun encourages such an interpretation: 'One chooses to stay at home and fight one's enemies, even though it means risking one's life.'

The Border Watch

The publication of *Islændingenes færd*, then, can be seen as an act (however modest) of Danish resistance against the German occupation during World War II. It was designed and introduced as a work which would help the Danes to endure and eventually to overcome their alien aggressors. But there were other ideological or political issues at stake. The potential unity of the Scandinavian countries had become highly topical in Denmark during the German occupation and is of consequence for any analysis of *Islændingenes færd*. Partially, this emphasis was a response to the Nazi ideas about *Germanic* heritage and race addressed in Chapter 1; the Danes maintained that they were a *Nordic* nation, culturally distinct from their southern neighbors. Many of them also believed (as did both German and British politicians) that, after the war, Europe would consist of a few dominating empires. Denmark's best and perhaps only possibility to maintain its identity and sovereignty was within a political unity of Scandinavia (cf. Gudme, 1940; Nielsen and Gudme, 1943). The sources of these ideas included nineteenth-century Romanticism and German philosophy. In Denmark, they were originally expounded by people like N.F.S. Grundtvig and N.M. Petersen but such concepts as 'Nordic unity' had been developed through the folk-high-schools and Scandinavian student movements (cf. Engberg, 1980).

For decades, the differentiation between the Germanic and the Nordic heritage had been particularly important for the Danes in relation to the controversial borderland of Slesvig (Schleswig) with its mixture of speakers of Danish and German. For many Danes, these borders were initially the borders between Scandinavia and continental Europe. After two wars between Denmark and the Austrian-led German confederacy, in the middle of the nineteenth century, the duchy had been annexed to Prussia in 1866, but at the end of World War I, Slesvig was divided between the two nations. The Danish-speaking majority of the northern part wanted to unite with Denmark, while the majority of German-speaking inhabitants in the southern part resolved to stay with Germany. With Hitler's rise to power in 1933, German claims for Northern-Slesvig were raised again, heightening the nationalistic tension in the area (cf. Rerup, 1982).

Throughout these developments, several Danish movements had fought for the maintenance of Danish/Nordic identity with the people of Slesvig, or Sønderjylland as the Danes customarily referred to it. In the 1920s and 1930s, Vilhelm la Cour was an active party in this debate, editing the journal *Grænsevagten* (*The Border Watch*) and writing a voluminous history of Sønderjylland. In the years of 1928–30, he also edited *Edda og Saga,* an anthology of Danish translations from Old Icelandic literature, including abridged versions of Petersen's translation of *Njáls saga* and other Icelandic sagas. In his short introduction to the volume, La Cour acknowledged that nobody wanted any longer to deprive the Icelanders and their kinsmen in Norway of the credit for creating this literature, but the Danes were nonetheless grateful for these narratives' portrayal of the Danish national character. Although 'the Nordic bond' was not the literal unity earlier generations had dreamt of, La Cour (1928–30: 7–8) contended, it was still a reality of communal strength – 'our root in a common language and a common ancestry'.

The issue of Slesvig and the theme of Scandinavian heritage was always topical within the folk-high-school movement. The first Danish folk-high-school was founded by Grundtvig in Rødding in

Slesvig in 1844, but moved to Askov, north of the new borders, after Denmark's defeat by Germany in 1864. The rise of National Socialism in Germany, with its emphasis on 'Volk' and the Aryan Germanic heritage, forced the people of the folk-high-schools to make a clear distinction between their own nationalistic agenda and the Nazi ideology. In simplified terms, their definition was that the Nordic identity was one characterised by personal freedom and Christian compassion in contrast to the militant totalitarianism advocated by Hitler and his regime (cf. Nissen, 1992). Arne Sørensen energetically participated in this discourse, writing as early as 1933: 'We shall not trade away Grundtvig for Hitler' (Halvorsen, 1982–83: 1:74). His work, *Det moderne Menneske*, can be sensed as an extension of that statement and the founding of Dansk Samling as its political realisation. Having spent a great deal of time in Sønderjylland and even having attended some courses at the folk-high-school in Askov, Sørensen was sensitive to the situation of the area. The German occupation of Denmark, in his view, initially meant that the whole country had suddenly become subjected to the circumstances which the inhabitants of the Danish borderlands had suffered for decades: 'We have all become Sønderjyllanders', he stated soon after the German invasion in 1940 (Halvorsen, 1982–83: 2:75). Partially, Sørensen (1942: 10) blamed the disunity of Scandinavia for this state of affairs – 'if the Nordic countries do not join hands, they will be sacrificed, one by one, to the superpowers' politics', he wrote in a pamphlet published by Det tredje Standpunkts forlag. However, he did not envision the creation of a Scandinavian empire but a decentralised alliance of independent equals, each country maintaining its cultural and political distinctiveness. Under Sørenson's editorship, *Det tredje Standpunkt* tirelessly advocated the unity of Scandinavia in the first years of the German occupation (cf. Wøller, 1940; Kruse, 1940). Sørensen's plan to publish N.M. Petersen's translations in 1942 can be construed as a part of the same engagement.

The previous fall, Petersen's 150th birthday had been noted in a number of newspaper articles, many of which characterised this first professor of old Nordic languages and literatures at the University of Copenhagen as a special 'Danish and Nordic personality', to quote one of the titles (Linneball, 1941; Nielsen, 1941; Fischer, 1941). All of these articles made a special note of Petersen's influential translations of the Icelandic sagas; one of the writers even proposed that a new edition was needed (Frederiksen, 1941: 6). It was in the spirit of these celebratory articles and in keeping with Sørensen's publication agenda that Bjarni M. Gíslason laid particular emphasis on the character of Petersen and his ideas about Nordic identity in relation to the publication of *Islændingenes færd.* Gíslason's discussion of Petersen also imitated La Cour's approach to Grundtvig in the introduction to Saxo.

In his promotional article in *Det tredje Standpunkt,* Gíslason (1942b, 165) explained how Petersen – this 'dry' scholar and writer – had been able to produce saga translations in a 'vibrant, juicy, melodious, and powerful language':

> The reason for his success is surely that he put all his heart into his work. Denmark's unfortunate years after England's attack on Copenhagen and the country's poverty after the Napoleonic wars filled him with pain and worry. He transformed that pain into affection for the Nordic Middle Ages, for everything that was Danish and Nordic. Just like Grundtvig and Ingemann, he tried to awaken the people by showing them their own past.

Gíslason (1942a: 10) developed the same argument more effectively in the introduction to *Islændingenes færd,* amplifying Petersen's lifelong endeavor to 'arouse affection for the Nordic past'. In this context, Gíslason (1942a: 13–14) quoted Petersen directly:

> The Nordic people had an indelible consciousness of their identity as people of the North and, as such, they were sharply distinct from other people in the South and the East. Still today this consciousness has not been erased. The fact that one can, irrespective of political distinctions, seriously conjecture a closer unity of all the Nordic countries which would serve as a stronghold against much too overwhelming alien influence, shows indeed, better than anything else, that it must be something Nordic which has never been torn apart.

Commenting on this paragraph, Gíslason (1942a:14) echoed Sørensen's writing on the same topic, as he maintained that Petersen's ideal had been an 'united but *diversified* Scandinavia'.

As far as the distinction between Scandinavia and continental Europe is concerned, Gíslason noted with a certain astuteness that Petersen had been opposed to French and German influence on the Danish language. Furthermore, Gíslason (1942a: 14–15) stressed that cultural affinity could not be constrained by 'the conditions and the limitations of an outer, alien world' or produced with political alliance; 'spiritual kinships' alone were able to instigate people's volition to live in a community. Although the context of this discussion was the development of Scandinavianism before the twentieth century –

and the failure of Scandinavian royal and political powers to unite the Nordic countries, either with force or treaties – it also communicated something about the alien force which was setting conditions upon Denmark and defining its borders in 1942.

But while the similarity between the times and the ideas of Petersen and the situation in Denmark in 1942 was slightly veiled in Gíslason's (1942a: 8) argument, his depiction of the sagas as a genre which related the make-up of 'our Nordic nature' decisively fused past and present. The times in which this literature came into being, Gíslason (1942a: 7) wrote, were not 'less filled with conflicts than ours'. The basic difference between these two periods, he explained, was that while material controversy (politics and economics) characterised the twentieth century, a contest between heathen and Christian beliefs (religion) had characterised the saga epoch. Better than anything else, the sagas' descriptions of this medieval spiritual contest enabled the modern Danes to realise the positive merging of the Nordic and the Southern in their own culture. One could, of course, be Nordic without being Christian and vice versa, Gíslason (1942a: 9) explained, but it had been the combination of the two which had transformed 'the heathen, Nordic outlook from being a *self-contained impulse* into universal principle, based on a human empathy [Medmenneskelighed]'. In these paragraphs, Gíslason echoed the arguments which the people of the folk-high-schools had been elaborating since 1933. His concept of 'Medmenneskelighed' even vibrates with an echo from Sørensen's early writings, with their Christian emphasis on the 'Menneske' (individual human being).

'One is Attached to the Land'

It certainly seem that Bjarni M. Gíslason's introduction to *Islændingenes færd* conformed to the publishing agenda and the techniques that Det tredje Standpunkts forlag developed in response to the German occupation of Denmark during World War II. That agenda, in turn, harmonised with the policy of resistance carried out by Danish Samling (and its underground groups) and with the general views of the folk-high-school movement towards the borderland in Sønderjylland and the unity of Scandinavia. Nonetheless, additional information regarding Gíslason's own nationality and his borderline status in Denmark allows us to distinguish some ambiguities in his writings.

A native of Iceland, Gíslason moved to Denmark in 1933, attending courses in several folk-high-schools in Sønderjylland in the following years. From 1935 to 1937, he was a student in Askov feeling the pulse of the Danish/Nordic revival in the area and the competing German policy of expansion (Engberg, 1978: 7–8). In the folk-high-school circles, he met a prevailing appreciation for old Icelandic literature and culture. He responded to that interest with publications and talks on Icelandic topics, advocating the cultural unity and co-operation between the Scandinavian countries while defending Iceland's political separation from Denmark (Gíslason, 1937; 1946; cf. Gunnarsson, 1992).

Iceland acquired sovereignty in 1918, after more than five hundred years of Danish rule. At the same time, the country was granted the right to cancel all political ties with Denmark after 1943, but acording to the 1918 treaty, the two nations continued to have the same king, dual citizenship, and a common foreign policy. As a result of the German occupation of Denmark on April 9, 1940, the Danish King and the Danish Foreign Office were, practically speaking, removed from power. The following day, the Icelandic parliament resolved that it would appropriate these powers. A year later, it concluded that, since Denmark had not been able to fulfill its obligations established in 1918, the Icelandic government was of the opinion that the treaty of the two nations had already been terminated. Consequently, the parliament founded the office of Governor and proclaimed the foundation of the Icelandic Republic. Many Danes thought it was unworthy of the Icelanders to cancel the ties with Denmark during the German occupation and felt that these matters should wait until the war was over (cf. Skúlason, 1994). However, one of the reasons for the rush was that Icelanders feared that a continuing federation with Denmark would sooner or later lead to German intervention in Icelandic matters (cf. Þorsteinsson and Jónsson, 1991: 401–19).

In 1941, Gíslason wrote a short article in Danish about the military defences of Iceland in which he complained that the Danes did not have an understanding of Iceland's development towards full independence. Instead, Gíslason (1946: 23) argued, the Danes were contaminated in this matter by 'an unsound federal-patriotism', as they maintained that the Icelanders were too few and ineffective to take care of their own matters and the country's military defense. He countered that, in reality, the Danes had never been able to defend Iceland due to the country's isolation and the Danish authorities' lack of interest. The contemporary military-Romanticism of united Scandinavia did not propose any change in that respect. Gíslason (1946: 26) suggested that rather than reacting to their own 'great humiliation' by talking superficially about how few and feeble the

Icelanders were, the Danes should unite with the other Nordic nations: 'Our vigor and morale are grounded on ideals which have moved Scandinavia consistently further away from heathen despotism towards humane recognition of each other's rights. That is our strength today.' Indirectly, Gíslason implied that some Danes still thought about Iceland in the way which the Germans thought of occupied Denmark.

If we review the introduction to *Islændingenes færd* from this perspective, it becomes clear that Gíslason's emphasis on the concept of freedom reflected not only on the German occupation of Denmark but also on Icelandic history. The 'years of severe hardship' that, in his presentation, had made the Icelanders turn back to the sagas, maintaining 'the faith in the freedom', were the centuries of Danish rule in the country. According to Gíslason, it was time for the Danes to turn the tables, to let go of self-serving motives and comply with the Nordic 'universal principle based on a human empathy'. The 'united but diversified Norden' he anticipated at the end of his introduction was a unity of independent nations, where Iceland was one among equals. In short, as the Danes appreciated their own desire for freedom, so too should they understand and respect Iceland's.

Gíslason's summary of *Njáls saga* in the promotional article for *Islændingenes færd,* which appeared in *Det tredje Standpunkt,* also acquires a new significance if we read it in view of his position as an Icelander in Denmark. Earlier, the decision of Gunnar of Hlíðarendi to stay at home and to fight his enemies was interpreted as a Danish model of behavior during the German occupation. Since this summary was originally published in 1937 under the title 'Edda og Saga', as a part of the collection *Glimt fra Nord* (Gíslason, 1937), we have to acknowledge that such a message of resistance may hardly have been on the author's mind when he wrote the chapter originally (although he might have seen the paragraph's inspirational potential when he included it in his 1942 article for *Det tredje Standpunkt*). It is more likely that Gíslason's romanticised description of Gunnar's region incorporated his own contemporary feelings towards Iceland: 'One is attached to the land. [. . .] Here, one has such a strong affection for the pasture, that one does not want to leave, even after having been exiled.' The irony is that Gíslason had left his native soil when he wrote these lines, without even being exiled.

But while his identification with Gunnar was contradictory in this respect, Gíslason's life-long endeavor to promote the Icelandic perspective among the Danes – one of the causes he fought for was the return of Icelandic manuscripts from Denmark to Iceland (cf.

Gunnarsson, 1992) – can be seen as his way of 'fighting the enemies' all the same, making up for his departure. This is Poul Engberg's (1978: 24) view as he recalls how Gíslason annually visited the classes at the Snoghøj folk-high-school in Denmark and told the students an Icelandic saga:

> He did that in the free and personal manner of the story-tellers on the Icelandic farms. Some of the most beautiful words in the sagas are the words of Gunnar of Hlíðarendi, when his friends encouraged him to move from his farm to save his life from the rascality of his enemies. He decided to stay, despite the risk, saying: 'So lovely is the hillside that it has never before seemed to me as lovely as now, with its pale fields and mown meadows; and I will ride back home and not go anywhere at all.' Although Gíslason has lived in Denmark for many years, his bond with the Icelandic people and nature is as firm and unbreakable as that of Gunnar of Hlíðarendi.

From Engberg's description one can infer that, by telling the story of Gunnar and other saga heroes, Gíslason matched Gunnar's example of 'staying at home', spiritually if not physically. Hence, the initial moral of the story was not that one should stay at home and fight the enemies but participate in the maintenance and the continuous dissemination of the saga tradition. In Bjarni Gíslason's case, narration replaced action.

Hierarchy of Constraints

The publishing of *Islændingenes færd* in Denmark in 1942 and 1943 enables us to distinguish the hierarchy of constraints influencing the textual (re)production within a literary system. This hierarchy is unusually well-manifested in the present case as it is represented by three different nationalities. The German censor constrained the publishing activities of the Danish publisher Arne Sørensen, just as the publishing agenda of Det tredje Standpunkts forlag predetermined the promotional writings of Icelander Bjarni M. Gíslason, enclosed with the publication in question. As we have seen, the publications of Det tredje Standpunkts forlag, including *Islændingenes færd*, generally conformed to the constraints of the censor while concurrently, on a different (disguised) level, challenged the German presence in Denmark during World War II. In the writings of Gíslason, one is moreover able to detect a third level of signification, reflecting the sensitive political ties between Iceland and Denmark in this period. In this respect, *Islændingenes færd* brings us to different fronts of the Danish 'borders': its political borders with Iceland and its geographical borders with Germany. From a slightly different angle, however, this is a question of boundaries as much as literal borders. What kind of boundaries – sociological, ideological, economical, cultural and racial – should be affirmed internally between the 'Nordic' nations of Scandinavia and between them and other 'Germanic' nations in Europe?

As a final methodological concern, it should be stressed that there is little way of knowing whether or not the Danish readership perceived these volumes of Icelandic sagas as a reaction to the German occupation. In addition to such material as forewords and introductions, book reviews are usually the most significant documentation one has in order to formulate ideas about the contemporary reception of a literary work. In the case of *Islændingenes færd*, however, the only published review was written by Gíslason himself! It appeared in *Aalborg Amtstidene* in 1944, a few months after the third and final volume of N.M. Petersen's translations had been released by Det tredje Standpunkts forlag. The first half of the review was identical to the opening of Gíslason's promotional article in *Det tredje Standpunkt*, but in the second half, he turned a critical eye on the edition, clarifying that he was only responsible for its introduction. He approvingly mentioned that names of places had been modernised in the new edition, but he opposed the Danish ending 'sen' of male family names where the Icelandic ending 'son' in his view would have been more appropriate. This point crystallises the different views of Arne Sørensen and Bjarni M. Gísla-son towards the sagas.

Gíslason's main complaint, however, was that two family sagas which N.M. Petersen translated were left out of the 1942–43 edition: *Grettis saga* and *Gísla saga Súrssonar*. The reason for this, he explained, was that Sørensen and his crew based their work on Guðbrandur Vigfússon's edition of Petersen and not on the more recent and complete edition of Finnur Jónsson and Verner Dahlerup. In spite of these objections, Gíslason (1944: 4) concluded his review on a reassuring and familiar note, stating that, although Petersen had shortened many of the sagas, his translations were real masterpieces: 'Each and every Dane, conscious of his Nordic background, should have them in his home.'

Chapter 5

Norwegian Liberation

Language and Nationality

The publication of N.M. Petersen's saga-translations in Denmark during World War II, discussed in Chapter 4, has a great deal in common with the publication of a particular translation of *Njáls saga* published in Norway during the second half of the nineteenth century. Like *Islændingenes færd,* Karl L. Sommerfelt's *Njaals Saga* was designed to appeal to a wide audience, to strengthen the readers' sense of nationality and to denounce foreign influences on the domestic culture. The irony is that, while the Danish publication was in part a reaction to the German military occupation of Denmark, Sommerfelt's 1871 translation defied a long-standing Danish influence on Norwegian culture and literature. More specifically, it was meant to supplant Petersen's Danish translation of *Njáls saga* on the Norwegian bookmarket. This sense of challenge is tentatively conveyed in the opening of Sommerfelt's (1871: iii) preface: 'Having taken on the task of translating *Njáls saga,* which has been available for a long time now in the translation of the Danish professor N.M. Petersen, I feel obliged to give my reasons.'

Concurrently, Sommerfelt's work provides us with an interesting example of what G.C. Kálmán (1986: 117) has termed as 'borderline cases of translation'. Elaborating Roman Jakobson's (1959: 233) well-known definition of intralingual, interlingual and intersemiotic translation, Kálmán highlights the uncertain status of pseudo-translations, auto-translations and phonetic transcriptions. He also discusses various borderline types of intralingual translations, considering both the dimensions of synchronicity (translation from one dialect to another) and diachronicity (modernisation or archaisation of a text). Due to the uncertain difference between the Danish and the developing Norwegian languages in the 1870s, Sommerfelt's translation seems to belong to yet another category. Its borderline status stems from the ambiguous identity of the target language. Surely the translator claimed to be producing a Norwegian text but in modern bibliographies and library catalogues, it is generally regarded as a Danish translation of the saga.

Targeting the Audience

Sommerfelt's translation was issued in 1871 by Selskabet for Folkeoplysningens Fremme (The Society for the Advancement of Public Enlightenment, hereafter SFF). The Christiania (now Oslo) based society had been founded twenty years earlier and was the first Norwegian organisation on a national scale devoted to the enlightenment of the general public. It was influenced by eighteenth-century Enlightenment ideas, but it also responded to the liberal tides stemming from the European revolutions of 1848. Hence, Hartvig Nissen, one of SFF's founders, argued that the only way to save the masses from becoming blind puppets in the hands of the collusive powers was 'to propagate bourgeois Enlightenment to a constantly widening circle' (Sømme, 1951: 9). Furthermore, the laws of SFF spelled out that its educational goals should be 'the awakening, the amplification, and the ennoblement of the national spirit' (Folkevennen, 1871: 651). These goals were to be reached with the publication of a periodical, which received the name *Folkevennen* (*The People's Friend*), as well as the publication and circulation of other literature that served SFF's objectives. Sommerfelt's translation was one of two supplementary volumes accompanying *Folkevennen* in 1871.

The hey-day of SFF was between 1860 and 1870, when *Folkevennen* attracted almost 5000 subscribers or members. The majority came from the growing Norwegian middle-class (government officials, teachers, students, clerks) rather than the targeted working-class and the rural population. Nevertheless, many of the supplementary volumes reached a wider audience, such as Hanna Winsnes' *For fattige Huusmødre* (*For Poor Housewives*), which was printed in 20,000 copies in the 1860s (Sømme, 1951: 12–14). In 1871, there were still around 3800 members who received *Folkevennen* and the two supplementary volumes for a modest subscription. A further 1200 copies of *Njaals Saga* were printed for the general market (Folkevennen, 1872: 210–11).

In his preface, Sommerfelt indicated that the Norwegian readership had already been exposed to *Njáls saga* in N.M. Petersen's 1841 Danish translation. Presumably, this translation satisfied both Danish and Norwegian readers who simply wanted to read the saga for its plot. For Norway, however, there were other factors to be taken into consideration. The first explanation (or excuse) Sommerfelt (1871: iii) gave for his challenge to Petersen's text was of an economic nature: 'The saga, in the form in which it has been hitherto available to the public, has been relatively so expensive that the price alone has blocked it from getting any general circulation.' In keeping with the publishing agenda of SFF, *Njaals Saga* was intended for a different and supposedly less exclusive market than Petersen's translation, that is, to a general audience and not just those who were financially well off. This sense of readership was sharpened by the Gothic letter-type used for Sommerfelt's translation. In the second half of the nineteenth century, the Latin letter-type had been slowly succeeding the Gothic letter-type as the accepted standard in Danish and Norwegian printing. Accordingly, Guðbrandur Vigfússon replaced the Gothic letter-type of the original edition of *Historiske fortællinger* with the more prestigious Latin letter-type, when he revised Petersen's translation in the 1860s. In Norway, however, the Gothic letter-type was still retained by patrons of popular literature, such as SFF (Tveterås, 1964: 142–44).

A more significant and complicated explanation relates to the nationalistic agenda of the publishers, an aspect that must be discussed in the context of Norwegian nineteenth-century history and culture. In 1814, after over four hundred years of dynastic union, Norway politically cut ties with Denmark and accepted a more autonomous dynastic union with Sweden. Linguistically, the ties with Denmark had left the Norwegians without an official voice of their own. The official written language was Danish, which was 'felt by most people to be common to both nations, equally distant from the spoken dialects of both' (Haugen, 1966: 29). The spoken language varied from (a) regular Danish, which was used by Danish officials and merchants, and in the theatre (many actors came from Denmark), and (b) a literary standard (Norwegian reading pronunciation of Danish) used on solemn occasions by Norwegian born pastors and officials, to (c) the colloquial standard of the educated class, (d) several urban substandards of the working class, and finally to (e) various rural dialects (Haugen, 1966: 31–32). Consequently, it was neither a simple nor a swift process to define what the term 'Norwegian' meant. Despite substantial attempts to institutionalise the Norwegian language, Danish continued to be the dominant literary language in Norway for most of the nineteenth century.

The period 1814–1884 witnessed the birth of Norwegian literature and the gradual growth of the Norwegian publishing industry (cf. Dahl, 1981). Yet, it is obvious that a clear distinction between the literary systems of Denmark and Norway had still not been developed by 1871, the time of Sommerfelt's translation. Otherwise, he would not have felt the need to justify the publication of his translation of *Njáls saga* against Petersen's. The crucial point of Sommerfelt's preface, however, was that the distinction between the two literatures needed to be sharpened and even redefined. Acknowledging its advantages,

Sommerfelt (1871: iii–iv) yet doubted that Petersen's translation would 'gratify a Norwegian reader'; this, he added, 'is not the fault of the translator, but of the Danish language. Though they are related, it is apparent that Danish and Norwegian are in certain respects two different languages, representing two different nationalities.'

Sommerfelt readily admitted that the difference between the two languages would not have been of consequence in certain other fields of writing. It did not matter, for instance, in which of the two languages the Norwegians read books on scientific subjects. Both Danish and Norwegian, he explained, were equally poor in scientific vocabulary. *Njaals Saga*, on the other hand, belonged to the delicate sphere of Norwegian nationality as it contained scenes and descriptions which illuminated Norway's historical past – or, as Sommerfelt (1871: iv) put it, 'the daily life of our ancestors', their 'habits, customs, and characteristics'. Hence, he concluded, in order to retain 'the familiarity, the deserved authenticity' of the text, it was essential to present the saga to Norwegian readers – actually to any nation in a similar situation – in their native language. In this respect, the publication of *Njáls saga* in Norway can be seen as serving the SFF's agenda of awakening, amplifying and ennobling the Norwegian national spirit.

Norwegian Saga Series

Sommerfelt's discussion of the Icelandic sagas and Norway's historical past ('the lives of our ancestors') is by no means unique. As noted in earlier chapters, many nations emphasised their racial kinship with the ancient Icelanders and interpreted the sagas accordingly. With nineteenth-century Norwegians, however, the kinship emphasis was particularly relevant as it is generally accepted that Iceland was settled mostly by Norwegians between the years 800 and 1000 AD. In fact, a number of family sagas are preoccupied with the migration and its diverse consequences (cf. Kristjánsson, 1988: 203–17). *Njáls saga*, although less concerned with Norway than are many other sagas, frequently traces the genealogy of individual characters back to Norwegian ancestors. Both during and after the period of migration, economic, political and cultural contacts with Norway were important for the Icelanders. In *Njáls saga*, these contacts are variously explored. Two scenes deserve to be mentioned in that context: Early in the saga (Ch. 3–6), we read of Hrútur Herjólfsson's visit to Norway and his intimate relationship with Queen Gunnhildur, mother of King Haraldur Grayfur. Later (Ch. 100–105), we learn of King Ólafur Tryggvason's successful efforts to convert the people of Iceland to

Christianity. These and other references to Norwegian history and politics rationalise Sommerfelt's claim for 'the familiarity, the deserved authenticity' of his Norwegian text.

At this point, it may be useful to recall the link between the family sagas and another genre of medieval Icelandic literature – that of the kings' sagas ('konungasögur'). While Norway (with several other northern countries) is peripheral to the plot of *Njáls saga* and other family sagas, the kings' sagas are mainly concerned with the biographies and reigns of Norwegian and occasionally Danish kings. As mentioned in Chapter 1, the most important collection of kings' sagas is Snorri Sturluson's *Heimskringla*, containing sixteen sagas of Norwegian history from mythological antiquity through 1177 (cf. Kristjánsson, 1988: 147–78). In the seventeenth century, these texts became the primary sources of Norwegian history, and they are believed to have been crucial to the development of Norwegian national identity over the next two hundred years. Peder Claussøn Friis' translation, *Snorre Sturlesøns Norske Kongers Chronica*, originally printed in 1633 and reprinted in 1757, was especially important in that context (cf. Sturluson, 1900: xxxix–xl). Already in the eighteenth century, Norwegian writers also produced important original literary works inspired by *Heimskringla*. Johan Nordahl Brun's play, *Einer Tambeskielver* dating from 1772, was for instance 'a major factor in securing a presence for Snorri in eighteenth-century Norwegian literature' (Hagland, 1994: 30).

Even though the kings' sagas and the 1871 Norwegian translation of *Njáls saga* may seem to be two separate undertakings, the connection is evident. Toward the end of his preface, Sommerfelt thanked one particular member of SFF's directorate, historian Oluf Rygh, for his responsive editorial guidance. To Professor Rygh, Sommerfelt (1871: vi) wrote,

> I owe many hints, much information and many explanations, which have significantly influenced both the translation itself and the notes, several of which are his, just as I am indebted to him for his kind assistance with the supplementary chronological table at the end and the metrical interpretation of the Darraðarljóð.

Rygh, who was elected the vice-chairman of SFF in 1871 (Folkevennen, 1872: 209), was a prolific saga translator and had published two of his saga translations, *Sagaen om Gunnlaug Ormstunge og Skalde-Ravn* and *Sigmund Brestessøns Saga* as supplementary volumes to *Folkevennen* (Rygh, 1859; 1861). Hence, it is likely that it was under his auspices that *Njaals Saga* was originally accepted or chosen as a supplementary volume to *Folkevennen* in 1871.

Rygh himself was under the decisive influence of his former teacher, saga translator and historian Peter Andreas Munch. Originally, Munch published translations from Snorri Sturluson's *Heimskringla* and several family sagas in the 1830s and 1840s. But his most successful publication was *Norges Konge-Sagaer* (*Norway's Kings' Sagas*), an extensive collection of sagas recording Norwegian history from earliest times to 1177 (Munch, 1859; cf. Knudsen, 1923: 33). With Munch's death in 1863, Rygh succeeded his mentor as lecturer in history at the University of Christiania. Along with his teaching responsibilities, Rygh also inherited Munch's unfinished translation of the kings' sagas dealing with the period from 1177 (these were published in the years 1869 and 1871). By comparing Sommerfelt's preface with the writings of Munch and Rygh, one recognises how the Norwegian translation of *Njáls saga* not only supplemented the publishing agenda of SFF but extended a tradition of saga translations in nineteenth-century Norway. At least three points of resemblance of the former to the latter can be noted:

(1) In his challenge to N.M. Petersen's translation, Sommerfelt consciously followed Munch in his criticism of N.F.S. Grundtvig's Danish translation of *Heimskringla* dating from 1818. After discussing the difference between the two languages and the possible effects of a Danish saga translation on Norwegian readers, Sommerfelt (1871: v) turned to Munch as his authority: 'Without doubt, Professor P.A. Munch had this in mind in the preface to his translation of Snorri, when he commented on Grundtvig's translation of the same work, and said: "It is possibly a genuine Danish, but it is not a genuine Norwegian".' Interestingly enough, however, when Munch (1845) started translating family sagas, he chose texts that had not appeared in N.M. Petersen's collection (*Gísla saga Súrssonar* and *Hænsna-Þóris saga*). It was Rygh (1859) who set the example for saga translations that challenged Peterson's work with his *Sagaen om Gunnlaug Ormstunge*.

(2) Discussing the price of Petersen's translations in his preface to *Njaals Saga*, Sommerfelt paraphrased the preface to *Gisle Sursons Saga* in which Munch (1845: 1:preface) argued that earlier translations of the family sagas had been 'too expensive and not very accessible to the general public'. Munch's aim, like Sommerfelt's, was to make this literature available to 'readers of all classes'.

(3) Sommerfelt's discussion of *Njáls saga's* position within the sphere of Norwegian national literature can be traced back to Munch's translation of the family sagas, which had been announced in the series *Sagaer eller Fortællinger om Nordmænds og Islændernes*

Bedrifter i Oldtiden (*Sagas or Narratives about the Ventures of the Norwegians and the Icelanders in Ancient Times*). By emphasising the Norwegian origin of the saga heroes, Munch was clearly suggesting that the Icelandic family sagas, similar to the kings' sagas, documented early Norwegian history. In this spirit, Munch (1845: 1:preface) referred to the family sagas as being 'truly national literature'. Similarly, he made the point that Gísli Súrsson had been born and raised in Norway before settling in Iceland (1845: 1:iii). Following Munch in this respect, Rygh (1859: 4) stressed in his introduction to *Sagaen om Gunnlaug Ormstunge* that almost all the settlers of Iceland had been Norwegians, and to the present day, he added, the Icelanders 'have done the most to preserve our ancestors' spiritual property'.

With his translations of *Gíslas saga* and *Hænsna-Þóris saga*, Munch (1845: 1:preface) had announced his plan to publish 'a series of saga-translations' in inexpensive volumes, each containing at least one unabridged saga. For one reason or another, he finished only the first two volumes. But the project prevailed under the patronage of SFF, first in the two saga-translations by Oluf Rygh, and later through Rygh's support for the publication of Karl L. Sommerfelt's translation of *Njáls saga*.

A Borderline Case of Translation

Sommerfelt's preface clearly formed a part of a particular Norwegian discourse that was engaged in defining the role of Icelandic medieval literature in Norway in the nineteenth century. As pointed out, the motive behind translating the sagas was to make them available to all Norwegians in their native diction. From a broader perspective, however, these publications reflect contentions between the interrelated literary systems of Denmark and Norway, contentions that are inseparable from Norway's complex and controversial linguistic politics.

Ever since 1814, the year in which Norway got its own constitution, Norwegians had been carrying forward their political and economic separation from Denmark into the vast field of culture. In that context, the linguistic question was crucial, psychologically reflecting the nation's general search for identity. Originally, the language reform was ignited by the apparent threat of Swedish influence – in accepting the dynastic union with Sweden, the Norwegians had mandated that governmental affairs should be conducted 'in Norwegian'

(Haugen, 1966: 29–30). However, as the decades passed, the issue evolved into a debate about different dialects and ways of construing a Norwegian literary standard. In simplified terms, two different views were on the forum in the period between 1840 and 1870; 'fornorskingslina', which argued that the Norwegian literary language should be deduced from the Danish standard, and 'nyskapingslina', which argued that the Norwegian literary language should be recreated on the basis of the Norwegian dialects and even from the Old Norse language preserved in the Icelandic sagas (Almenningen and others, 1981: 60). The difference between these two approaches was far from clear; those who followed 'fornorskingslina' typically spiced their Danish with words and phrases from the Norwegian dialects and even at times with words from the sagas.

It is not immediately obvious where Sommerfelt stood in the linguistic debate but he was most certainly convinced that the Danish literary standard was inadequate. Characterising the Norwegian reader of *Njaals Saga*, Sommerfelt (1871: iv–v) wrote in his preface:

> Though unfamiliar with the original, he will easily perceive that the Danish language is too weak to communicate the strength, the vigour and the crispness of the expression, the pride and the courage of the characters and the scenes, which are authentic to the saga; one will sense that the narrative has not quite attained its potential, that it has lost its ancient flavour, its freshness and vitality.

In the light of Sommerfelt's earlier statement about Danish and Norwegian being two different languages, 'representing two different nationalities', his characterisation of the defects of Danish hinted at a profound distinction between the two nations (Danish: weakness; Norwegian: strength). To a degree, the aim of his rhetoric was to boost the ego of his countrymen, loading the Norwegian identity with positive values, at the expense of the Danish.

It is possible to associate these ideas with the native Romantic nationalism of the preceding decades which had celebrated the Norwegians as being racially and culturally the purest or the most authentic branch of the Germanic tribe (Sanness, 1959: 56–58). As far as language is concerned, such ideas can be traced to the writings of German philosophers such as Johann Gottlieb Fichte (1978: 60–72), who in his *Reden an die Deutsche Nation* (*Addresses to the German Nation*, 1806–1807) argued that a foreign influence on a nation's language eventually would result in the moral decay of that nation. However, the evidence of Sommerfelt's preface essentially exposes his insecurity in relation to the literary dominance of the Danish language and the canonised status of Petersen's translation.

In this context of linguistic difference, Sommerfelt (1871: iv) compared Petersen's Danish translation of *Njáls saga* to a hypothetical Danish translation of works by Norwegian writers:

> One can imagine Asbjørnsen's and Moe's fairy tales or Bjørnson's narratives, for example, being recast in a Danish form. Even in the hands of the most skilled Danish narrator and stylist, I venture to say, they would have suffered an immeasurable loss in the eyes of every Norwegian reader. The narrative would be deprived of its fresh fragrance, its naturalness, and hence its sympathetic power. Admittedly, the saga in question is not national [Norwegian] to the same degree as these other works but, like the whole of Icelandic saga literature, it has for us the deep national interest which will always be an attribute of tales that remind a nation of the life and achievements of its ancestors.

This comparison between *Njáls saga* and the collections of Asbjørnsen and Moe fixes Sommerfelt's translation within the Norwegian linguistic debate. The fairy tale collection of Peter C. Asbjørnsen and Jørgen Moe, *Norske Folkeeventyr* dating from 1842–1844, is generally regarded as the first systematic program of 'fornorsking' in Norwegian literature. In this widely popular publication, Danish spelling-rules were observed while sentence structure, certain grammatical features, and individual words were adopted from the 'gold-mines of the popular dialects' (Almenningen and others, 1981: 63). Examples of the Norwegian flavour included the use of a double article ('the evil stepmother': Danish: 'den slemme Stedmoder'; Norwegian: 'den slemme Stedmoder*n*') and the post-nominal position of personal pronouns ('my cow', 'his horse': Danish: 'min Ko', 'hans Hest'; Norwegian: 'Koen min', 'Hesten hans'). On the other hand, the editors' own commentary was written in regular Danish.

The style of *Norske Folkeeventyr* is believed to have influenced leading contemporary Norwegian writers such as Bjørnstjerne Bjørnson and Henrik Ibsen. Their works were also directly inspired by the Icelandic sagas, both in terms of style and motifs. Bjørnson's first play, *Mellem Slagene* dating from 1856, was a Norwegian historical drama based on Snorri Sturluson's *Heimskringla*. Later came *Halte-Hulda*, echoing themes from *Njáls saga* and other ancient Icelandic works. In 1857, Ibsen wrote *Hærmændene paa Helgeland*, a play borrowing motifs from *Völsunga saga*, *Egils saga*, *Laxdæla saga*, and *Njáls saga*. In *Kongsemnerne*, dating from 1863, Ibsen also turned to Snorri Sturluson (cf. Dahl, 1981: 168–223). As for stylistic influences of the Norwegian fairy tales and the Icelandic sagas on these authors, Bjørnson's early prose narratives ('Bjørnsons Fortællinger', as Sommerfelt called them) provide the classical examples. Bjørnson debut as a prose writer was the 1856 short story 'Aanun'. It opened much like an Icelandic saga: 'Lasse hedte en Mand', ('Lasse was a man's name', echoing the saga refrain 'Mörður hét maður'; Dahl, 1981: 174–78). The setting, on the other hand, was a nineteenth-century farm in rural Norway, and the language in many respects was similar to the simple oral style of the fairy tales. In the following years, Bjørnson wrote a series of stories with the same setting, the best known of these being *Synnøve Solbakken* dating from 1857. Even though his style gradually became more personal, it continued to owe much to both the sagas and the fairy tales. Sentences were simple and to the point, and subordinate clauses, which were characteristic of the Danish literary language, unusually rare. At times, Bjørnson also put verbs at the beginning or at the end of sentences, contrary to the Danish tradition ('that, which shall grow': Danish: 'det som skal voxe'; Norwegian: 'det som voxe skal'). Additionally, he used to a certain extent the Norwegian double definite article and various particular Norwegian expressions (cf. Seip, 1916).

One of Bjørnson's aims with his 'Bondefortællinger' ('Farmers' narratives') was to reveal the continuity between the old Nordic people and contemporary Norwegian farmers (Halvorsen, 1951: 212). That point was understood by his contemporaries. In a review of *Synnøve Solbakken*, critic Paul Botten-Hansen claimed that Bjørnson's aim was to 'renew the saga or employ its characteristics in the field of the novella'. In Botten-Hansen's estimation, Bjørnson had succeeded, 'insofar as the underlying tone and the simplicity of language were concerned' (Øyslebø, 1982: 27). While Bjørnson was later reluctant to admit any direct debt to the collection of Asbjørnsen and Moe, he always identified the Icelandic sagas as having been a major influence on his writing (Dahl, 1981: 176–77).

Born in 1832, Bjørnson originally read the kings' sagas in the translations of Jacob Aall, published between 1838 and 1839, and the family sagas in N.M. Petersen's translations. He also read the saga translations of P.A. Munch (Halvorsen, 1951: 211). A native of Norway, Aall was one of the pioneers in importing expressions from the Norwegian dialects into the Danish literary language used in Norway. He and Johan Storm Munch originally applied that technique to a series of translations of selections from the Icelandic sagas, including *Njáls saga* (Aall, 1819), that were published in the periodical *Saga* in 1816–1820 (cf. Johnsen, 1946). Later, when Aall published his translations of *Heimskringla* and some other kings' sagas, he criticised Grundtvig's Danish translation of Snorri Sturluson's work and discussed the ways Norwegian might be used without offending the accepted taste and general comprehension (cf. Jakobsen, 1980). Already in his texts, one finds Norwegian expressions like 'Buskap' ('farming') and linguistic features like 'sønnen din' ('your son'; Dahl, 1981: 27).

P.A. Munch took a similar course with his saga translations in the 1850s. His work as a translator was closely related to his general interest in the debate about the Norwegian language, an interest which can be traced back to his first translations from *Heimskringla* in 1832 (cf. Raabe, 1941). Over the next thirty years, Munch voiced his opinions on the language question on numerous occasions. Even though his language policy was inconsistent and at times paradoxical, his most important translations can be said to follow a moderate 'fornorskings' plan, which aimed at 'bursting' the borders of the Danish literary language (Knudsen, 1923: 33, 134). In Munch's earliest translations, one finds various Danish archaisms and remains of the technical saga vocabulary. The sentence structure is also influenced by the source text. However, in spite of the existence of distinct expressions from Norwegian dialects, Munch regularly chose more literary and Danish words. He wrote, for example, 'Faarehyrde' rather than 'sauegjæter' ('a shepherd') and 'Øxnene' rather than 'oksene' ('the oxen'). Nonetheless, there are some notable exceptions; the Norwegian word 'Tun' replaces, for instance, the traditional Danish expression 'Gaardsmarken' ('the field'). In Munch's later translations, these exceptions became more of a rule: 'Arbeidstræl' becomes 'Verktræl' ('a slave') and 'på Gjestebud' becomes 'paa Veitsler' ('at a feast'), while many of the Danish archaisms disappear (Knudsen, 1923: 32–33, 142–43).

With his preface to *Njaals Saga*, Sommerfelt aligned himself linguistically with the 'fornorskingslina' of writers such as Bjørnson and Munch. A brief comparison between his text and N.M. Petersen's Danish translation of the saga is, nonetheless, needed to determine how far Sommerfelt goes in his linguistic reform. For that comparison, I have chosen the description of the killing of Höskuldur Þráinsson Hvítanesgoði, Njáll Þorgeirsson's step-son:

> På denne tid vågnede Höskuld Hvidenæsgode; han for i sine klæder; og tog den kappe over sig, som Flose havde givet ham; han tog en kornkurv i den ene hånd, sværdet i den anden, gik hen til gærdet, og gav sig til at så. Skarphedin og de andre havde overlagt, at de skulde alle bære våben på ham. Skarphedin sprang op fra gærdet; men da Höskuld så ham, vilde han flygte. Men

> Skarphedin løb imod ham, og sagde: 'Tænk aldrig på at fly, Hvidenæsgode!' og hug til ham, og traf ham i hovedet, så han sank i knæ. Höskuld udbrød i det han faldt: 'Gud hjælpe mig og tilgive eder!' Da løbe de alle mod ham, og bare våben på ham. (Petersen, 1862–68: 2:209)

> Ved denne Tid vaagnede Høskuld Hvitanæsgode. Han for i sine Klæder og tog over sig Kappen Flosenaut. Han tog sin Saaløb i den ene Haand og Sværdet i den anden, og gik derefter ud paa Jordet for at saa. Skarphedin og de Andre havde aftalt, at de alle skulde give ham Saar. Skarphedin sprang op bag Gjærdet. Da Høskuld saa ham, vilde han tage Flugten; men Skarphedin løb ind paa ham og sagde: 'Tænk ikke paa at rømme, Hvitanæsgode!' hug til ham og traf ham i Hovedet, saa at han sank i Knæ. I det Samme han faldt, sagde han: 'Gud hjælpe mig og tilgive Eder!' De løb nu alle ind paa ham og saarede ham. (Sommerfelt, 1871: 199)

> [About that time Höskuldur Hvítanesgoði awoke; he put on his clothes and covered himself with his cloak, Flosi's gift. He took his seed-basket in one hand and his sword in the other and went to his field and started sowing. Skarphéðinn and the others had agreed that they would all give him a wound. Skarphéðinn sprang up from behind the wall. When Höskuldur saw him, he wanted to turn away but Skarphéðinn ran up to him and spoke: 'Don't bother taking to your heels, Hvítanesgoði' – and he struck with his sword and hit him in the head, and Höskuldur fell on his knees. He spoke this: 'May God help me and forgive you.' (Ch. 111)]

It should be noted, first of all, that the difference in capitalisation and in spelling between the two translations (å and ö in Petersen's become aa and ø in Sommerfelt's) is directly related to the two different letter-types used in these translations. This difference is not found between Sommerfelt's text and the first edition of Petersen's translation, dating from 1841, which has the Gothic letter-type. In short, Sommerfelt observed Danish spelling rules and word forms. The only exception was his use of 'ta' in 'Hvi*ta*næsgode' (Danish: 'Hvi*de*næsgode') which was, in the tradition of P.A. Munch, influenced by the Norwegian dialects and gives the text a significant Norwegian flavour.

Generally, however, differences are not so much between Danish and Norwegian expressions, but typically between two different Danish expressions ('overlagt'/'aftalt', 'flygte'/'tage Flugten', 'løb imod ham'/'løb ind paa ham', 'ikke'/'aldrig', 'fly'/'rømme', 'så'/'saa at', 'mod ham'/'ind paa ham', 'udbrød'/'sagde'). The most typical

Norwegian words in Sommerfelt's text are 'Saaløb' and 'Jordet', replacing Petersen's Danish words 'kornkurv' og 'gærdet'. Again in the tradition of Munch, Sommerfelt also preserved the technical saga word 'Flosenaut', while Petersen spelled out its meaning ('som Flose havde givet ham'). Regarding the sentence structure, Sommerfelt's Norwegian: 'I det Samme han faldt, sagde han' can be contrasted with Petersen's more traditional Danish order: 'Höskuld udbrød i det han faldt'. However, unlike the form of language used in Bjørnson's prose-narratives and in the fairy tales of Asbjørnsen and Moe, Sommerfelt seems to have avoided purely Norwegian characteristics such as the double definite article (he writes 'den ene Haand' and not 'den ene Haanden') and post-nominal differences (he writes 'sine Klæder' and 'Ved denne Tid' and not 'Klæderne sine' and 'Ved denne Tiden').

The paragraph under observation does not support Sommerfelt's suggestion that the 'Norwegian language' was stronger or more suitable than regular Danish for the translation of Icelandic sagas. In fact, the difference between the two translations is so slight that one is tempted to deduce that Sommerfelt translated his text directly from Petersen's translation, only with secondary observance of the original Icelandic. If that was the case, Sommerfelt's work with *Njáls saga* might be seen as an example of what G.C. Kálmán (1986: 120) refers to as *synchronic intralinguistic translation*, applying to instances when a text is translated from one dialect to another, but also – and more appropriately for our discussion – when translation or transcription is produced 'according to (co-existent, synchronic) stylistic norms' within the same single language. On the other hand, Sommerfelt's secondary observance of the Icelandic 'original' is clearly manifested by expressions such as 'Flosenaut' (Icelandic: 'Flosanaut') and 'Jordet', which in this context improves Petersen's inaccurate 'gærdet' ('the wall') as a translation of 'gérdisins' ('the field'). In the same paragraph, he retained 'gærdet'/'Gjærdet' as a translation of 'gardinum' ('the [stone] wall'; cf. Olavius, 1844: 257). Details of this sort may encourage us to judge the 1871 *Njaals Saga* simply as a translation from Icelandic into Danish. But in view of the translator's claim for a Norwegian nationality of his text, one is inclined to put it into the category Kálmán (1986: 118) so distinguishes: 'there is something wrong or special about the language used'. His examples include bilingual poems, calligraphic texts and sound-poetry, but in the present example, the language allegedly used did not (yet) exist.

It is interesting to observe here that Sommerfelt (1871: v), in the aforementioned preface, implied that the Norwegian language of his translation was after all destined for controversy:

> Now there are unquestionably many, who will find my labours have not achieved the desired ends, in comparison to Petersen's [translation]; in other words that it might resemble genuine Norwegian to a greater extent. On the other hand, others will perhaps think that I have gone too far in employing unusual expressions. Here it must be remembered that our taste is so variable with regard to linguistic features ['gestalter'], that it will hardly be in any way possible to please all readers.

This comment reveals how far the Norwegian nation was from reaching a consensus on what the term 'Norwegian language' should mean in 1871. It should also be noted that Sommerfelt's language in the preface was not 'Norwegian', but a form of literary Danish, which was considerably influenced by German at the time. Consequently, contrary to his expressed intention, Sommerfelt's preface demonstrated exactly how little the Norwegian literary language had developed from the dominant Danish over the period from 1814.

Coloniser and Colony

In the discussion above, it has been argued that Karl L. Sommerfelt's translation of *Njáls saga* was published in 1871 with the intention of acquainting the general Norwegian reading public with a remote period in Norwegian history and, as a result, of strengthening national pride. The publication was an expansion of a particular strand of saga translations in Norway, which was deliberately meant to contrast with earlier Danish saga translations. In that respect, it followed a general development in Norwegian publishing and culture in the nineteenth century, striving for autonomy from a wide-reaching Danish influence.

The most important issue at stake in the Norwegian liberation of the saga was the linguistic question. A key to Norwegian national identity was a clear sense of a language which united the people and defined Norway's borders with other nations. In the long and complex development of the Norwegian language in the nineteenth century, literary translations played a significant role (cf. Skard, 1968). In their attempt to negotiate two languages, translators may grant themselves more freedom than other language-users to erase or extend the limits of the target language. In Norway, translations from the Icelandic sagas were an optimal medium for such an expansion since the sagas contained a language which people in Norway once spoke; while it, therefore, had some common characteristics with the Norwegian dialects, it was, at the same time, different from the dominant Danish literary standard.

The literary system in Norway in this period fits perfectly Itamar Even-Zohar's description of a young literary system in the process of being established. Under such circumstances, Even-Zohar (1990: 46) tells us, it is characteristic that translated literature should not only be an integral system within the literary system, but also 'as a most active system within it'. This is confirmed by the fact that leading Norwegian writers, including Ibsen and Bjørnson, deliberately borrowed themes and stylistic features from the saga corpus (cf. Mjöberg, 1967–68).

But as a final twist to this analysis of Sommerfelt's translation, it is tempting to draw attention to an article by F. Roll, which was published in the 1872 issue of *Folkevennen*. Entitled 'Norge i 1871' ('Norway in 1871'), it served as an annual report on main events and developments in Norway for the previous year. Admittedly, the publication of Sommerfelt's translation was not mentioned in this context, but the author spent considerable space describing how merchants in the Norwegian city of Bergen had, in 1871, started trading with Iceland after a long period of Danish monopoly that had been centred in Copenhagen. Stressing that monopolised trading had been eliminated, 'everywhere among the more enlightened nations', Roll (1872: 249) went on to detail the financial success of the Bergen merchants during this first year and expressed the hope that other contacts with Iceland would be re-established as a consequence: 'Of course we have other things to trade than just lumber and wool. There are those who have already started to anticipate that Iceland should come back to us and be united with Norway as in earlier times.' Roll added that, irrespective of how appealing that thought might appear to his countrymen, the matter would depend on whether both parties had something to gain.

This discussion of (inter)national trading and Iceland's possible unity with Norway provides us with an additional perspective on Sommerfelt's translation and his definition of *Njáls saga* as a piece of Norwegian national literature. Interestingly, it also echoes the words of Oluf Rygh, Sommerfelt's patron and the vice-chairman of SFF, who, in an epilogue to his 1861 translation of a part of *Færeyinga saga*, complained that Norwegian businessmen had not yet taken advantage of the new Danish laws regarding free trade in the Faroes. Both with respect to the countries' geographical distance from each other and the supply of raw material (such as lumber and iron), Norway was in Rygh's (1861: 88) view much better qualified than

Denmark to trade with the Faroes: 'It will perhaps be possible in the course of time to renew the old but frequent communications between Norway and the Faroes and for old acquaintances to meet again.'

The period of 'old but frequent communications' between the two nations, which Rygh was referring to, is that in which *Færeyinga saga* takes place. The Faroes, like Iceland, had been mostly settled by Norwegian immigrants in the ninth century. The country became a tax-colony of the Norwegian king in 1035 and then, along with Norway, a part of the Danish kingdom in 1380. When Norway accepted dynastic union with Sweden in 1814, the Faroes continued to be a part of Denmark. Rygh (1861: 61) lamented that development in the opening of his epilogue: 'This country is lost to Norway, just like so many others which it once had the power both to populate and to maintain.' The same concerns made up the conclusion of Rygh's (1861: 102) epilogue:

> In 1814, when the king of Denmark signed the peace-treaty of Kiel and gave away his right to Norway, he excluded Norway's irrefutable tax-colonies, Iceland, Greenland, and the Faroes. As a result, the final bond which connected the Faroeses with their old native soil was broken.

It looks as if the publication of Rygh's saga translation was designed as a step towards renewing this ancient bond between the Faroes and Norway or, more accurately, to re-establish Norway as the 'native soil' ('Moderland') for the inhabitants of Iceland, Greenland and the Faroes. Ideas of this sort cannot be found in Sommerfelt's preface to *Njaals Saga*. Rygh's involvement with the publication nonetheless suggests that the 1871 Norwegian translation of *Njáls saga* may have been published in hope of a more comprehensive unity between Iceland and its 'Moderland' of Norway.

Part IV

Njáls Saga **in Icelandic**

Chapter 6

Icelandic Saga Laws

Patronage and Politics

Of the numerous rewritings of *Njáls saga* produced in Europe and North-America in the past two hundred years, few texts offer such a fascinating insight into the configuration and function of literary patronage as the 1944 Icelandic edition edited by Magnús Finnbogason. The peculiar context of this edition not only reveals Icelanders' archetypical attachment to their sagas; its history also reveals how the rewriting of literature, however ancient, can be motivated and affected by various contemporary political interests. Sponsored by the Icelandic state in the year the nation declared full political independence from Denmark, this edition was meant to appeal to the communal sensibility of its readers. On the other hand, the parliamentary debate preceding its publication exposes fierce tensions between conservative and progressive members of a society at economic and cultural crossroads. Significantly, the course of action was determined by the desire of individual parliamentary members to control the rewriting of Icelandic medieval literature.

Addressing the mechanisms of power active in this case, the following chapter reinforces the claim of Translation Studies that any form of rewriting is a manipulatory process, a process also involving various extra-literary litigants. As discussed in the introduction, André Lefevere (1992: 15) suggested the term literary patrons in this context, defining it as 'the powers ... that can further or hinder the reading, writing and rewriting of literature'. Such a power can be exerted by persons, groups of persons (a political party for instance), a social class, a royal court, publishers or the media; but often, it operates by means of specific institutions, such as academies, bureaux of censorship, critical journals and the educational establishment. In many instances it is not easy to identify the contribution of patrons on publications but in the case of the 1944 Icelandic edition that presence was far from being disguised. On the opening page, readers were informed that the edition had been produced under the aegis of the Icelandic parliament. As further confirmation of the state's involvement, readers could note that the saga was published by Bókaútgáfa Menningarsjóðs og Þjóðvinafélagsins (The Publishing House of the Icelandic Cultural Fund and the Patriotic Society), which was in part a governmental institution; moreover that it was printed by the state printing firm of Gutenberg.

According to Lefevere, patronage consists of three interactive elements: *ideology, economics,* and *status.* In the following, we will see how each of these elements affected the 1944 *Njáls saga,* but we will also go beyond these terms and detect the personal interests some parlimentary members had invested in the matter. However useful the concept of patronage proves to the analysis of rewriting, this chapter emphasises the necessity *also* to identify the individuals disguised behind various institutions of patronage.

The Ideology of Obstruction

In the field of rewriting, Lefevere emphasises, *ideology* acts as a constraint on the choices a literary patron makes (what should and shouldn't be published) and on the development of both form and subject matter (how should it be edited and presented). Ideology, in this context, should not be taken in a sense limited to the political sphere. Quoting Fredric Jameson, Lefevere (1992: 16) defines the concept as 'that grillwork of form, convention, and belief which orders our actions'.

As for the ideology of the 1944 *Njáls saga,* Vilhjálmur Þ. Gíslason's (1944: xvi) introduction spelled out its purpose: 'It is essential now for [Icelandic] nationality and national development that the sagas should be thoroughly read and respected.' Later in his introduction, Gíslason added that the 1944 edition was expected to be better qualified for wide circulation than previous editions. Even though he concluded that the aim of the publication was both to open up the saga's 'wonderlands' to young readers and to give older readers an opportunity to experience its charm anew, the official ideology of the edition was not so much to gratify individual readers as to underpin and promote a sense of national identity and unity among the citizens of the Icelandic state. Gíslason's stress on the urgent need for the new edition ('It is essential now . . .') evidently refered to Iceland's declaration of independence from Denmark in 1944 and the continued Allied occupation of Iceland, by then in its fourth year. Whilst the Allied military presence was generally regarded by the Icelanders as preferable to the alternative of German invasion, it was nevertheless understandable that the indigenous population should be concerned about 'national development' at a time when the nation was in daily contact with English-speaking troops (cf. Þorsteinsson and Jónsson, 1991: 398–419).

Establishing the virtues of *Njáls saga* in ideological and nationalistic terms, Gíslason (1944: v) asserted in his introduction that the Icelandic family sagas in general were 'among the best and the most valuable resources of Icelandic culture'. In that context, he refered to their subject-matter, narrative technique and vocabulary, and their lasting influence on a variety of readers, scholars and artists as well as the general public. *Njáls saga*, Gíslason (1944: xiii) continued, was the most comprehensive and 'in many ways the richest' of the family sagas; its many surviving manuscripts testifying to the saga's popularity from the earliest times. From his argument, one can infer that the 1944 publication was intended and expected to maintain the beneficial influence of the sagas in an independent Iceland and to help to secure the stability of a society that was in many ways at a cross-roads.

Irrespective of the particular circumstances of 1944, the nation had made remarkable economic, social and cultural changes since the turn of the century. In 1901, 80% of Icelanders were living in rural areas, with 70% of the total work-force employed in agriculture. By 1940, only 35% of the inhabitants remained in the countryside; the rest had moved to coastal towns and villages. Most strikingly, in this period, Reykjavík had been transformed from a small town of 6700 inhabitants (8.5% of the population in 1901) into a small city of almost 40,000 citizens (31.5% of the population in 1940; Hagstofan, 1967: 19–35). In the face of these major changes, it is as if Gíslason sought to represent *Njáls saga* as a source of cultural reassurance and stability. No matter how much the world turned and tumbled, the 1944 edition would help to ensure that the Icelanders could continue to read and respect their native cultural resources.

However, in the discussions and debates which led up to this state-sponsored edition, supporters in the parliament did not draw particular attention to the views that later found expression in Gíslason's introduction. Instead they emphasised that the state edition should be seen as a response to another edition of *Njáls saga*, proposed to be edited by Halldór Laxness, one of Iceland's leading novelists, and published by Ragnar Jónsson, Laxness' permanent publisher. As summarised in a statement accompanying the original parliamentary proposal, the background to the whole affair was a complex one: In the autumn of 1941, Ragnar Jónsson announced the publication of an abridged version of *Laxdæla saga* in modern Icelandic spelling (Vísir,

1941), this at a time when the long-accepted custom had been to print saga-editions in the so-called normalised ancient spelling. This plan met with passionate opposition, first expressed in several newspaper articles and eventually in law (no. 127, Dec. 9, 1941) granting to the Icelandic state the copyright for all Icelandic texts written before 1400 (Alþingi, 1942: 1:56–57). Individuals interested in publishing editions of these works now needed to apply for authorisation to the Minister of Education.

Before this law came into operation, Jónsson and his collaborators – his co-publisher Stefán Ögmundsson and editor Laxness – had been able to publish their edition of *Laxdæla saga*. However, they confronted and challenged the new law in 1942 by publishing *Hrafnkatla* (*Hrafnkels saga Freysgoða*) in a modern spelling edition, without obtaining the now necessary permission. As a result, they were prosecuted and convicted; each of them was sentenced to either a fine of kr. 1000 or a prison sentence of 45 days. They immediately appealed against the sentence on the grounds that it violated constitutional provisions relating to the freedom of the press (Hæstiréttur, 1943: 237–44). As a matter of principle, they could not acknowledge the literary patronage of the Minister that had been institutionalised in 1941.

While their case was being heard in the superior court in the spring of 1943, the Icelandic parliament had to vote on further proposed legislation which sought to invalidate the 1941 copyright law (Alþingi, 1943–46: 3:168–220). Before producing its report, the commission appointed to discuss this proposal sought academic advice from three professors of Icelandic studies at the University of Iceland. Together, these scholars wrote a report, claiming that even though it was desirable to protect old texts from potential damage and distortion in new editions, the copyright laws themselves were in many ways imperfect. They also indicated that examination of Laxness' edition of *Laxdæla saga* had revealed serious flaws. The editor had modernised some of its vocabulary, had omitted old words and inserted new ones at various points in the text, and had omitted or reorganised sentences or even whole chapters from his source edition. All these changes, the professors concluded, had distorted the substance and character of the saga (Alþingi, 1943–46: 1:719–20). On April 2, the parliament agreed to postpone revisions of the copyright law on the grounds that the government was then in the midst of preparing a comprehensive *corpus juris* addressing questions of artistic and literary copyright in Iceland. However, it also resolved that the revised law should have the power to prevent publication of 'distorted' editions of early Icelandic literature (Alþingi, 1943–46: 1:764). At the heart of the matter was the very liberty of rewriting. Laxness' editions, falling into Roman Jakobson's (1959: 233) category of intralingual translations, violated the sacredness of the saga literature.

The following week, it was announced that Ragnar Jónsson and Halldór Laxness were preparing a new modern-spelling edition of *Njáls saga*, having obtained the required authorisation from the Minister of Education. It was in response to this announcement that three members of the lower house of the parliament – Helgi Jónasson, Ingólfur Jónsson and Sveinbjörn Högnason – put together a proposal for the state edition of the saga, submitting it for discussion on April 9. Drawing on the unfavorable comments which Laxness' edition of *Laxdæla saga* had received from the university professors, the three parliamentary members argued in their statement that Laxness' *Njáls saga* would be similarly and seriously impaired. Hence the need for state involvement:

> We, who cherish *Njáls saga*, want to ensure by this parliamentary proposal that the people [of Iceland] have the chance of owning the saga in an inexpensive, good-quality edition, free from the fingerprints of those who want to drag everything into the gutter and who will not spare even our most valuable works of art, such as *Njála*, from that fate. (Alþingi, 1943–46: 1:803)

The agenda of those responsible for the proposal seems clear. Dissatisfied with the performance of the Minister of Education, they wanted the parliament to (re)assume the role of a literary patron. Their aim was to obstruct the rewriting and reading of literature; the idea with the parliamentary intervention was to prevent (or, as they saw it, to protect) the Icelandic nation from reading Laxness' version of *Njáls saga*. The metaphors in the proposal characterised Laxness' rewritings as profane, even bestial, while the saga itself was a feminised image of purity and value.

Economics of Symbolic Capital

For a fuller understanding of the parliament's sensitivity to the publication of unauthorised saga editions, it is helpful to examine the second of the three features which Lefevere identifies as constitutive elements in literary patronage, that of *economics*. In his definition, this element usually involves the writer (or translator, editior or whatever) enjoying some form of financial support from the patron; but in the case of the 1944 *Njáls saga*, there were additional factors involved.

In his 1944 introduction, Vilhjálmur Þ. Gíslason did not make direct reference to the economic aspects of the state edition, but it is interesting to note the kind of imagery in which his references to the sagas were expressed. We read of sagas as 'resources' and of *Njáls saga* as the 'richest' of these resources. In employing these formulaic metaphors, Gíslason echoed the proponents' statement, in which the saga was referred to as one of the 'most valuable' works of Icelandic art. This imagery of value or wealth was more fully developed in a speech by one of the bill's three sponsors, Helgi Jónasson:

> We Icelanders have to admit that we are poor and few in number and we do not enjoy much material wealth, but we do have one asset – our old literature. It must be almost without parallel that a small nation such as ours should possess the kind of pearls beyond price which our ancient literature represents. (Alþingi, 1943–46: 4:191)

For this reason, Jónasson continued, it was a delicate matter when any editor sought to change the language or the subject matter of a saga. He went on to criticise certain aspects of Laxness' 1941 edition of *Laxdæla saga*: not only had the text of the saga been distorted but the whole book had been badly printed on poor-quality paper. It was obvious, he concluded, that the publication of the saga had been undertaken for profit and not for the worthier purpose of 'increasing the value' of Icelandic literature (Alþingi, 1943–46: 4:192).

It may be helpful to apprehend Jónasson's argument in view of Pierre Bourdieu's analysis of the different powers or forms of capital which are efficient in a given social universe. In addition to *economic* capital, Bourdieu (1987: 4) identifies three other forms: '*cultural* capital or better, informational capital' and then the very strongly correlated '*social* capital, which consists of resources based on connections and group membership, and *symbolic* capital, which is the form the different types of capital take once they are perceived and recognized as legitimate'. Evidently, Jónasson perceived the sagas as being tokens of symbolic capital. In his view their 'value' was expected to be at least preserved, if not enriched, through the scholarly and presentational quality of any published edition. Furthermore, if the sagas were indeed national cultural treasures, their symbolic capital had to be widely and equally distributed. Laxness' project was seen as violating both of these principles, comprising a poorly produced edition with the whole enterprise driven by the desire to make a personal profit. Under state sponsorship, in contrast, the nation as a whole would benefit. Readers were getting *Njáls saga*, a literary pearl beyond price, expertly edited and produced for the lowest possible charge.

As far as traditional economics are concerned, the point needs to be made that, by recommending that *Njáls saga* be published by Menningarsjóður and Þjóðvinafélagið, the parliament was plugging into an established system of subscribers or members (Alþingi, 1943–46: 1:803). The arrangement had been established by the publishing board of Menningarsjóður in 1940; members would receive seven books annually in return for a modest subscription. This offer proved so popular that, by the end of the first year, the number of subscribers was sufficently large to allow the company to print 12,000 copies of each of these seven books, apparently a record in the history of Icelandic publishing (Guðmundsson, 1985: 91). For a country of 120,000 citizens (Hagstofan, 1967: 20), it meant that the publications of Bókaútgáfa Menningarsjóðs og Þjóðvinafélagsins entered a significant proportion of Icelandic homes. Distributed in this way, the 1944 *Njáls saga* was indeed better qualified for wide circulation than any previous editions.

But despite these advantages, individual parliamentary members found various faults with the whole plan. According to the proposal, the government was called upon to 'encourage' Menningarsjóður and Þjóðvinafélagið to publish a good popular edition of *Njáls saga* (Alþingi, 1943–46: 1:803). Questions were soon raised about the government's authority for such intervention in the decisions of the publishing board. Although the board had been appointed by the parliament and included several of its members, Bókaútgáfa Menningarsjóðs og Þjóðvinafélagsins was supposedly responsible for its own operations. It certainly ought not to be subject to government interference, argued the Minister of Education, Einar Arnórsson, who had authorised Laxness' edition. On the other hand, he added, if governmental encouragement merely involved granting Menningarsjóður and Þjóðvinafélagið the required authorisation for publishing the saga – that would hardly be a problem (Alþingi, 1943–46: 4:193). As a second concern, Barði Guðmundsson pointed out that Hið íslenzka fornritafélag (Early Icelandic Text Society; hereafter Fornritafélagið) also had plans to publish *Njáls saga*. Its scholarly editions were subsidised by the state and sufficiently well-respected for the 1941 copyright law uniquely to exempt the society from having to apply for permission to publish Icelandic works written before 1400 (Alþingi, 1942: 1:57). Guðmundsson said he could not support the proposed state edition since it would involve Fornritafélagið in a huge financial loss on its own edition of the saga (Alþingi, 1943–46: 4:196). Thirdly, Sigfús Sigurhjartarson stressed that a satisfactory popular edition of the saga from 1942 (edited by Guðni Jónsson) was still in circulation. In his view, this edition already represented just the alternative to Laxness' proposed edition which the parliament sought to establish (Alþingi, 1943–46: 4:199).

In response to these criticisms, Helgi Jónasson explained that governmental encouragement certainly included Einar Arnórsson's authorisation of the state edition but could also extend into other areas. He noted, for instance, that war-time conditions made supplies of paper difficult to obtain, while the printing presses themselves were so busy that it took a long time to have anything published at all. In all these matters, the government's support could be helpful. Jónasson went on to read a statement signed by ten of the seventeen members of the other chamber of the parliament, in which they voiced their support for the proposed edition of Bókaútgáfa Menningarsjóðs og Þjóðvinafélagsins. Additionally, they expressed their willingness to increase the grant which Fornritafélagið received from the state as compensation for any loss which the society might suffer from the state edition of *Njáls saga* (Alþingi, 1943–46: 4:196–97).

It is clear from this discussion that some very unusual economic conditions were to attend the publication of the state sponsored edition of *Njáls saga*. There seems not to have been a particular public demand for the edition, and the capacity of the war-time printing industry was in any case severely limited. On the premise that cultural values had priority over market forces, not to mention shortage of raw materials, government involvement was expected to bestow important economic privileges on the new edition. Furthermore, Helgi Jónasson acknowledged that it might also prove damaging (with any luck) to the profitability of the proposed edition of Halldór Laxness (Alþingi, 1943–46: 4:215).

Status Non-Grado

In this analysis we have been observing a literary patron operating in a defensive way. The fundamental motive behind governmental support of the 1944 *Njáls saga* was not so much that Icelanders should buy and read the state edition, but rather that they should not buy or read Laxness' edition. This same pattern of priorities surfaces again when we mark the element of *status* involved in this affair. The point was not primarily that the Icelandic parliament should sponsor the publication of sagas but rather that Laxness and his patron should not be doing so.

In André Lefevere's (1992: 16) definition, status implies the very acceptance of patronage; 'intergration into a certain support group and its lifestyle, whether the recipient is Tasso at the court of Ferrara, [or] the Beat poets gathering around the City Lights bookstore in San Francisco'. The concept thus intersects with Bourdieu's broader terms of cultural and social capital – the fundamental resources of social power. From this perspective, it is noteworthy how Helgi Jónasson and his followers in the parliament qualified themselves as elected representatives of Icelandic voters. Jónasson claimed, for instance, that while the Minister of Education, Einar Arnórsson, had not broken any laws in authorising Laxness' edition of *Njáls saga*, he had nevertheless consciously defied the will of the parliament, 'and, I venture to assert, the will of the great majority of the [Icelandic] nation'. In his conclusion, Jónasson added that the proposed state edition would represent *Njáls saga* 'as we wish to have it and as the nation wishes to have it ' (Alþingi,1943–46: 4:192–93). In this case, social capital was being directly indicated and utilised. (Surprisingly, Jónasson did not make a note of the fact that Minister Arnórsson had been Laxness' father-in-law for a decade, between 1930 and 1940 (cf. Jónsson, 1982: 1:564).)

The main thrust of Jónasson's argument was, however, systematically to question Laxness' status as a saga editor. In analysing his strategy, we need to look again at the written submission of the three university professors which dealt both with the 1941 copyright law and Laxness' *Laxdœla saga*. According to the copyright law, the Minister of Education *could* authorise editions of Icelandic works written before 1400 to follow 'normalised ancient spelling' (Alþingi, 1942: 1:57). In their written submission, the university professors opposed this attempt to impose such a system of spelling since no such system, they claimed, could ever represent exactly the forms and sounds of the ancient language. Indeed, they argued, the modern Icelandic spelling sanctioned by law from 1929 (and which Laxness had used in his editions) was in some respects closer to the 'linguistic origins' of Icelandic than the system used in the scholarly editions of Fornritafélagið. In both cases, we should note, texts of old manuscripts were being rewritten; like Laxness' editions, the editions of Fornritafélagið are unmistakably intralingual translations.

Furthermore, the university men acknowledged that even the oldest preserved saga manuscripts were already rewrites. They emphasised the variety of changes that Icelandic medieval texts had undergone in the thirteenth and fourteenth century. Some of these changes, they said, had even led to improvements in particular texts; younger versions of some sagas were quite properly chosen for publication rather than older ones. The quality of an edition could rest as much on aesthetic merit as on fidelity to some supposed but lost, original text.

In this context, the scholars expressed doubts as to the qualifications and capacity of the Ministry of Education to make judgements about which editorial changes to old saga texts would or would not endanger the nation's cultural or linguistic health. They concluded: 'If it is considered necessary to supervise the publication of older works of literature, as many people tend to feel, it seems more natural that such works should be placed in the hands of scholars and writers appointed for that task, whose knowledge and taste can be trusted' (Alþingi, 1943–46: 1:720). Questioning the very element of status inherent in the 1941 law, the scholars were not only referring here to their own cultural capital (their educational credentials and university positions), but also to that of writers like Laxness.

Proposing the state edition, Helgi Jónasson avoided direct quotation from these paragraphs in the scholars' report. It seems, however, that his approach was determined by these very comments. On the one hand, he admitted that the system of spelling in saga editions was a matter of individual taste; on the other hand, he questioned Laxness' status as a saga editior. Jónasson quoted a statement, dating from the fall of 1941, in which Laxness had claimed that the only proposed change in his forthcoming edition of *Laxdæla saga* was to modernise the spelling. In view of the fact that his editorial interventions had been rather more wide-ranging, Jónasson argued that Laxness' claims could not be relied on. Citing the negative verdict which the university scholars had reached, he went on to suggest that the writer's aesthetic taste could not be trusted either, but it may be noted that Laxness' writing style and the personal rules of spelling he used in his own work had been a subject of heated criticism in the preceding years (cf. Höskuldsson, 1973). Finally, Jónasson referred to the ruling of the lower courts over Laxness' edition of *Hrafnkatla*, implying that the novelist's character was not beyond reproach (Laxness had been sentenced to either a fine of kr. 1000 or a prison sentence of 45 days for his involvement with that edition). According to the university professors, the editing of old texts should be left to established experts, scholars and writers. Jónasson's strategy, in short, was to undermine Laxness' authority – his cultural capital – and to claim that he was bound to 'deform' *Njáls saga* (Alþingi, 1943–46: 4:191–93).

Patronage and Geography

Thus far in the discussion of the 1944 *Njáls saga*, it has been described how the Icelandic parliament was seeking to regulate the editing and dissemination of early Icelandic literature during the years of World War II. But there are additional strands in this complex debate which have not yet been discussed. One of these pertains to the traditional definition of *Njáls saga* as a piece of local history, particularly the history of Rangárvallasýsla, the district in which a substantial part of the saga takes place. (Symbolically, the heraldry of the district portrays the weapons of Gunnar Hámundarson and Skarphéðinn Njálsson as described in the saga.)

Indeed, the three men who were officially responsible for the 1943 parliamentary proposal all lived in Rangárvallasýsla: Helgi Jónasson, who was a farmer at Stórólfshvoll in Fljótshlíð, and Ingólfur Jónsson, who lived in the small town of Hella, were the two elected representatives of the district, while Sveinbjörn Högnason, although representing the neighboring district of Vestur-Skaftafellssýsla, was a clergyman in Rangárvallasýsla, living at Breiðabólsstaður in Fljótshlíð (Alþingi, 1943–46: 3:916). Their involvement with *Njáls saga* reproduced the 1941 parliamentary discussions on the proposed copyright law, triggered by Laxness' *Laxdæla saga*. Then the importance of sagas' local links was clearly revealed by Þorsteinn Þorsteinsson, a judge and revenue officer of the Dalasýsla district, who spoke in support of the copyright proposal:

> The district with which I am involved has been struck by a disaster. Its major saga, *Laxdæla saga*, has been published in a 'modern' spelling edition, without introduction, index or explanatory notes; it is more or less deformed. I have no wish for other districts to be stuck in the same muddy stream and I think it is right to block it at its source. (Alþingi, 1942: 2:107)

Þorsteinsson stressed that the family sagas were 'ancient, classical' historical documents. Accordingly, he criticised Laxness for deleting from his *Laxdæla saga* edition detailed information about genealogies and places of residence.

Although the supporters of the state edition of *Njáls saga* did not present themselves so explicitly as spokesmen for their district, their collaboration suggests that they were initially fighting for the interests of their fellow residents in the region which is the principal location for the saga. In this context we may note the arguments of Helgi Jónasson, who shared Þorsteinn Þorsteinsson's basic views on the nature of the sagas as historical documents. Jónasson criticised Laxness' very poor (as he regarded it) preface, in which *Laxdæla saga* was characterised as being historically unreliable – a kind of 'a fabrication' (Alþingi, 1943–46: 4:192). He also stressed that the genealogies were indispensable for a proper understanding of the feuds in the sagas: 'The men of the past killed other men for family reasons and not for fun' (Alþingi, 1943–46: 4:197). This remark is certainly valid for many scenes in the sagas, but it also needs to be understood that by no means all genealogies are important to the plot. For twentieth-century residents of Rangárvallasýsla, however, genealogies had an independent validity as links between living individuals or locations and the ancient saga narrative. Apparently, Laxness' rewritings threatened the way in which these people identified, geographically at least, with the sagas and their characters.

The genealogy of Gunnar Hámundarson in *Njáls saga* (Ch. 19) is representative of Helgi Jónasson's concerns. First, Gunnar's maternal lineage is outlined, revealing how he is related to Unnur Marðardóttir. Subsequent events in the saga are determined by Gunnar's service to Unnur, and it is necessary for readers to understand on what grounds she asks for his assistance when she has problems of her own. Gunnar's paternal lineage is then traced; he is the son of Hámundur Gunnarsson. Right at the end of the narrative (Ch. 148), this information will prove illuminating when Valgerður Þorbrandsdóttir, the daughter of Hámundur's sister, becomes involved in the plot. The description of the rest of Gunnar's paternal line, in contrast, serves to explain elements in his character (as presented), rather than the course of events. Among his relatives are the law-speaker Hrafn Hængsson, suggesting that powerful intellectual qualities run in the family, and Ormur the Strong, indicating corresponding powerful physical qualities. Finally, one branch of the family tree leads us to a particular place-name in Rangárvallasýsla: we are told that the farm Gunnarsholt derived its name from Gunnar's grandfather, Gunnar Baugsson. Although such knowledge does not in itself illuminate the narrative significantly, it was an important historical background for the people of Rangárvallasýsla in the 1940s, not least for those who lived at Gunnarsholt.

For a more immediate link between person and place we recall that Helgi Jónasson lived at Stórólfshvoll. According to the saga (Ch. 19), Stórólfur Hængsson was the great-grandfather of Gunnar Hámundarson, being the brother of Hrafn Hængsson and the father of Ormur the Strong. Clearly, Jónasson was not at all keen to have that topological connection between himself and the mighty Gunnar of Hlíðarendi removed from *Njáls saga* in Laxness' edition. Indeed, his performance in the parliament suggests that the twentieth-century chieftain of Stórólfshvoll had inherited some of the qualities of advocacy which characterised Stórólfur's brother, Hrafn Hængsson, the law-speaker.

Icelandic Saga Politics

Even though the proposal for the state edition of *Njáls saga* initially served the interests of a specific district in southern Iceland and its inhabitants, it should be underlined how the opposition to the proposal in the parliament ran as much along political as geographical lines. The twelve 'no' voters in the lower house of the parliament included all the seven representatives of the Socialist Coalition (Sameiningarflokkur alþýðu, Sósíalistaflokkur; hereafter SAS). Similarly, the seven members of the upper house not to sign the statement in support of the proposal included the three representatives of SAS; one of them was Kristinn E. Andrésson, the man who had asked for the invalidation of the 1941 copyright law only a few days before the parliament became preoccupied with *Njáls saga* (Alþingi, 1943–46: 4:196, 220–22).

It is also significant that, in the discussion about the state edition, Laxness' editorial plans were consistently supported and defended by three members of SAS – Áki Jakobsson, Einar Olgeirsson, and Sigfús Sigurhjartarson – all of whom maintained that the proposal for the state edition was part of an elaborate political plot, devised by a member of the upper house of the parliament, Jónas Jónsson. Jakobsson said that the purpose of the state edition was to 'persecute' Laxness and also conceivably to denigrate SAS (Alþingi, 1943–46: 4:202). Olgeirsson suggested that this tendency to limit people's freedom of action was no new phenomenon in Icelandic politics: Jónas Jónsson had, for example, recommended that Laxness' novels should be banned in Iceland on the grounds that they were full of Communist propaganda (Alþingi, 1943–46: 4:204). Jónsson had also drawn up a proposal, accepted by a majority vote in the parliament, which would have prevented people with 'particular political opinions', as Olgeirsson expressed it, from being employed by the state or from enjoying state financial support (Alþingi, 1943–46: 4:205). Finally, Sigurhjartarson recalled that Jónsson, in an extended crusade against Icelandic Socialists, had persuaded a majority of parliamentary members to support a statement claiming that it was disgraceful that they should have to share the parliamentary floor with SAS representatives (Alþingi, 1943–46: 4:212). In the course of their speeches, the representatives of SAS referred to the advocates of the state edition as Jónas Jónsson's disciples, but two of the three proponents – Helgi Jónasson and Sveinbjörn Högnason – were members of the farmers oriented Framsóknarflokkur (The Progressive Party), in which Jónsson was a leading figure.

It is beyond the scope of this study to trace the twists and turns that the debate between the Socialists and their adversaries took in Iceland in the 1930s and 1940s, but ever since the foundation of Kommúnistaflokkur Íslands (The Icelandic Communist Party) in 1930, Jónas Jónsson had been one of the fiercest opponents of this 'dictatorial pest' (Guðmundsson, 1985: 87; cf. Friðriksson, 1993). Exercising his power as Minister of Education in the early 1930s, he had, for instance, introduced measures whereby students who advocated Communist doctrines should be excluded from higher education. The revival of publishing activities administered by the state's cultural fund, Menningarsjóður, and its cooperation with Þjóðvinafélagið (an independent cultural society) was, similarly, Jónsson's response to the success of Mál og menning, a literary society originally established in 1937 by a group of Socialists, mostly writers (cf. Ólafsson, 1990). Under his leadership, Bókaútgáfa Menningarsjóðs og Þjóðvinafélagsins adopted the subscription system used by Mál og menning, which by 1939 had already attracted a few thousand members. One of Jónsson's declared aims was to balance the Communist propaganda which, he claimed, Mál og menning was distributing in Iceland with financial aid from Moscow.

On a number of occasions during this period, there were confrontations between Jónas Jónsson and Halldór Laxness. Although not a registered member of SAS, Laxness was an outspoken Socialist, an admirer of Stalin's Soviet Union, one of the founders of Mál og menning, and active member on its editorial board. In the 1940s, he worked closely with Kristinn E. Andrésson, who edited the journal *Tímarit Máls og menningar* and who became a representative of SAS in the parliament in 1942. While Jónsson criticised Laxness for his political views and for writing perverted anti-national novels that advocated Communism (Jónsson, 1942), Laxness attacked the publishing agenda of Bókaútgáfa Menningarsjóðs og Þjóðvinafélagsins. Laxness (1942: 228–29) also attacked Jónsson personally for his editorial role in some of the books published by Bókaútgáfa Menningarsjóðs og Þjóðvinafélagsins. Their quarrel additionally related to changes in the law, passed in 1939, which entrusted to parliamentary Education Commission (Menntamálaráð) responsibility for distributing the annual state grants to the arts.

In January 1941, Jónas Jónsson published a long newspaper article, discussing the publishing policy of Bókaútgáfa Menningarsjóðs og Þjóðvinafélagsins. He refered to a recent survey indicating that the Icelandic family sagas were not to be found on the bookshelves of the majority of Icelandic homes. His sense was that the average person could not afford to buy the expensive editions of Fornritafélagið, the only saga editions in print at this time. Jónsson proposed that, if the price could be lowered by almost half, Menningarsjóður would be happy to work with Fornritafélagið and distribute the sagas through its subscriber network. If such an arrangement could not be established, he concluded, Bókaútgáfa Menningarsjóðs og Þjóðvinafélagsins would have to address in some other way the urgent need for inexpensive editions of the family sagas (Jónsson, 1941a). Apparently, some negotiations between Fornritafélagið and Menningarsjóður did take place (cf. Alþingi, 1942: 2:87), but at the time when the debate on the state edition of *Njáls saga* began in 1943, these had resulted merely in the Menningarsjóður decision to begin publication of saga editions in full 'conformity' with the interest of Fornritafélagið (Alþingi, 1943–46: 4:196).

In the meantime, however, the announcement of Laxness' forthcoming edition of *Laxdæla saga* had upset Jónas Jónsson's plan. In a long news-paper article appearing in October 1941, Jónsson (1941b) condemned the proposed publication enterprise of the 'Communists': 'There is no doubt, that, if the Icelandic Communists get the opportunity to publish the old literature, they will attempt to offend general taste and national sensibility in whichever way they believe will produce the best result on every occasion.' He emphasised that Fornritafélagið and the parliament (through Menningarsjóður) were already employing qualified editors whose task was to increase the circulation of the sagas. 'Communist' intervention was, in his view, unnecessary as well as undesirable; Laxness' editions would represent merely 'a caricature' of the sagas, works that, along with the Bible and the psalms of the Icelandic seventeenth-century poet Hallgrímur Pétursson, had for centuries formed the foundations of Icelandic culture. Jónsson's argument clearly forshadows some of the views we have already detected in Helgi Jónasson's parliamentary speaches and Vilhjálmur Gíslason's introduction to the 1944 *Njáls saga.* The sagas were seen as Iceland's sacred texts, a key to the psyche of the nation, and there was an urgency to prevent Laxness from distorting them. But Laxness' questionable status, in Jónsson's definition, stemed solely from his dubious political views. Even though publisher Ragnar Jónsson was by no means a Socialist, Jónas Jónsson seemed determined that the actual patron of Laxness' saga editions was the Icelandic Communist Party, superintended by Comintern.

Two weeks after Jónas Jónsson's article appeared, members of his party introduced the 1941 copyright law into the lower house of the parliament; the proposal was presented on November 4, but not debated until November 10 (Alþingi, 1942: 2:83). As with the proposal for the state edition of *Njáls saga* in 1943, Jónsson was not an official sponsor of the copy-right law, but in both these cases his adversaries claimed that they could sense his controlling hand. As for his personal interest in the state edition, it may have been significant that two months prior to the parliamentary debate in 1943, the power-structure in Menntamálaráð had changed with the appointment of a number of new board members. At the very first meeting of this new board, Jónsson was replaced as chairman by Valtýr Stefánsson, a delegate of the conservative Sjálfstæðisflokkur ('Independent Party'), who had been very critical of his predecessor. Consequently, Jónsson's influence on the board diminished at once (Guðmundsson, 1985: 95). Two of the other five board members, Kristinn E. Andrésson and Barði Guðmundsson, were also members of the parliament; they had both been opposed to the idea of the state edition.

It is conceivable that Jónsson, in the (for him) unfamiliar role of underdog in Menntamálaráð, designed the parliamentary proposal in order to mobilise the publishing outlet of Bókaútgáfa Menningarsjóðs and Þjóðvinafélagsins against all odds and thus to regain the saga publishing initiative from Laxness. There were even some advantages in this procedure. An edition of *Njáls saga* was bound to have more prestige and to carry less the aura of a personal or political vendetta, were it to be authorised by the Icelandic parliament – the elected voice of the national will – rather than appearing as an edition authorised by the controversial Jónas Jónsson. From a broad perspective, the political nature of the whole case implies that Jónsson, with a majority of parliamentary members, suspected that those who controlled the editing of the sacret sagas had acquired the very power to control the Icelandic nation.

Paths of Power

Some months after the Icelandic parliament had agreed to the state edition of *Njáls saga*, the Icelandic Superior Court acquitted Halldór Laxness, Ragnar Jónsson and Stefán Ögmundsson in the *Hrafnkatla* case on the grounds that the 1941 copyright law violated constitutional provisions relating to the freedom of the press (Hæstiréttur, 1943: 237–39). In this respect, the literary patronage of the parliament was defeated. It succeeded, however, in another respect: Bókaútgáfa Menningarsjóðs og Þjóðvinafélagsins, backed up with considerable governmental grant, published its *Njáls saga* in 1944.

In the light of the preceding discussion, Vilhjálmur Þ. Gíslason's introduction to the state edition might be characterised as extremely diplomatic and prudent. Gíslason provided a summary of the various views which people, mostly scholars, had expressed about the nature of the Icelandic family sagas in general and *Njáls saga* in particular. In controversial matters, of which there were many, he did not take sides but rather encouraged those readers who might be interested in specific issues to consult scholarly works. Gíslason (1944: xvi) also indicated that a more detailed bibliographical review was likely to appear elsewhere, thus drawing attention to the forthcoming Fornritafélagið edition.

As far as practical editorial policy was concerned, Gíslason's introductory essay incorporated a statement written by the text editor, Magnús Finnbogason, who claimed that the saga appeared in the volume in modern spelling, but with word-forms and linguistic features of thirteenth-century Icelandic duly preserved in all major respects. With the verses, however, the ancient spelling had been retained, since most of these verses, Finnbogason explained, were older than the saga's narrative prose. He did not mention the controversy in the parliament over Laxness' proposed edition, but he was clearly following the editorial line set out by the three university professors, who had offered their testimony during the parliamentary debate.

In his statement, Finnbogason also made clear that the publishing board of Bókaútgáfa Menningarsjóðs og Þjóðvinafélagsins had appointed a special editorial board for this project which had cooperated with him on the publication. The board consisted of Vilhjálmur Þ. Gíslason, who was also a board member of Menningarsjóður, Þorkell Jóhannesson, a librarian at the National Library, and Bogi Ólafsson, who had a degree in English and German. Finnbogason himself, like Gíslason and Jóhannesson, had a degree in Icelandic language and literature (cf. Jónsson, 1982). This powerful group was to ensure that the state edition of *Njáls saga* could not be accused, as Laxness' editions had been, of insufficient cultural capital. On the other hand, we may sense a continuing tendency to avoid responsibility for this controversial publication: apparently Jónas Jónsson asked his fellow party-members to ask the parliament to ask Bókaútgáfa Menningarsjóðs og Þjóðvinafélagsins to publish *Njáls saga*. The publishing-board had then asked a selected group of scholars to prepare the edition and they, in turn, had asked Magnús Finnbogason to become the editor. This complex mechanism reveals the subtle workings of power in this extraordinary case of literary patronage.

In the state edition, *Njáls saga* was neither presented nor rejected as a reliable historical document but it complied perfectly with the requirements of those who wanted to read it as the history of a particular district. In the middle of the introduction, a pull-out map of Rangárvallasýsla and its neighbouring district could be consulted, showing the geographical location of major farms and other sites mentioned in the saga. Interestingly, the position of Stórólfshvoll, the farm of Helgi Jónasson, was also shown on the map, even though the farm is quite irrelevant to the plot of the saga. Somewhat in keeping with the sense of the saga as a national possession, a fold-out map of Iceland and a series of photographs from various saga-sites could also be found in the volume, linking Iceland's overall geography with the narrative. Explanatory notes and an index confirmed that the saga was indeed more than a 'fabrication'.

Our inquiry into the patronage of the 1944 edition of *Njáls saga* has shown a discrepancy between the official ideology, suggested by Vilhjálmur Þ. Gíslason's introduction, and the complex motivations that led to its eventual publication. In his introduction, Gíslason (1944: vii) mentioned the lively interest the author of *Njáls saga* seems to have taken in laws and legal procedures. Gíslason was careful not to exhibit any such interest himself. His voice is impersonal and detached – almost as if seeking to conceal those political and personal controversies which had led to the Icelandic parliament playing the improbable role of saga patron.

Chapter 7

Intersections

Njáls Saga *and Urban Development*

In Chapter 6, we observed how Halldór Laxness' proposed edition of *Njáls saga* provoked the Icelandic parliament to sponsor its own edition of the saga in 1944. Laxness' *Brennunjálssaga* was published a year later. These two publications represent conflicting views on Iceland's literary heritage and culture in this period, with the parliamentary edition embodying the conservative tradition which Laxness challenged. In this chapter, the affair will be reviewed from Laxness' point of view, but apart from the political issues involved, his saga editions were correlated to important developments in the field of saga scholarship in Iceland, with the historical veracity of the sagas being seriously undermined.

Furthermore, it will be outlined how these developments concurrently affected the rewriting of *Njáls saga* on the face of Iceland's capital, through the naming of individual streets. In the introduction, the existence of *Njalsgade* (Njáll's Street) in Copenhagen was briefly commented on, but in contemporary Reykjavík, there are no less than six streets taking names from characters of the saga. It is tempting to approach these streets in view of Itamar Even-Zohar's ideas about the fate of canonised literary texts in a culture. In his *Polysystem Studies*, Even-Zohar (1990: 44) points out that these texts hardly ever circulate on the market as integral texts; when they have been 'stored in the historical canon', they are often distributed as textual fragments, i.e. quotations, short parables and episodes. Thus the *Iliad* is a wooden horse, *Don Quixote* is an old knight fighting windmills, and *Hamlet* is a young man holding a skull saying: 'To be or not to be' (two episodes of Shakespeare's play united in one). Highlighting the socio-cultural message of such textual fragments, Even-Zohar (1990: 44) suggests that one may treat them 'as a ready-made inventory for daily communication, or as a permanent *background* against which new texts and fragments can be generated and compared'. He adds that a semiotic approach would treat these fragments

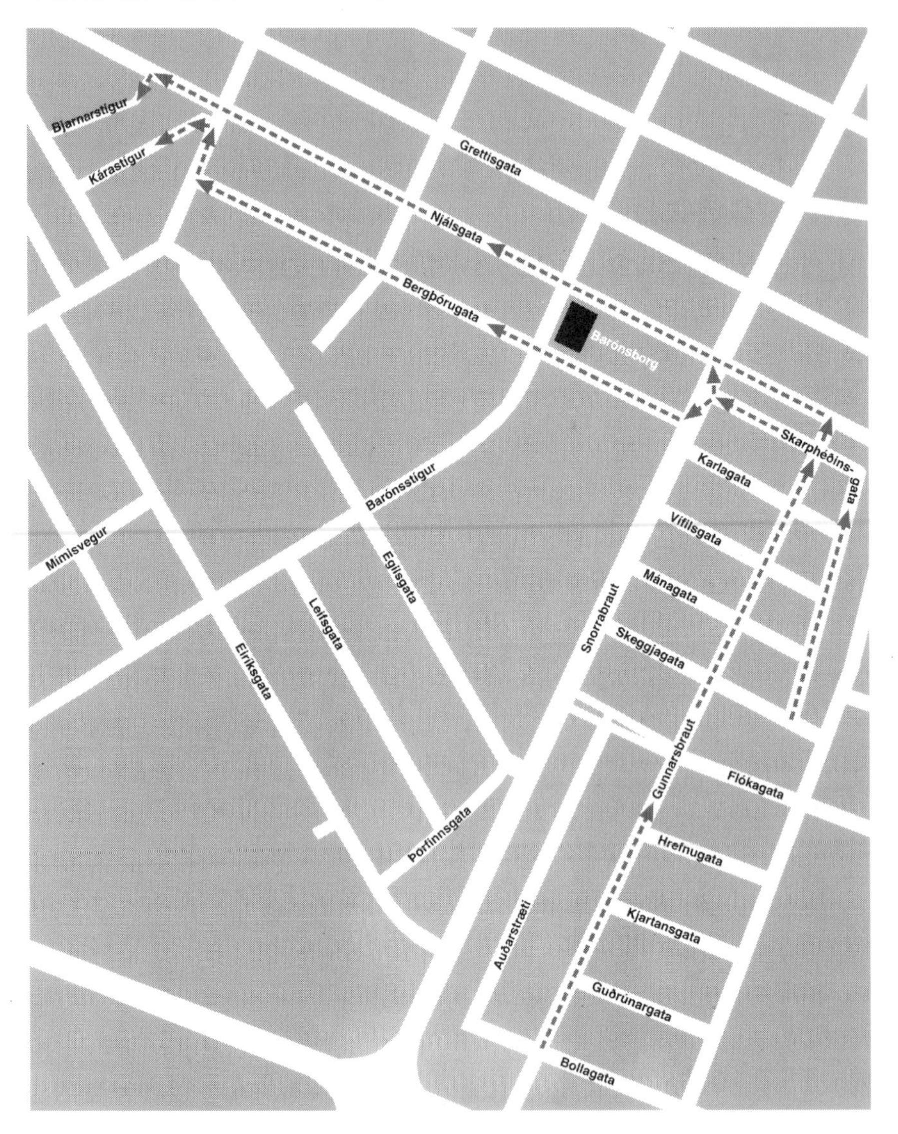

Figure 5 *Njáls saga* on the city map of Reykjavik; illustration by Bjarni Hinriksson

> not simply as a neutral stock, but as one which helps society maintain its *models of reality*, which in their turn govern the models of interpersonal interaction. They thus constitute a source for the kinds of *habitus* prevailing in the various levels of society, helping to preserve and stabilize it.

Inspired by Even-Zohar's discussion, the social role of the sagas will be central to the following analysis of *Njáls saga's* presence in Reykjavík. In particular, the focus is placed on the intersection of Njálsgata (The Street of Njáll) and Snorrabraut (The Avenue of Snorri), where two leading figures of Icelandic literary history meet. These figures are Njáll Þorgeirsson and Snorri Sturluson, the assumed author of *Heimskringla, Snorra-Edda,* and possibly even *Egils saga.* Corresponding intersections can be found both north of Njálsgata, where Snorrabraut crosses Grettisgata, and south of Njálsgata, where Snorrabraut meets Skarphéðinsgata, Bergþórugata and Egilsgata. Using perspectives suggested by these intersecting streets, we shall survey the development of saga-rewriting in Iceland, from its preoccupation with saga heroes to its enthusiasm for saga authors. Theoretically, this chapter unites the principles of Translation Studies, that have formed the basis of this study, with those of Semiotics, identifying the literary text on the intricate crossings of society and signification.

The Streets of *Njáls Saga*

The social significance of the saga hero in Iceland has been subject to considerable change over the centuries. In Chapter 1, two major stages in that development were detected. Already in the thirteenth century, the hero was defined by observance to his personal merits, most importantly his physical strength. It was in this tradition that Þorkell Elfaraskáld composed his verse about the valiant defence of Gunnar Hámundarson and his consequent death. Icelandic poets of every century have followed this lead, partially to strengthen the spirit of the Icelanders during periods of physical hardship, often brought about by cruel nature (cf. Ólason, 1989: 209). A similar approach was explicit in the works of Arngrímur Jónsson from around 1600. Jónsson placed the saga heroes alongside kings and members of the royal courts in contemporary European works of history, creating substitutes for Iceland's non-existent aristocracy (Benediktsson, 1957: 46–61). He also presented the period of the saga heroes as Iceland's Golden Age. In its description of Gunnar Hámundarson's corn-field, for instance, Njáls saga supplied Jónsson with a criterion for the contemporary state of Icelandic agriculture when no grain was being produced (Jonae, 1951: 49).

The Romantic poetry of Jónas Hallgrímsson implied a new definition of the saga heroes in Iceland during the nineteenth century. According to him, it was not enough to be physically or even mentally strong; you also had to love your native soil. Said Hallgrímsson (1838: 34; 1997) in his poem 'Gunnarshólmi': 'For Gunnar felt it nobler far to die / than flee and leave his native shores behind him.' The concept of the Golden Age was also redefined in this period: the times in which the sagas take place were now preceived as the epoch of political independence. Like most other Golden Ages, it also held out a promise of a new Golden Age, somewhere in the near future, and this time featuring a politically independent Iceland.

These two sides of the saga hero were united during the first decades of this century within the popular Ungmennafélagshreyfing (Icelandic Youth Movement). The main emphasis was on physical training and competing in sports, but an underlying concern was to strengthen the patriotic sense of Icelandic youth (Hreinsson, 1992: 10). Íþróttasambandið Skarphéðinn (The Skarphéðinn Athletic Club), established in 1911, may be taken as the literary embodiment of this unity. Here, Skarphéðinn Njálsson of *Njáls saga* – 'a big and strong man and a good fighter. He swam like a seal and was swift of foot' (Ch. 25) – was fixed as the idol of young athletes in Árnessýsla and Rangárvallasýsla, those districts in southern Iceland many nineteenth-century British travellers knew as 'Njal's Country'.

In essence, the cultural significance of the saga heroes was being 'translated' into the urban environment through those streets in Reykjavík taking their names from particular saga characters. Njálsgata and Grettisgata (from Grettir Ásmundarson of *Grettis saga*) are the oldest of these; the first houses at their western ends were built soon after 1900 (Líndal, 1987: 1:168; 2:190). Egilsgata, on the other hand, belongs to the youngest of these streets, named in 1932 after Egill Skallagrímsson of *Egils saga* (Líndal, 1987: 1:117). It is difficult to determine who suggested these names; it seems the tradition was gradually formed as Reykjavík grew towards the east but, as noted in Chapter 6, it was transformed in this period from a small town into a small city.

Interestingly, the placement of the streets named after the characters of *Njáls saga* reflects aspects of the narrative. Bjarnarstígur, for instance, keeps a low profile behind Kárastígur, just as Björn Kaðalsson from Mörk shielded himself behind Kári Sölmundarson in a well known scene in the saga (Ch. 150). Similarly, Bergþórugata and Njálsgata lie side by side, mirroring Bergþóra and Njáll in their bedstead during the burning of Bergþórshvoll (Ch. 129). From this perspective, significant threads between the saga heroes and the twentieth-century inhabitants of Reykjavík were preserved – indeed, the latter group was destined to symbolically follow the footsteps of their heroic ancestors. In this context, we may recall how the heroes of *Njáls saga* served as models of behaviour in various other cultures, whether in Victorian Britain, early twentieth-century United States or German occupied Denmark during World War II.

For centuries, the sagas had been a natural part of Icelanders' local geography and history. In the 1920s, saga scholar Björn M. Ólsen (1937–39: 41) pointed out that the verisimilitude of the setting had probably influenced these native saga readers to assume also a verisimilitude for the plot. As mentioned in Chapter 1, this factor instigated the archaeological research at Bergþórshvoll where the aim was to read *Njáls saga* from the 'original'; the landscape against which the saga events are played out. With street names, such as Njálsgata and Bergþórugata, an attempt was made to recreate the saga's topology within the growing city. This form of rewriting, just like the parliamentary edition of *Njáls saga* discussed in Chapter 6, can be seen as a response to radical social changes in Iceland during the first decades of the twentieth century. It was deemed important to maintain a continuity between traditional cultural values and the modern urban ones; what way was better than through the use of names which would recall for the people of Reykjavík the (fading) connection with their heroic past?

The Nationalistic Agenda

At this stage (or street-corner), it is appropriate to turn the focus for a while towards Halldór Laxness' 1945 edition *Brennunjálssaga* and sustain the analysis of the saga's symbolic capital from Chapter 6. The discussion there was partially based on a close reading of Vilhjálmur Þ. Gíslason's preface to the 1944 parliamentary edition of *Njáls saga*. Unlike Gíslason, Laxness did not write a preface or an introduction to *Brennunjálssaga*. Nonetheless, the large format, the elaborate lay-out and the expensive gilded leather binding of his edition conveyed a clear message regarding the merit of the narrative it contained. And that message was accented by the editor in Laxness' (1945: 415) epilogue:

> Many have regretted the fact that the books, which we truly regard as the most valuable classical works of Icelandic fiction –

> the best of our old sagas – are not available in suitable publications which are both befitting to the needs of the modern reader, as well as costly objects insofar as workmanship is concerned, just as books were in ancient times, equally appropriate as a gift and a delightful domestic possession which book-lovers and friends of good fiction would be equally proud to have.

Laxness' edition of the saga was intended to meet this need. Publisher Ragnar Jónsson, Laxness (1945: 415) explained, had particularly prescribed that 'while considering the limitations implicit in the Icelandic printing industry during this first year of the republic, no costs were too great in the effort to make the edition as elaborate as possible'.

Familiar themes of the Icelandic saga discourse surface in these quotations. One notes, for instance, formulaic metaphors of the sagas as objects of value and of *Njáls saga* as being one of the most valuable works of Icelandic literary history. In this respect, the 1945 edition can be observed in view of Helgi Jónasson's comments during the 1943 parliamentary debate regarding the paper and the quality of printing in Laxness' earlier *Laxdœla saga*. There was little chance that anyone would criticise *Brennunjálssaga* for poor presentational quality. However, while Jónasson's main concern was that the sagas' cultural value be confirmed by the printing and paper, Laxness additionally emphasised the connection between his edition and the manuscript tradition ('books in ancient times'). Furthermore, appealing to his readers' sense of nationalism, Laxness (1945: 415) pointed out how foreign nations had published their greatest literary works in magnificent editions, 'and we cannot permit ourselves anymore to be inferior to them when we publish those works which we correctly consider to be the acme of Icelandic art, both past and present'.

This comparison between past and present, Iceland and other nations, had been variously developed by Laxness in the 1940s. Consider, for instance, his article on the political relations between Denmark and Iceland and the repatriating of Icelandic manuscripts from Danish libraries. Defining the importance of the manuscripts and the ancent literature for Icelandic nationality, Laxness (1946: 78) claimed: 'We have never had any credentials except for [our] literature and it is only on its account that we pass for a people.' Similarly, Laxness (1946: 66) stressed in the conclusion of his 'Minnisgreinar um fornsögur' ('Notes on Ancient Sagas'), that the sagas were solely responsible for the fact 'that we are an independent nation today'. Comments of this sort, however overstated, are closely related to the views that were expressed by members of the Icelandic parliament in 1943 and echoed by Vilhjálmur Þ. Gíslason in the preface to the 1944 edition of *Njáls saga*. They suggest an ideological consensus between Laxness and his adversaries over the cultural and social importance of the sagas for the independent republic of Iceland. The dispute was over *how* the sagas' relevance could be best maintained.

A key to Laxness' response to that question can be found in his epilogue to *Brennunjálssaga*, where he alluded to his edition as one being 'well-suited to the needs of the modern reader'. This point, echoing familiar concerns of Allen French's *Heroes of Iceland*, leads us back to the original rationale for Laxness' and Ragnar Jónsson's controversial publication of *Laxdæla saga*, as stated in one of the newspapers in 1941: 'The plan is to publish the Icelandic family sagas in a new edition, with the language put in a modern dress and with long and dry genealogies deleted' (Vísir, 1941). According to this statement, archaic language and irrelevant genealogies were the two elements of traditional saga editions which Laxness and Jónsson found ill-suited to the needs of modern Icelandic readers.

With reference to the analysis of French's *Heroes of Iceland* in Chapter 3 and the fact that Laxness did not abridge *Njáls saga* in his 1945 edition, we only focus here on his interest in modernising the saga language. That interest can be traced back to an article he wrote in 1935 on orthography in saga editions. Laxness' (1962: 123) purpose was to point out that the 'normalised ancient spelling', generally used in such editions, both falsified the texts of the original manuscripts and prevented modern readers from discovering and enjoying the literature:

> The normalised spelling, this loathsome Esperanto of linguists, repels the reader from the sagas, as all lifeless rules are bound to do but, with normal spelling, it becomes clear to everyone that the writing style of the sagas is not an extinct phenomenon but our own language, which we use at this very moment, a beautiful and a dynamic modern tongue.

The stimulus for Laxness' discussion seems to have been the publishing activity of Fornritafélagið (The Early Icelandic Text-Society), which had started out in 1933 with Sigurður Nordal's edition of *Egils saga Skallagrímssonar*. According to Nordal's (1933: c) introduction, these publications were primarily intended for Icelandic readers 'who value our ancient works without having obtained any particular education in the field'. Still, Nordal (1933: xcix) explained, the orthography was 'normalised mostly in accordance with the tradition of non-diplomatic editions'. Such a system of spelling had originally been designed by European nineteenth-century saga scholars, who wanted to systematise the irregular spelling within the Icelandic manuscript corpus, but one questionable pretext for this form of rewriting was that it was said to reflect, even better than the spelling of the manuscript in question, the qualities of the ancient language (cf. Helgason, 1958: 15–24).

It is certainly possible to regard the Fornritafélagið editions, the 1944 *Njáls saga*, and Laxness' *Brennunjálssaga* as intralingual translations into three different 'dialects'. First, the editors of Fornritafélagið rewrote the texts of the ancient Icelandic manuscripts according to international, academic spelling convention. The text in their editions is slightly divergent from modern Icelandic, both in terms of orthography and word forms. Secondly, Magnús Finnbogason defined his 1944 *Njáls saga* as a modern spelling edition, but the contrast to the Fornritafélagið editions primarily entailed the orthography of two characters (ǫ → ö, oe → æ). Finally, Laxness conformed entirely to the twentieth century Icelandic language and spelling by modernising also various word forms and linguistic features ('ek' (I) → 'ég', 'ok' (and) → 'og', 'maðr' (man) → 'maður', 'lǫgligir' (legal) → 'löglegir').

In a harsh criticism of Finnbogason, Laxness characterised his rival's system of spelling as a corruption which resembled neither the normalised spelling of the Fornritafélagið series, nor modern orthography, let alone the ancient Icelandic language. In Laxness' (1946: 245) view, Finnbogason wanted to give the public a false impression of how the Icelanders spoke and wrote in ancient times. Laxness' own aim was to give his readers the (equally false?) impression that the Icelandic language had not changed significantly over the centuries. The fundamental issue was whether the sagas should sound and look like ancient or modern texts. On the one hand, these were indeed ancient works. A normalised system of spelling, however corrupted, clearly made that impression. On the other hand, a modern spelling edition spoke directly to the modern reader, solidifying a continuity and a contact between past and present.

In view of Laxness' appeal for the return of the Icelandic manuscripts from Denmark, it may be noted how he also cleverly defined the modern spelling of his saga editions as a 'matter of Iceland's defence'. The normalised spelling, Laxness (1941: 7) asserted, had been invented 'by foreign editors of these works', partially for the purpose of refuting that they had been written in Icelandic; 'it was an attempt to disconnect our ancient literature from Iceland and – especially – Icelandic contemporary culture'. From this perspective, Laxness claimed that the normalised spelling would give the world – and even general Icelandic readers – the impression that the sagas were Old Norse (Scandinavian) or even Norwegian literature, rather than specific products of Iceland. That was a serious matter for a small nation which had never had 'any credentials' except for its literature. Previous chapters suggest the causes of this cultural anxiety; Norwegians, Danes, Germans and British Victorians – even a 'native' American such as Allen French – had all claimed the Icelandic sagas as a part of their cultural heritage. In contrast, modern spelling saga editions were designed to prove that the sagas had indeed been written in Icelandic, by Icelanders, and could even only be appropriately read and respected by them.

New Heroes: The Saga Authors

Halldór Laxness' efforts to 'modernise' the saga language in his *Brennunjálssaga* seem to have complemented the topographical rewriting of saga in Reykjavík in the first decades of the twentieth century. However, more needs to be said about that connection. Earlier, it was pointed out that street names such as Njálsgata and Bergþórugata celebrated the traditional saga heroes. Laxness, on the other hand, did no such thing in his own writings. An avid critic of romanticised heroes such as Gunnar Hámundarson and Skarphéðinn Njálsson, he admired the sagas far more for their artistic qualities than their sometimes violent ethics. In this respect and despite divergent policies in the spelling of saga editions, Laxness was in agreement with Sigurður Nordal and some other contemporary Icelandic scholars – an unofficial group generally referred to as the Icelandic School in saga studies. Let us momentarily perceive the Reykjavík municipality from their aestetic viewpoint.

In 1935, the Mayor of Reykjavík appointed a committee 'to make proposals for names of new streets and plazas, at the request of the planning-committee' (Borgarskjalasafn, 1955). The following year, the committee presented its first suggestions for names of streets east of Snorrabraut (which was called Hringbraut at this time) and south of Njálsgata:

> We have chosen the names of ancient individuals for the streets, since streets with corresponding names can be found on two sides of this neighbourhood. Next to Njálsgata, two names are taken from *Njáls saga*, then four names are from Ingólfur's settlement and finally five names [come] from *Laxdæla saga*. Flóki's name is inserted in between. (Sigurðsson and others, 1936)

This proposal was accepted by the Reykjavík planning committee and the city council in 1937 (Halldórsson, 1937). Hence, five names related to the early settlement of Iceland were added to the city plan (Skeggjagata, Vífilsgata, Karlagata, Mánagata, Flókagata), along with six names relating to specific saga characters (Auðarstræti, Guðrúnargata, Kjartansgata, Bollagata, Hrefnugata, Skarphéðinsgata, Gunnarsbraut). These last two honour *Njáls saga's* Skarphéðinn Njálsson and Gunnar Hámundarson.

Following the tradition of Njálsgata, Bergþórugata, Kárastígur and Bjarnarstígur, the relative position of these two streets correspond to specific patterns in the saga. Hence, Skarphéðinsgata lies like a branch which extends the area between Njálsgata and Bergþórugata, thus reminding us that Skarphéðinn was the offspring of Bergþórá and Njáll. Gunnarsbraut, on the other hand, stretches towards the south, intersecting Njálsgata and crossing Skarphéðinsgata. This pattern allowed pedestrians to trace the plot of *Njáls saga*, which opens with the tale of Gunnar. So we start from the south end of Gunnarsbraut and move towards Njálsgata (Ch. 1–77). Then we follow Njálsgata towards the west in the direction of the burning (Ch. 78–132). The walk ends properly in the area of Kárastígur and Bjarnarstígur, insinuating that Kári and Björn are portrayed in the final part of the saga (Ch. 150) (cf. Figure 5 on p. 138).

It may seem that these new names were in no way different from those dated from 1900–1932, but when one realises who sat on the Reykjavík naming committee in the 1940s, second thoughts emerge. Interestingly, the three committee members were all affiliated with the University of Iceland: Pjetur Sigurðsson was the university secretary, Ólafur Lárusson was a professor in the law department, and finally Sigurður Nordal was a professor of Icelandic studies (Borgarskjalasafn, 1955). In view of his scholarly interests and authority, Nordal most probably edited this annex to the urban saga corpus. His presence on the naming committee encourages us, at least, to approach these Reykjavík street-names as a side-product of the Icelandic School.

Traditionally, the Icelanders who had read *Njáls saga* and other family sagas as a reliable narrative of an oral tradition hardly envisioned the 'original' text as having been created by an individual author. The plot of the saga, they assumed, was a devise of the divine force that shapes history. Inspired by nineteenth-century saga scholars such as Andreas Heusler and Albert Ulrich Bååth, the members of the Icelandic School renounced this natural connection between sagas and reality. Instead, they referred to the sagas as human *constructions*. In his 1940 *Hrafnkatla*, a study of *Hrafnkels saga*, Sigurður Nordal (1940: 3) expressed, for instance, his conviction that the saga owed 'its final cast and refinement' to an author, implying the work of a smith or a craftsman. Nordal's student and colleague, Einar Ólafur Sveinsson (1943: 21) wrote similarily in his *Á Njálsbúð, bók um mikið listaverk* (*At Njáll's Booth, A Study of a Literary Masterpiece*):

> All things *are* made out of some substance, and there is no evidence of anyone, except the Lord Almighty, creating something out of nothing. Human originality is different; it can rather be compared to the art of gold-making, transforming lead into gold. And that was something which the author of *Njáls saga* had mastered.

Finally, Laxness (1945: 417) developed a similar metaphor in his epilogue to *Brennunjálssaga*, when he described how the author connected various themes in his narrative, creating 'a construction, which in many ways resembles the Gothic cities of his time, in some ways even the architecture of Gothic cathedrals'. These words acquire added significance in view of the fact that in Laxness' lifetime his hometown of Reykjavík had, symbolically at least, started to mimic the 'construction' of *Njáls saga*.

As far as Laxness' direct ties with the Icelandic School are concerned, his epilogue to *Brennunjálssaga* clearly presented the narrative as being an original work of fiction. In particular, Laxness (1945: 415) explained how this view had influenced his editorial policy:

> Historical and linguistic notes were ignored in this publication. The former were left out since people do not confuse this work of fiction with history any longer; yet the book itself is an important record of thirteenth-century cultural history. With regard to the language, the continuity of Icelandic culture is such that few if any Icelandic works of fiction are more modern than *Brennunjálssaga*. One can hardly find a new modern Icelandic novel which has fewer perplexing words and phrases for the majority of readers than this book and the ancient sagas in general.

It is interesting to note how Laxness poses here his major challenge to traditional saga views as an accepted fact but, as observed in Chapter 6, there were positively influencial members in the Icelandic parliament who still confused 'this work of fiction with history'. Laxness (1945: 416) qualified his assertion later in the epilogue, where he complained that the majority of saga scholars had based their research of the text 'on the misconception that *Brennunjálssaga* was a work of history, though incomplete and questionable'. The only exception, he added, was Einar Ólafur Sveinsson's *Á Njálsbúð*.

Additional evidence for tying Halldór Laxness' saga editions with the ideas and works of the Icelandic School can be provided (cf. Helgason, 1998: 115–31). For instance, Laxness' claim that *Brennunjálssaga* was linguistically comparable to 'a modern Icelandic novel' echoed the tone of *Hrafnkatla*, where Sigurður Nordal (1940: 79) had encouraged other saga scholars to 'make a distinction between the old excesses of the sagas, the dead knowledge, and their eternally young soul'. By modernising the language and ignoring historical and linguistic notes in his own saga editions, Laxness was trying to make precisely this distinction. But the clearest sign of this link between him and the Icelandic School is in an article from 1941, where Laxness (1942: 331) proudly acknowledged having, in preparation for his *Laxdæla saga*, consulted 'some of the leading academics and intellectuals in the country, and some of our best linguists'. He mentioned specifically the names of saga scholars Jón Helgason and Sigurður Nordal in this context, noting: 'the latter has supported me in this work with good counsel'.

In recent decades, it has been pointed out how the ideas of the Icelandic School were in many ways a logical step in the development of Icelandic nationalism in the twentieth century (cf. Halldórsson, 1978; Sigurjónsson, 1984; Ólason, 1984). According to Jesse L. Byock (1994: 181): 'The literary basis of the sagas equipped Iceland with a cultural heritage worthy of its status as an independent nation.' In particular, Byock outlines some of the premises for Sigurður Nordal's approach to the sagas. First, Nordal's emphasis on the family sagas as works of thirteenth-century *Icelandic* authors rather than products of an oral tradition, can be seen as a response to the claims of some Danes, Norwegians and Swedes, who approached this literature as part of a common Scandinavian cultural heritage. In this respect, the ideas of the Icelandic School and the modern spelling of Laxness' saga editions served a common objective. Secondly, Byock (1994: 184) suggests, the aim of the Icelandic School was to place the sagas, 'reinterpreted in light of standard European concepts of literary development ... among the artefacts of European high culture'. Unlike the Victorian nineteenth-century, with George Webbe Dasent proudly comparing his 'Burnt Njal' to the works of Thucydides, Tacitus, Clarendon, and Hume, the men of the Icelandic School compared the family sagas to the works of Dante, Shakespeare and Kleist. Einar Ólafur Sveinsson was particularly active with such comparisons, both in his *Á Njálsbúð* and in separate articles dealing with topics such as the similarities between Clytemnestra and Hallgerður Höskuldsdóttir. Notably, Sveinsson (1956: 95) did not ground his analysis on Homer's characterisation of the Greek heroine, as Dasent might have done, but on the tragedy *Agamemnon*, by 'the great poet' Aeschylus.

One of the obstacles in articulating this new concept was the mystery surrounding the identity of 'the great saga poets'. This was indeed a serious problem, as these men were expected to succeed the acclaimed saga heroes in terms of importance. Discussing the consequences of his *Hrafnkatla* study, Sigurður Nordal (1940: 76) wrote: 'As for national pride, one can say that the injury possibly inflicted upon the fame of fighters and strong men of the saga-age will be mended by new heroes, who hitherto have been kept in the background: the saga authors. Is that such a bad substitution?' In answering Nordal's question, it might be said that it was a bad substitution as long as these authors continued to be anonymous. Making reference to Michel Foucault's well-known essay 'What is an Author?', Ástráður Eysteinsson has raised this point in relation to the sagas, suggesting that the term *family sagas* ('Íslendingasögur') has served somewhat as a qualifying label in the absence of authors' names. Eysteinsson (1990: 174) also hints that Snorri Sturluson, the best-known author of Icelandic saga writing, was seen as representative for all the other unknown authors. Nordal, we need to remember, was instrumental in reinforcing Sturluson's reputation as an author in the twentieth century, originally with his book *Snorri Sturluson* (Nordal, 1920), and then later in his introduction to *Egils saga Skallagrímssonar*, where he argued for Sturluson's authorship (Nordal, 1933).

This fact leads us once more towards the Reykjavík city map. The weakness in linking street names like Gunnarsbraut and Skarphéðinsgata with the ideas of the Icelandic School is that these names celebrate the fighters and strong men for whom Nordal wanted to replace with the saga authors. On the other hand, there were certainly some difficulties involved in naming a street after anonymous authors, like that of *Njáls saga*. However, the naming of Snorrabraut (The Avenue of Snorri) seems to represent the final touch. Originally, that street formed a part of Hringbraut, a long circular avenue intended to envelop the centre of Reykjavík. As early as 1936, the city had crossed over the eastern borders represented by Hringbraut. However, it was not until 1948 that the Reykjavík planning committee asked the naming committee to propose new names for different parts of Hringbraut. In its response from February 20, the naming committee suggested that 'the most eastern part of Hringbraut should be named Snorrabraut, since neighbourhoods with names of ancient individuals are on both sides of it' (Sigurðsson, 1948). With the naming of Snorrabraut, committee-member Nordal was able to secure Snorri Sturluson a seat of honour in the company of saga heroes, initially changing the gravity of street names in this area. Before 1948, Njálsgata and Gunnarsbraut connected the saga streets. Since 1948, the neighbourhood has been united by Snorrabraut, symbolising the role of the *author* as the creator and the unifying principle of Icelandic saga literature.

It must be observed at this stage that no topic relating to *Njáls saga* had been more popular with Icelandic saga scholars and readers during the first half of this century than that of the author's unknown identity. Leading the debate was historian Barði Guðmundsson. In a series of articles from 1937 to 1955, Guðmundsson (1958) interpreted *Njáls saga* as a *roman á clef* of the Icelandic thirteenth century, arguing that it was written by Þorvarður Þórarinsson from Valþjófsstaður in Fljótsdal. Einar Ólafur Sveinsson (1937) and some others (i.e. Vilhjálmsson, 1948) were of different opinion, proposing various candidates for this honourable office. For the present purposes, the most interesting nomination came from Helgi Haraldsson, a farmer at Hrafnkelsstaðir in the southern part of Iceland. In a newspaper article published on April 9, 1948 (six weeks after the naming committee proposed the name of Snorrabraut), Haraldsson made a strong objection to Guðmundsson's theory about Þorvarður Þórarinsson's authorship. Instead he suggested that Snorri Sturluson had written *Njáls saga*. Haraldsson referred to several accepted facts about Sturluson's life in support of his theory. For instance, Sturluson got his education at Oddi in Rangárvallarsýsla, a place where the written and oral sources of *Njáls saga* would have been readily available to him. Yet, despite this argument, Haraldsson (1948: 4–6) suspected that the Reykjavík academic community would not be easily convinced:

> I know the scholars will not accept Sturluson as the author of *Njáls saga*. On the other hand, they have often agreed that Sturluson was the most brilliant genius in Scandinavia in his time. If he was not the author of *Njáls saga*, then this statement is incorrect, because then there would be another one his equal.

Apparently, Haraldsson's analysis presupposed the following syllogism: Sturluson was the greatest writer of medieval Iceland, *Njáls saga* is the greatest work, hence Sturluson must be the author of *Njáls saga*. Haraldsson's view on the authorship issue was in no way characteristic of the views of the Reykjavík naming committee or of Icelanders in general. His argument gives us, nontheless, a fair impression of the literary prestige of both *Njáls saga* and Snorri Sturluson in 1948, and also – and this is the main point – of the ideology invested in the intersection of Njálsgata and Snorrabraut.

The Story of Burnt Saga

In these last two chapters, we have seen how Halldór Laxness' saga editions challenged the dominant conception of the sagas in Iceland in the 1940s. At least three traditional views were at stake. The sagas were regarded as:

(1) ancient historical documents,
(2) sacred texts, and
(3) forming the center of the Icelandic literary system.

In his *Laxdæla saga* edition, Laxness contested the first two views. In his opinion, the only way to secure the canonised status of the sagas was to rewrite and abridge them in accordance with the poetics of the contemporary novel. In his later editions, especially in the expensive publications of *Brennunjálssaga* and *Grettis saga,* Laxness seems to have acknowledged the sacred status of the sagas, but it is also possible that he was giving in to the pressure of his publisher, and even of his ally, Sigurður Nordal.

The compromise between the views of Laxness and Nordal can undoubtedly also be related to the fact that the two men had a common cause in a larger crisis: Jónas Jónsson was their common enemy. As was noted in Chapter 6, Jónsson's involvement with the spelling and publication of the sagas complemented his intervention in the distribution of the annual state grants to the arts and the wide-reaching cultural influence of the Menntamálaráð. We should not forget that Sigurður Nordal was one of Jónas's *persona non grata.* The reason for their personal animosity was that, in Jónsson's view, Nordal had allied himself with the 'Communists', initially in 1939 when he decided to publish one of his works with Mál og menning, but more seriously in early 1940s when Nordal and numerous Icelandic artists protested against the dealings of Menntamálaráð (cf. Friðriksson, 1993: 208–18).

The political aspects of this confrontation were explored in Chapter 6. Nonetheless, a few words should be added regarding the cultural implications of this conflict. A vital concept in Jónas Jónsson's crusade against the 'Communists' was the term 'anti-national'. He criticised Halldór Laxness for writing perverted anti-national novels and claimed that with their saga editions, the 'Communists' wanted to offend Icelandic national sensibility. In this period, Jónsson also denounced many modern Icelandic painters and sculptors for producing 'degenerate' works of art; essentially anti-national imitations of modern French art (Friðriksson, 1993: 196–207). His discourse resembles the campaign against degenerate art in Hitler's Germany a few years earlier. In 1942, Jónsson went as far as organising an exhibition of degenerate Icelandic art in the state's possession in the parliamentary building, imitating the Nazi 'Degenerate Art' exhibition of 1937 held in Munich.

Interestingly, the painters who had works in Jónas Jónsson's 1942 exhibition included Þorvaldur Skúlason and Gunnlaugur Ó. Scheving, two of the three painters who later illustrated Laxness' edition of *Brennunjálssaga*. All of the three painters (Snorri Arinbjarnar was the third one), Halldór Laxness and Sigurður Nordal along with sixty-one other Icelandic artists and writers, protested against the dealings of the Menntamálaráð and Jónas Jónsson soon after the degenerate art exibition in 1942 (Alþýðublaðið, 1942). This information may further explain the violent reaction of Jónas Jónsson to Laxness' saga editions. In his eyes, this mixture of sagas and 'degenerate art' represented an impossible union between the sacred and the profane.

In contrast to the photographs and maps in the 1944 state edition of *Njáls saga*, the illustrations of the three artists in the 1945 *Brennunjálssaga* certainly supported Laxness definition of the saga as a modern work of art. The expressionist illustrations of Þorvaldur Skúlason are particularly enticing in that context, as they challenge most explicitly the preference of Jónas Jónsson (and that of many of his contemporaries) for realism. Following the style in his paintings, Skúlason draws simple forms (the motifs are almost two-dimensional), and his choice of scenes and perspectives is inventive (cf. the cover of this book). In his epilogue to *Brennunjálssaga*, Laxness (1945: 415) drew special attention to the illustrations, stating that he was convinced that some of them would

> eternally endure as artistic accomplishments, valued equally to the immortal text which they are created to serve. Icelandic youth will get used to these illustrations . . . and learn to appreciate them while reading this ancient book, the most modern of all books, and in their old age they will cherish their memory with the memory of the saga itself.

In the same ways as the grand publication of *Brennunjálssaga* was designed to complement Iceland's ancient book making, the art of the modern illustrators was meant to equal the art of the saga author. The sagas were indeed sacred relics, Laxness seems to be saying, but so was contemporary Icelandic art. The time had come to join (if not to substitute) the sagas at the centre of the Icelandic cultural system. Twice in his epilogue, Laxness made references to the creation of *Njáls saga* and Iceland's loss of independence in the thirteenth century. These two events seemed to have been mysteriously related. The 1945 *Brennunjálssaga* was supposed to signify a new beginning. Not only had Iceland regained its political independence in 1944; the Golden Age of high-culture was with the Icelanders again.

In later years, it has been suggested that Halldór Laxness, partially with his saga editions, but specifically with his controversial but now acclaimed novels, has taken the place of the saga authors as the Icelandic national and cultural hero (cf. Eysteinsson, 1990: 177; Helgason, 1998: 185–97). Laxness' career, especially after he received the Nobel Prize for literature in 1955, may in fact be interpreted as proof of Iceland's cultural Golden Age of great artists in modern times. To some degree, his novels have replaced the sagas in the seat of honour on Icelandic book-shelves. According to data supplied by anthropologist Richard F. Tomasson (1975: 90), there was, in the 1970s, little 'to support the contention that many Icelanders continue to read the Sagas or are involved with their classical literature'. On the other hand, Tomasson found that Halldór Laxness was not only the best known contemporary Icelandic writer at the time, but also the most respected living Icelander. Snorri Sturluson, by comparison, came in ninth place of the most respected deceased Icelanders, sharing that seat with parliamentary member Jónas Jónsson.

Tomasson's testimony gives us a perspective on Friðrik Þór Friðriksson's (1980) *Brennu-Njáls saga*, the last rewriting of the saga that we will oberseve. In this twenty minute long film, done by one of Iceland's leading film-makers early in his career, one sees two hands turning over the pages of Laxness' 1945 *Brennunjálssaga*. The illustrations in this edition make it easier for the audience to realise the silent unfolding of the narrative – the only sound is strange music in the background. After about eight minutes, at the chapter concerning the burning of Bergþórshvoll, the music stops. We see the book from a different perspective. The reader in the film, represented by the two hands, lights a match and sets the book afire. It burns for the next eight minutes to distorted sounds of drums and screams. Bells are heard in the distance. For the last four minutes the perspective is changed once more. No sound is heard; the burning book fades away.

Acknowledgements

The present book is a product of a decade of research and writing on the reception of the Icelandic sagas in modern times. This research originally began in Maria Tymoczko's course in Translation Theory in 1989, when I was as a graduate student at the University of Massachusetts at Amherst. Since then, I have had opportunity to develop my ideas in a dissertation, several scholarly papers and a book-long study in Icelandic. During this period, my work has been supported by grants from the Icelandic Science Fund, Gjöf Jóns Sigurðssonar and the research funds of the University of Massachusetts.

Sincere thanks go to Maria Tymoczko, Gary Aho, William Moebius and Frank Hugus for their invaluable academic guidance and friendship, and to Edwin Gentzler and Susan Bassnett who have supported the project through to its final form. Additionally, I owe particular thanks to numerous friends and colleagues for their encouragement and help at various stages of the writing and rewriting of this book. I am especially grateful to Ástráður Eysteinsson, Rossella Bernascone, Gerður Harpa Kjartansdóttir, Guðni Elísson, Guðrún Nordal, Gunnar Sigurðsson, Sabine Groote, Terry Gunnell, Astrid Kjetså, Þórir Jónsson and Andrew Wawn.

Special appreciation goes to my parents, Helgi Hákon Jónsson and Birna Gunnarsdóttir, and to my brother, Hannes Snorri Helgason, who have always shown me complete support in my academic pursuit. Finally, my warmest thanks go to my wife, Fríða B. Jónsdóttir, and our children, Marteinn Sindri and Katrín Helena, for making it worthwhile.

Two chapters in this book have been published in earlier English versions. Chapter 4 was published in 1994 as 'On Danish Borders: Icelandic Sagas in German Occupied Denmark' in *Contemporary Sagas*, Preprints for The Ninth International Saga Conference (Reykjavík: The Ninth International Saga Conference, pp. 408–22). Chapter 6 was published the same year as '"We who cherish Njáls saga" The Alþingi as Literary Patron' in *Northern Antiquity: The Post-Medieval Reception of Edda and Saga* (ed. Andrew Wawn, Enfield Lock: Hisarlik Press, pp. 143–61). I am grateful for permission to reuse this material.

Note on the text

Except for *Njáls saga,* translations from languages other than English are my own, unless otherwise noted. English quotations from the saga are based on the translation of Cook (1997); to avoid confusion I use modern Icelandic spelling for the names of characters. Icelandic quotations (occasionally shown in parenthesis within the English quotations) are from Thorsson (1991). The titles of individual sagas (saga traditions) are written in modern Icelandic, except where I am referring to specific editions and translations with alternative titles.

References

Aall, Jacob (trans.) (1819) Oversættelse af en Deel af Niala Saga. *Saga, et Fjerdingsars Skrift* 2, 1–138.

Aasmundstad, Olav (trans.) (1896) *Njaala elder Soga um Njaal Torgeirson og sønerne hans*. Kristiania: Norske samlaget.

Aho, Gary (1982) William Morris and Iceland. *Kairos* 1 (2), 102–33.

Aho, Gary (1993) 'Með Ísland á heilanum.' Íslandsbækur breskra ferðalanga 1772 til 1897 (trans. Jón Karl Helgason). *Skírnir* 167 (Spring), 205–58.

Almenningen, Olaf, Thore A. Roksvold, Helge Sandøy and Lars L. Vikør (eds) (1981) *Språk og samfunn gjennom tusen år*. Oslo: Universitetsforlaget.

Alving, Hjalmar (1935–45) *Isländska sagor*. 5 vols. Stockholm: Bonnier.

Alþingi (1942) *Alþingistíðindi 1941. Fimmtugasta og áttunda löggjafarþing*. 4 vols. Reykjavík: Ríkisprentsmiðjan Gutenberg.

Alþingi (1943–46) *Alþingistíðindi 1942–43. Sextugasta og fyrsta löggjafarþing*. 4 vols. Reykjavík: Ríkisprentsmiðjan Gutenberg.

Alþýðublaðið (1942) 66 listamenn kæra formann menntamálaráðs fyrir alþingi. *Alþýðublaðið* (16 April), 2 and 7.

Andersson, Theodore M. (1964) *The Problem of Icelandic Saga Origins: A Historical Survey* (Yale Germanic Studies 1). New Haven and London: Yale University Press.

Anko, Bostjan (trans.) (1970) *Saga o Njalu* (Knjiznica kondor, izbrana dela iz domace in svetovne knjizevnosti 115). Ljubljana: Mladinska Knjiga.

Ásmundarson, Valdimar (ed.) (1894) *Njáls saga* (Íslendinga sögur 10). Reykjavík: Sigurður Kristjánsson.

Bakker, Matthijs and Ton Naaijkens (1991) A Postscript: Fans of Holmes. In Kitty M. van Leuven-Zward & Ton Naaijkens (eds) *Translation Studies: The State of the Art. Proceedings of the First James S. Holmes Symposium on Translation Studies* (pp. 193–208). Amsterdam & Atlanta, GA: Rodopi.

Barthes, Roland (1975) *The Pleasure of the Text* (trans. Richard Miller). New York: The Noonday Press.

Bartholini, Tomæ (1689) *Antiqvitatum Danicarum de causis contemptæ a Danis adhuc gentilibus mortis libri tres*. Hafniæ: Joh. Phil. Bockenhoffer.

Bassnett, Susan (1991) *Translation Studies* (revised edition). London and New York: Routledge.

Bassnett, Susan (1993) *Comparative Literature. A Critical Introduction*. Oxford UK & Cambridge USA: Blackwell.

Bayerschmidt, Carl F. and Lee M. Hollander (trans.) (1955) *Njál's Saga*. New York: New York University Press for The American-Scandinavian Foundation.

Bååth, A.U. (trans.) (1879) *Nials Saga, med eitt tillägg, Darrads-sången* (Isländska sagor i svensk bearbetning för allmän läsning). Stockholm: Jos. Seligmann & C:is Förlag.

Bååth, A.U. (1885) *Studier öfver kompositionen i några isländska ättsagor.* Lund: Gleerupska Universitets-Boghandeln.

Benediktsson, Jakob (1957) *Arngrímur Jónsson and His Works.* Copenhagen: Ejnar Munksgaard.

Benediktsson, Jakob (1981) Den vågnende interesse for sagalitteraturen på Island i 1600–talet. *Maal og minne* (3–4), 157–70.

Benét, William Rose (ed.) (1965) *The Reader's Encyclopedia* (second edition). New York: Thomas Y. Crowell Company.

Bergmann, Árni (1995) Niðjar Óðins, hetjur og skáld. *Skírnir* 169 (Fall), 223–61.

Bernárdez, Enrique (trans.) (1986) *Saga de Nial* (Clasicos Alfaguara 38). Madrid: Ediciones Alfaguara.

Bjarnason, Óskar (1995–96) Altisländische Literatur und deutscher Nationalismus. Zur Edda- und Sagarezeption 1900–1933. Unpublished M.A. thesis, Albert-Ludwigs-Universität zu Freiburg i. Br.

Blicher, Steen Steensen (1940) Tale, drømt at være holden i Stændersalen. *Det tredje Standpunkt* 4 (2), 49–51.

Bollason, Arthúr Björgvin (1990) *Ljóshærða villidýrið. Arfur Íslendinga í hugarheimi nasismans.* Reykjavík: Mál og menning.

Bonus, Arthur (ed.) (1907–9) *Isländerbuch.* 3 vols. München: Georg D.W. Callwey.

Borgarskjalasafn (1955) A note signed P.M. to the mayor of Reykjavík regarding the Reykjavík naming committee (21 February). Borgarskjalasafn Reykjavíkur, Reykjavík.

Borges, Jorge Luis (1983) The Garden of Forking Paths (trans. Donald A. Yates). In *Labyrinths: Selected Stories & Other Writings* (pp. 19–29). New York: Modern Library.

Bottomley, Gordon (1909) *The Riding to Lithend.* Sussex: At the Pear Tree Press.

Bourdieu, Pierre (1987) What makes a social class? On the theoretical and practical existence of groups. *Berkeley Journal of Sociology* 32, 1–18.

Boyer, Régis (trans.) (1976) *La saga de Njall le brûlé.* Paris: Aubier Montaigne.

Breiðfjörð, Sigurður (1839) *Ljóða Smámunir, samt Emilíu Raunir* (Annar ársflokkur). Viðeyar Klaustri: Helgi Helgason.

Brenner, Oscar (1878) *Über die Kristni-saga: kritische Beiträge zur altnordischen Literaturgeschichte.* München: Christian Kaiser.

Brooks, Peter (1992) *Reading for the Plot. Design and Intention in Narrative.* Cambridge, MA: Harvard University Press.

Burritt, Elihu (1841) Icelandic Literature: Translations, with Introductory Notes. *The American Eclectic: Or Selections from the Periodical Literature of all Foreign Countries* 1 (January), 99–111.

Burton, Richard (1875) *Ultima Thule; or, A Summer in Iceland.* London: William P. Nimmo.

Byock, Jesse L. (1994) Modern Nationalism and the Medieval Sagas. In Andrew Wawn (ed.) *Northern Antiquity. The Post-Medieval Reception of Edda and Saga* (pp. 163–87). Middlesex: Hisarlik Press.

Böðvarsson, Jón (ed.) (1968–69) *Brennu-Njáls saga.* 2 vols. Reykjavík: Prentsmiðja Jóns Helgasonar.

Carlyle, Thomas (1840) *On Heroes, Hero-Worship and the Heroic in History.* London: Chapman and Hall.

Clarke, M.L. (1959) *Classical Education in Britain 1500–1900*. Cambridge: Cambridge University Press.
Claussen, J. (trans.) (1878) *Die Nialssaga*. Leipzig: J.A. Barth.
Clay, Beatrice E. (1907) *Stories from the Saga of 'Burnt Njál'. The Story of Gunnar*. London: Horace Marshall & Son.
Collingwood, W.G. and Jón Stefánsson (1899) *A Pilgrimage to the Saga-Steads of Iceland*. Ulveston: W. Homes.
Comsa, Ioan (trans.) (1963) *Saga despre Njal: Gunnar si Njal*. Bucharest: Pentru Literatura Universala.
Cook, Robert (trans.) (1997) Njal's Saga. In Viðar Hreinsson, Robert Cook, Terry Gunnell, Keneva Kunz and Bernard Scudder (eds) *The Complete Sagas of Icelanders, Including 49 Tales*. Vol. 3 (pp. 1–220). Reykjavík: Leifur Eiríksson Publishing.
Cox, George W. and Eustace Hinton Jones (1872) *Tales of the Teutonic Lands*. London: Longmans, Green, and Co.
Dahl, Willy (1981) Tid og tekst 1814-1884. *Norges litteratur*. Vol. 1. Oslo: H. Aschehough & Co.
Dareste, Rodolphe (trans.) (1896) *La saga de Nial*. Paris: E. Leroux.
Dasent, George Webbe (trans.) (1861) *The Story of Burnt Njal or Life in Iceland at the End of the Tenth Century*. 2 vols. Edinburgh: Edmonston and Douglas.
Delabastita, Dirk (1990) Translation and the Mass Media. In Susan Bassnett and André Lefevere (eds) *Translation, History and Culture* (pp. 97–109). London and New York: Pinter Publishers.
Det tredje Standpunkt (1940–43) *Det tredje Standpunkt* 4–7.
Einarsson, Bjarni (1974) On the role of verse in saga-literature. *Mediaeval Scandinavia* 7, 118–25.
Engberg, Poul (1978) *De islandske håndskrifter og dansk folkelighed*. Ry: Foreningen Fri nordisk Folkehøjskole.
Engberg, Poul (1980) *Grundtvig og det folkelige oprør*. København: Samleren.
Engelhardt-Pabst, Helene von (1909) *Gunnar von Hlidarendi. Isländisches Epos in 36 Gesängen*. 2 vols. Wien: Verlag von Hugo Heller & Co.
Even-Zohar, Itamar (1978) *Papers in Historical Poetics* (Papers on Poetics and Semiotics 8). Tel Aviv: The Porter Institute for Poetics and Semiotics.
Even-Zohar, Itamar (1990) Polysystem Studies. *Poetics Today* 11 (1).
Eysteinsson, Ástráður (1990) Er Halldór Laxness höfundur Fóstbræðrasögu? Um höfundargildi, textatengsl og þýðingu í sambandi Laxness við fornsögurnar. *Skáldskaparmál* 1, 171–88.
Faulkner, Peter (1980) *Against the Age: An Introduction to William Morris*. London: George Allen & Unwin.
Fichte, Johann Gottlieb (1978) *Reden an die Deutsche Nation*. Hamburg: Felix Meiner Verlag.
Finnbogason, Gunnar (ed.) (1977) *Njáls saga*. Reykjavík: Valfell.
Finnbogason, Magnús (ed.) (1944) *Njáls saga*. Reykjavík: Bókaútgáfa Menningarsjóðs og Þjóðvinafélagsins.
Fischer, Rasmus (1941) En elsker af Dansk Sprog og Literatur. *Aalborg Stiftstidende* (25 October), 8.
Folkevennen (1871) [General laws of Selskabet for Folkeoplysningens Fremme]. *Folkevennen* 20, 651.
Folkevennen (1872) Den aarlige General forsamling. *Folkevennen* 21, 209–14.

Forbes, Charles S. (1860) *Iceland: Its Volcanoes, Geysers, and Glaciers.* London: John Murray.
Frederiksen, Carl Johan (1941) En Fynbo bliver 150. N.M. Petersen: 24 Oktober 1791–1941. *Kristelig Dagblad* (23 October), 6.
French, Allen (1904) *The Story of Rolf and the Viking's Bow.* Boston: Little, Brown, and Company.
French, Allen (1905) *Heroes of Iceland.* Boston: Little, Brown, and Company.
French, Allen (1908) *Grettir the Strong.* Boston: Little, Brown, and Company.
French, Allen (1951) Allen French. In H. Haycraft and S.J. Kunitz (eds) *The Junior Book of Authors* (second edition) (pp. 132–34). New York: The H.W. Wilson Company.
Friðriksson, Adolf (1994) *Sagas and Popular Antiquarianism in Icelandic Archaeology* (Worldwide Archaeology Series 10). Aldershot, Brookfield USA, Hong Kong, Singapore, Sydney: Avebury.
Friðriksson, Friðrik Þór (1980) *Brennu Njáls saga* (filmstrip, 20 min). Reykjavík: Íslenska kvikmyndasamsteypan.
Friðriksson, Guðjón (1993) Ljónið öskrar. *Saga Jónasar Jónssonar frá Hriflu.* Vol. 3. Reykjavík: Iðunn.
Friðriksson, Halldór Kr. (1846) *Islandsk læsebog.* København: Jæger Skandinaviske Forlagshandel.
Gentzler, Edwin (1993) *Contemporary Translation Theories* (Translation Studies). London and New York: Routledge.
Gíslason, Bjarni M. (1937) *Glimt fra Nord. En bog om Island.* Ry: Skyttes forlag.
Gíslason, Bjarni M. (1942a) Fortale. In N.M. Petersen (trans.) *Islændingenes færd hjemme og ude* (fifth edition). Vol. 1 (pp. 5–15). København: Det tredje Standpunkts forlag.
Gíslason, Bjarni M. (1942b) Islandske Sagaer. *Det tredje Standpunkt* 5 (4): 150–70.
Gíslason, Bjarni M. (1944) Islandske Sagaer. *Aalborg Amtstidende* (5 February), 3–4.
Gíslason, Bjarni M. (1946) *Island under besættelsen og Unionssagen.* Aarhus: Forlaget Aros.
Gíslason, Konráð and Eiríkur Jónsson (eds) (1875) *Njála.* København: Thieles bogtrykkeri.
Gíslason, Konráð and Eiríkur Jónsson (eds) (1875–89) *Njála, udg. efter gamle håndskrifter.* 2 vols. København: Commission i den Gyldendalske Boghandel.
Gíslason, Vilhjálmur (1944) Formáli. In Magnús Finnbogason (ed.) *Njáls saga* (pp. v–xvi). Reykjavík: Bókaútgáfa Menningarsjóðs og Þjóðvinafélagsins.
Godard, Barbara (1990) Theorizing Feminist Discourse/Translation. In Susan Bassnett-McGuire and André Lefevere (eds) *Translation, History and Culture* (pp. 87–96). London and New York: Pinter Publishers.
Gourdault, Jules (trans) (1885) *Gunnar et Nial. Scénes et mæurs de la vieille Islande.* Tours: A. Mame.
Green, W.C. (1890) Two Sagas From Iceland. *Blackwood's Edinburgh Magazine* 148 (July–December), 103–14.
Gudme, Peter de Hemmer (1940) *Danmarks skæbne under Europas nyordning.* København: Gyldendal.
Guðmundsson, Barði (1958) *Höfundur Njálu. Safn ritgerða.* Reykjavík: Bókaútgáfa Menningarsjóðs.

Guðmundsson, Gils (1985) Jónas Jónsson og Menningarsjóður. *Andvari. Nýr flokkur* 27, 78–96.
Gunnarsson, Sigurður (1992) Bjarni M. Gíslason. In *Í önnum dagsins*. Vol. 2 (pp. 258–70). Reykjavík: Skógar.
Hagland, Jan Ragnar (1994) The Reception of Old Norse Literature in Late Eighteenth-Century Norway. In Andrew Wawn (ed.) *Northern Antiquity. The Post-Medieval Reception of Edda and Saga* (pp. 27–40). Middlesex: Hisarlik Press.
Hagstofan (1967) *Tölfræðihandbók* (Hagskýrslur Íslands 2 (40)). Reykjavík: Hagstofa Íslands.
Halldórsson, Óskar (1978) Íslenski skólinn og Hrafnkelssaga. *Tímarit Máls og menningar* 39 (3), 317–24.
Halldórsson, Pétur (1937) A note on names of new streets in Reykjavík (8 January). Borgarskjalasafn Reykjavíkur, Reykjavík.
Hallgrímsson, Jónas (1838) Gunnarshólmi. *Fjölnir* 4, 31–34.
Hallgrímsson, Jónas (1997) Gunnar's Holm. In *Selected Poetry and Prose* (trans. Dick Ringler). Web site ed. by Dick Ringler and developed by Peter C. Gorman (http://www.library.wisc.edu/etext//Jonas). Wisconsin: University of Wisconsin-Madison General Library System.
Halvorsen, E.F. (1951) Bjørnsons forhold til den nørrøne literatur. *Edda* 51, 211–19.
Halvorsen, Erik (1982–83) *Et moderne Menneske*. 2 vols. København: Samleren.
Hammershaimbs, V.U. (1855) *Færøiske Kvæder* (Nordiske Oldskrifter 12 (20)). Vol. 2. København: Nordiske Literatur-Samfund.
Haraldsson, Helgi (1948) Höfundur Njálu. *Tíminn* (10 April), 4–6.
Haugen, Einar (1966) *Language Conflict and Language Planing. The Case of Modern Norwegian*. Cambridge, MA: Harvard University Press.
Heger, Ladislav (trans.) (1965) *Sága o Njálovi*. In Vladimir Rocman (ed.) *Staroislandské ságy* (Lidové umění slovesné 9) (pp. 321–559). Praha: K.L.U.
Helgason, Grímur M. and Vésteinn Ólason (eds) (1973) *Íslendingasögur: Brennu-Njáls saga, Gunnars saga Keldugnúpsfífls, Flóamanna saga, Orms þáttur Stórólfssonar* (Íslenzkar fornsögur 8). Akranes: Skuggsjá.
Helgason, Jón (1958) *Handritaspjall*. Reykjavík: Mál og menning.
Helgason, Jón Karl (1998) *Hetjan og höfundurinn. Brot úr íslenskri menningarsögu*. Reykjavík: Heimskringla, háskólaforlag Máls og menningar.
Hermans, Theo (1985) Images of Translation. Metaphor and Imagery in the Renaissance Discourse on Translation. In Theo Hermans (ed.) *The Manipulation of Literature. Studies in Literary Translation* (pp. 103–35). New York: St. Martin's Press.
Heusler, Andreas (trans.) (1914) *Die Geschichte vom weisen Njal* (Thule, altnordische Dichtung und Prosa 4). Jena: E. Diederichs.
Heyse, Paul (1912) Gunnar. (Aus der Nialssage. 990). In *Epische Dichtungen. Lyrische und epische Dichtungen*. Vol. 1 (pp. 103–12). Stuttgart and Berlin: J.G. Cotta.
Hildebrand, Hans (1867) *Lifvet på Island under sagotiden*. Stockholm: Joseph Seligmanns Boghandel.
Hoff, Bartholomaeus and J.P.J. Hoffory (eds) (1877) *Udvalgte stykker af Njála til skolebrug* (Oldislandske læsestykker til skolbrug 2). København: Chr. Steen & Söns Forlag.

Hole, Richard (1789) The Tomb of Gunnar. *The Gentleman's Magazine and Historical Chronicle* 59 (Part the second), 937.

Holmes, James S. (1970) Forms of Verse Translation and the Translation of Verse Form. In James S. Holmes, Frans de Haan and Anton Popovic (eds) *The Nature of Translation* (pp. 91–105). The Hague: Mouton.

Holstein, Ludvig and Johannes V. Jensen (trans.) (1931) Njals saga. In *De islandske sagaer; paa dansk ved Selskabet til udgivelse af islandske sagaer.* Vol. 2 (pp. 29–243). København: Gyldendalske Boghandel, Nordisk forlag.

Hopp, Odd and Kaare Jargård (eds) (1953) *Njaals saga gjennom 40 år.* N.p.

Hreinsson, Viðar (1992) 2. landsmót UMFÍ í Reykjavík 17.–25. júní 1911. In Viðar Hreinsson, Jón Torfason and Höskuldur Þráinsson (eds) *Saga landsmóta UMFÍ 1909–1990* (pp. 13–24). Reykjavík: Jóhann Sigurðsson og Sigurður Viðar Sigmundsson.

Hæstiréttur (1943) *Hæstaréttardómar 1943.* Reykjavík: Hæstiréttur.

Höskuldsson, Sveinn Skorri (1973) Sambúð skálds við þjóð sína. In Sveinn Skorri Höskuldsson (ed.) *Sjö erindi um Halldór Laxness* (pp. 9–40). Reykjavík: Helgafell.

Ionam, Arngrimvm (1593) *Brevis commentarivs de Islandia.* Hafniæ: n.p.

Istvan, Bernáth (trans) (1965) *Vikingfiak: az ízlandi Njaudl-történet.* 2 vols. Budapest: Szépirodalmi Könyvkiadó.

Jabasvilma, Giorgi (1977) *Nialis saga: jueli islandiuridan targmna.* Tbilisi: n.p.

Jakobsen, Alfred (1980) Jakob Aals kongesagaoversettelse. *Det Kongelige Norske Videnskabs Selskabskrifter* 3, 1–10.

Jakobson, Roman (1959) On Linguistic Aspects of Translation. In Reuben Brower (ed.) *On Translation* (pp. 232–39). Cambridge, MA: Harvard University Press.

Jenkyns, Richard (1980) *The Victorians and Ancient Greece.* Cambridge, MA: Harvard University Press.

Jensen, Johan Fjord (1981) Kritik af Det tredje Standpunkt. In *Efter guldalder-konstruktionens sammenbrud.* Vol. 3. Århus: Modtryk.

Johannessen, Matthías (1958) *Njála í íslenzkum skáldskap* (Safn til sögu Íslands og íslenzkra bókmennta, annar flokkur 2 (1)). Reykjavík: Hið íslenzka bókmenntafélag.

Johnsen, Egil Eiken (1946) Om Jacob Aalls sagaoversettelse. *Maal og minne. Norske Studier,* 26–34.

Johnsonius, Jón (trans.) (1809) *Nials-saga. Historia Niali et Filiorum.* København: P.F. Suhmii, Arna-Magnæan Commission.

Jonae, Arngrími (1951) *Opera Latine Conscripta* (Bibliotheca Arnamagnæana 9). Vol. 1 (ed. Jakob Benediktsson). København: Ejnar Munksgaard.

Jónasson, Hermann (1912) *Draumar. Erindi flutt í Reykjavík í febrúar 1912.* Reykjavík: Ísafold

Jónsson, Finnur (ed.) (1908) *Brennu-Njálssaga (Njála)* (Altnordische saga-bibliothek 13). Halle a.S: M. Niemeyer.

Jónsson, Guðni (ed.) (1942) *Íslendinga sögur.* 12 vols. Reykjavík: Bókaverzlun Sigurðar Kristjánssonar.

Jónsson, Jónas (1941a) Þjóðarútgáfan. *Tíminn* (14 January), 18-20; (18 January), 26–28; (23 January), 34–35.

Jónsson, Jónas (1941b) Innsta virkið. *Tíminn* (24 October), 426.

Jónsson, Jónas (1942) Ljótleiki eða fegurð? *Tíminn* (9 May), 170–71.

Jónsson, Torfi (1982) *Æviskrár samtíðarmanna.* 3 vols. Hafnarfjörður: Skuggsjá.

Jørgensen, Keld Gall (1995) *Betydningens grænser. Oversættelsesvidenskab og saga.* København: Akademisk Forlag.
Kath, Lydia (1936) Hallgerd und Bergthora. In *Urmutter Unn. Geschichten um altnordische Frauen* (Trommlerbuch) (pp. 60–79). Berlin: Junge Generation Verlag.
Kálmán, G.C. (1986) Some Borderline Cases of Translation. *New Comparison* 1, 117–22.
King, Richard John (1874) The Change of Faith in Iceland. A.D. 1000. In *Sketches and Studies: Descriptive and Historical* (pp. 147–96). London: John Murray.
Kjær-Collection. A collection of letters Holger Kjær received from Icelandic informants in response to questionnaires he distributed in the 1920s. Reykjavík, Þjóðminjasafn Íslands.
Knudsen, Tryggve (1923) *P.A. Munch og Samtidens norske sprogstrev.* Kristiania: Gyldendalske boghandel.
Kress, Helga (1991) Staðlausir stafir. Um slúður sem uppsprettu frásagnar í Íslendingasögum. *Skírnir* 165 (Spring), 130–56.
Kristjánsson, Jónas (1988) *Eddas and Sagas. Iceland's Medieval Literature* (trans. Peter Foote). Reykjavík: Hið íslenska bókmenntafélag.
Kruse, Vinding (1940) Nordisk Aand. *Det tredje Standpunkt* 4 (2), 52–53.
La Cour, Vilhelm (ed.) (1928–30) *Edda og Saga.* København: Gyldendalske Boghandel, Nordisk Forlag.
La Cour, Vilhelm (1945) *For dansk domstol under besættelsen.* København: Samlerens forlag.
La Cour, Vilhelm (1959) *Vejs Ende. Træk fra min Manddoms afsluttende Kampaar.* København: P. Haase & søns forlag.
LaGumina, Salvatore J. and Frank J. Cavaioli (1974) *The Ethnic Dimension in American Society.* Boston: Holbrook Press, Inc.
Lang, Andrew (1891) The Sagas. In *Essays in Little* (pp. 141–52). New York: Charles Scribner's Sons.
Larsen, Martin (trans.) (1946) *Branden paa Bergtorshvol.* København: Athenæum.
Lawrence, Hannah (1861) [Review of *The Story of Burnt Njal.*] *British Quarterly Review* 34, 323–49.
Laxness, Halldór (ed.) (1941) *Laxdæla saga.* Reykjavík: Ragnar Jónsson, Stefán Ögmundsson.
Laxness, Halldór (1942) *Vettvángur dagsins. Ritgerðir.* Reykjavík: Heimskringla.
Laxness, Halldór (ed.) (1945) *Brennunjálssaga.* Reykjavík: Helgafell.
Laxness, Halldór (1946) *Sjálfsagðir hlutir. Ritgerðir.* Reykjavík: Helgafell.
Laxness, Halldór (1962) *Dagleið á fjöllum.* Reykjavík: Helgafell.
Lefevere, André (1982) Mother Courage's Cucumbers: Text, System and Refraction in a Theory of Literature. *Modern Language Studies* 7 (4), 3–20.
Lefevere, André (1985) Why Waste Our Time on Rewrites? The Trouble with Interpretation and the Role of Rewriting in an Alternative Paradigm. In Theo Hermans (ed.) *The Manipulation of Literature: Studies in Literary Translation* (215–43). New York: St. Martin's Press.
Lefevere, André (1987) 'Beyond Interpretation' Or The Business Of (Re)-Writing. *Comparative Literature Studies* 24 (1), 17–39.
Lefevere, André (1992) *Translation, Rewriting, and the Manipulation of Literary Fame* (Translation Studies). London and New York: Routledge.

Lefevere, André in collaboration with others (1995) Translators and the Reins of Power. In Jean Delisle and Judith Woodsworth (eds) *Translators Through History* (Benjamins Translation Library 13) (pp. 131–55). Amsterdam and Philadelphia, PA: John Benjamins Publishing Company and UNESCO Publishing.
Lefolii, Hans Henrik (1863) *Nials Saga*. Odense: Den Hempelske Boghandel.
Lehmann, Karl and Hans Schnorr von Carolsfeld (1883) *Die Njálssage insbesondere in ihren juristischen Bestandtheilen: ein kritischer Beitrag zur altnordischen Rechts- und Literaturgeschichte*. Berlin: R.L. Prager.
Levy, V. (ed) (1893) *Udvalgte stykker af Njáls saga*. København: V. Pio.
Lie, Hallvard (trans.) (1941) *Njåls saga*. Oslo: Gyldendal.
Lieder, Paul Robert (1920) Scott and Scandinavian Literature. *Smith College Studies in Modern Languages* 2 (1), 8–57.
Linneball, Poul (1941) En dansk og nordisk Personlighed. 150 Aaret for N.M. Petersens Fødsel. *Børsen* (28 December), 3.
Líndal, Páll (1987) *Reykjavík. Sögustaður við Sund*. 4 vols (ed. Einar S. Arnalds). Reykjavík: Örn og Örlygur.
Lock, Charles G. Warnford (1879) *The Home of the Eddas*. London: Sampson Low, Marston, Searle, Rivington.
Lohrmann, Heinrich Friedrich (1938) *Die altnordische Bauernsaga in der deutschen Erziehung*. Volkhafte Schularbeit. Erfurt: Kurt Stenger.
Lowe, Robert (1861) [Review of *The Story of Burnt Njal*.] *The Edinburgh Review or Critical Journal* 13 (January–April), 217–33.
Lundgreen-Nielsen, Flemming (1992) Grundtvig og danskhed. In Ole Feldbæk (ed.) *Folkets Danmark 1848–1940. Dansk Identitetshistorie*. Vol. 3 (pp. 9–187). København: C.A. Reitzels Forlag.
Lönnroth, Lars (1963–64) Kroppen som själens spegel – ett motiv i de isländska sagorna. *Lychnos. Lärdomshistoriska Samfundets Årsbok*, 24–61.
Lönnroth, Lars (1976) *Njáls Saga. A Critical Introduction*. Berkeley: University of California Press.
MacDougall, Hugh A. (1982) *Racial Myth in English History. Trojans, Teutons, and Anglo Saxons*. Montreal, Hanover, and London: Harvest House & University Press of New England.
Majstorovica, Stevana (trans) (1967) *Saga o Njalu* (Mala knjiga 92). Beograd: Nolit.
Malim, Herbert (1917) *Njal and Gunnar. A Tale of Old Iceland* (English Literature for Secondary Schools). London: MacMillan and Co.
Massachusetts Commission on Immigration (1914) *Report of the Commission on the Problem of Immigration in Massachusetts*. Boston: Wright & Potter Printing Co., State Printers.
Metcalfe, Frederick (1861) *The Oxonian in Iceland; or, Notes of Travel in that Island in the Summer of 1860, with Glances at Icelandic Folklore and Sagas*. London: Longmans, Green, Langman, and Roberts.
Mjöberg, Jöran (1967–68) *Drömmen om sagatiden*. 2 vols. Stockholm: Natur och kultur.
Morris, William (1898) Gunnar's Howe Above the House at Lithend. In *Poems By the Way & Love is Enough* (pp. 122–23). New York and Bombay: Longmans, Green, and Co.
Morris, William (1966) *Journals of Travel in Iceland 1871 1873. The Collected Works of William Morris*. Vol. 8 (ed. May Morris). New York: Russel & Russell.

Munch, Peter Andreas (trans.) (1845) *Sagaer eller Fortællinger om Nordmænds og Islænderes Bedrifter i Oldtiden.* 2 vols. Christiania: Johan Dahl.

Munch, Peter Andreas (trans.) (1859) *Norges Konge-Sager fra de ældste Tider indtil anden Halvdeel af det 13de Aarhundrede efter Christi Fødsel, forfattede af Snorre Sturlassøn, Sturla Thordssøn og flere.* Christiania: W.E. Fabritius og Georg E. Pettersen.

Müller, Ludvig Christian (1837) Njáls Saga. In *Islandsk Læsebog* (pp. 1–205). København: Gyldendal.

Müller, Peter Erasmus (1817) *Sagabibliothek, med Anmærkninger og indledende Afhandlinger.* Vol. 1. København: J.F. Schutz.

Niclasen, Bjarni (trans.) (1966) *Njáls søga.* Tórshavn: Keldan.

Nicolson, Alexander (1861) [Review of *The Story of Burnt Njal.*] *Macmillan's Magazine* 4, 294–305.

Nielsen, Erling and Peter de Hemmer Gudme (1943) *Ja til Norden.* København: Nyt nordisk forlag – Arnold Busck.

Nielsen, Jørgen (1941) Lidt om Historikeren og Sprogmanden N.M. Petersen i Anledning af 150-Aarsdagen efter hans Fødsel. *Sorø Amtstidende* (24 October), 7–8; (25 October), 9–10.

Nissen, Henrik S. (1992) Folkelighed og frihed 1933. Grundtviganernes reaktion på modernisering, krise og nazisme. In Ole Feldbæk (ed.) *Folkets Danmark 1848–1940. Dansk Identitetshistorie.* Vol. 3 (pp. 587–673). København: C.A. Reitzels Forlag.

Nordal, Sigurður (1920) *Snorri Sturluson.* Reykjavík: Þór B. Þorláksson.

Nordal, Sigurður (ed.) (1933) *Egils saga Skallagrímssonar* (Íslenzk fornrit 3). Reykjavík: Hið íslenzka fornritafélag.

Nordal, Sigurður (1940) *Hrafnkatla* (Studia Islandica 7). Reykjavík: Ísafoldarprentsmiðja; København: Ejnar Munksgaard.

Nordby, Conrad Hjalmar (1901) *The Influence of Old Norse Literature upon English Literature* (Columbia University Germanic Studies 113). New York: The Columbia University Press.

O'Donoghue, Heather (1991) *The Genesis of a Saga Narrative. Verse and Prose in Kormaks Saga* (Oxford English Monographs). Oxford, New York: Oxford University Press, Clarendon Press.

Olavius, Ólafur (ed.) (1772) *Sagan af Niáli Þórgeirssyni ok Sonvm Hans &c.* København: J.R. Thiele.

Olavius, Ólafur (ed.) (1844) *Sagan af Njáli Þorgeirssyni og Sonum Hans &c.* Videyjar Klaustri: M. Stephensen.

Omberg, Margaret (1976) *Scandinavian Themes in English Poetry, 1760–1800* (Aca Universitatis Upsaliensis. Studia Anglistica Upasaliensia 29). Uppsala: Almqvist & Wiksell.

Oswald, Elizabeth (1882) The end of the feud. A true story of Iceland. A.D. 1017. In *By Fell and Fjord* (pp. 174–75). Edinburgh and London: W. Blackwood & Sons.

Ólafsson, Örn (1990) *Rauðu pennarnir. Bókmenntahreyfing á 2. fjórðungi 20. aldar.* Reykjavík: Mál og menning.

Ólason, Vésteinn (ed.) (1979) *Sagnadansar.* Reykjavík: Rannsóknastofnun í bókmenntafræði, Menningarsjóður.

Ólason, Vésteinn (1984) Bókmenntarýni Sigurðar Nordals. *Tímarit Máls og menningar* 45 (1), 5–18.

Ólason, Vésteinn (1989) Bóksögur. In Frosti F. Jóhannsson (ed.) *Munnmenntir og bókmenning. Íslensk þjóðmenning.* Vol. 6 (pp. 161–227). Reykjavík: Þjóðsaga.

Ólsen, Björn M. (1937–39) *Um Íslendingasögur. Kaflar úr háskólafyrirlestrum* (Safn til sögu Íslands og íslenzkra bókmennta 6 (3)) (ed. Sigfús Blöndal and Einar Ólafur Sveinsson). Reykjavík: Hið íslenzka bókmenntafélag.

Paasche, Fredrik (trans.) (1922) *Njaals saga* (Islandske ættesagaer 1). Kristiania: Aschehoug.

Pálsson, Hermann and Magnus Magnusson (trans.) (1960) *Njal's Saga* (Penguin Classics). Middlesex: Penguin Books.

Pálsson, Hermann (1962) *Sagnaskemmtun Íslendinga.* Reykjavík: Mál og menning.

Pálsson, Hermann (1984) *Uppruni Njálu og hugmyndir.* Reykjavík: Bókaútgáfa Menningarsjóðs.

Peters, Absalom (1841) Introduction: – Plan of the Work Illustrated, – Obligations and Facilities of American Literature. *The American Eclectic: Or Selections from the Periodical Literature of all Foreign Countries* 1 (January), 1–14.

Petersen, N.M. (trans.) (1839–44) *Historiske fortællinger om islændernes færd hjemme og ude.* 4 vols. København: Det kongelige Nordiske Oldskriftselskab.

Petersen, N.M. (trans.) (1862–68) *Historiske fortællinger om islændernes færd hjemme og ude.* 4 vols (second edition, revised by Guðbrandur Vigfússon). København: Fr. Vøldikes forlag.

Petersen, N.M. (trans.) (1901) *Historiske fortællinger om islændernes færd hjemme og ude.* 4 vols (third edition, revised by Verner Dahlerup and Finnur Jónsson, the verses redone by Olaf Hansen). København: Det Nordiske forlag.

Petersen, N.M. (trans.) (1942–43) *Islændingenes færd hjemme og ude.* 3 vols (fifth edition). København: Det tredje Standpunkts forlag.

Petersen, N.M. (trans.) (1994) *Njals saga* (revised by Ellen Olsen). København: Sesam.

Phelps, William Lyon (1893) *The Beginnings of the English Romantic Movement. A Study in Eighteenth Century Literature.* Boston: Ginn & Company, Publishers.

Politiken (1979) *Besættelsen 1940–45. Politik, modstand, befrielse.* København: Politiken.

Ponzi, Frank (1986) *Ísland á nítjándu öld: leiðangrar og listamenn. 19th-Century Iceland: Artists and Odysseys* (trans. Ólafur B. Guðnason). Reykjavík: Almenna bókafélagið.

Raabe, Gustav E. (1941) *Det første Snorre-trykk. Litt bok-historikk.* Oslo: Cammermeyers Boghandel.

Rahbek, Knud Lyne (trans.) (1819–21) *Nordiske Fortællinger.* 2 vols. København: Dorothea Schultz.

Rask, Erasmus (1843) *A Grammar of the Icelandic or Old Norse Tongue* (trans. George Webbe Dasent). London: William Pickering; Frankfurt o/M: Jaeger's Library.

Rerup, Lorenz (1982) *Slesvig og Holsten efter 1830.* In Svend Ellehøj and Kristof Glamann (eds) *Danmarks Historie – uden for Danmark.* København: Politikens Forlag A/S.

Rolfsen, Nordahl (1888) *Vore Fædres Liv. Karakterer og Skildringer fra Sagatiden.* Bergen: Ed. B. Giertsens Forlag.

Roll, Ferdinant (1871) Norge i 1871. *Folkevennen* 20, 214–56, 321–52, 497–528.

Rosen, Wilhelm von (1969) Den politiske og ideologiske debat i den illegale presse og litteratur under Danmarks besættelse (TMs [photocopy]). The Royal Library, København.

Rygh, Oluf (trans.) (1859) *Sagaen om Gunnlaug Ormstunge og Skalde-Ravn* (supplementary volume to *Folkevennen* 8). Christiania: Selskabet for Folkeoplysningens Fremme.

Rygh, Oluf (trans.) (1861) *Sigmund Brestesøns Saga. Et Brudstykke af Færøingernes Saga* (supplementary volume to *Folkevennen* 10). Christiania: Selskabet for Folkeoplysningens Fremme.

Said, Edward W. (1979) *Orientalism*. New York: Vintage Books.

Sanness, John (1959) *Patrioter, Intelligens og Skandinaver. Norske reaksjoner på skandinavismen før 1848*. Oslo: Universitetsforlaget.

Saveth, Edward N. (1965) *American Historians and European Immigrants 1872–1925*. New York: Russell & Russell.

Saxo Grammaticus (1941) *Danmarks krønike* (trans. N.F.S. Grundtvig, ed. Vilhelm la Cour). København: Det tredje Standpunkts forlag.

Schier, Kurt (1996) Die Literaturen des Nordens. In Gangolf Hübinger (ed.) *Versammlungsort Moderne Geister. Der Eugen Diederichs Verlag – Aufbruch ins Jahrhundert der Extreme* (pp. 411–49). München: Diederichs.

See, Klaus von (1970) *Deutsche Germanen-Ideologie vom Humanismus bis zur Gegenwart*. Frankfurt a.M.: Athenäum.

See, Klaus von (1994) *Barbar Germane Arier. Die Suche nach der Deutschen*. Heidelberg: Universitätsverlag C. Winter.

Seip, Didrik Arup (1916) Stilen i Bjørnsons bondefortellinger. *Edda* 5, 1–21.

Sengupta, Mahasweta (1990) Translation, Colonialism and Poetics: Rabindranath Tagore in Two Worlds. In Susan Bassnett and André Lefevere (eds) *Translation, History and Culture* (pp. 56–63). London and New York: Pinter Publishers.

Sigurðsson, Pjetur, Ólafur Lárusson and Sigurður Nordal (1936) A letter to the mayor of Reykjavík (17 December). Borgarskjalasafn Reykjavíkur, Reykjavík.

Sigurðsson, Pjetur (1948) A letter to the Reykjavík planning committee (20 February). Borgarskjalasafn Reykjavíkur, Reykjavík.

Sigurjónsson, Árni (1984) Um hugmyndafræði Sigurðar Nordal. *Tímarit Máls og menningar* 45 (1), 49–63.

Simon, Sherry (1990) Translating the Will to Knowledge: Prefaces and Canadian Literary Politics. In Susan Bassnett and André Lefevere (eds) *Translation, History and Culture* (pp. 110–17). London and New York: Pinter Publishers.

Skard, Sigmund (1968) Frå framande bokheimar. In Bjarte Birkeland, Reidar Djupedal, Alf Hellevik, and Dagfinn Mannsåker (eds) *Det Norske Samlaget 1868–1968* (pp. 174–87). Oslo: Det Norske Samlaget.

Skúlason, Snorri Már (1994) Sambandsslitin í dönskum fjölmiðlum. Allt þjóðlífið grundvallast á lögbroti. *Morgunblaðið* (17 June), 48–49.

Sommerfelt, Karl L. (trans) (1871) *Njaals Saga* (supplementary volume to *Folkevennen* 20). Kristiania: Selskabet for Folkeoplysningens Fremme.

Steblin-Kamenskogo, M. Í. (1956) *Íslandskie sagi*. Moskva: Khudozhestvennaia literatura.

Stefánsdóttir, Elínborg and Gérard Chinotti (1975) *La saga de Njall le Brûlé*. Paris: Union générale d'éditions.

Stephenson, George M. (1926) *A History of American Immigration 1820–1924.* New York: Russel & Russel.

Storch, Vilhelm (1887) *Kemiske og mikroskopiske Undersøgelser af et ejendommeligt Stof: fundet ved Udgravninger, foretagne for det islandske Oldsagsselskab (fornleifafélag) af Sigurd Vigfusson paa Bergthorshvol i Island, hvor ifølge den gamle Beretning Njal, hans hustru og hans Sønner indebrændtes Aar 1011.* København: Det islandske Oldsagsselskab.

Sturluson, Snorri (1842) *The Prose or Younger Edda Commonly Ascribed to Snorri Sturluson* (trans. George Webbe Dasent). Stockholm: Norstedt and Sons; London: William Pickering.

Sturluson, Snorri (1900) *Kongesagaer* (trans. Gustav Storm). Christiania: J.M. Sternersen & Co. Forlag.

Sveinsson, Einar Ólafur (1933) *Um Njálu.* Reykjavík: Bókadeild Menningarsjóðs.

Sveinsson, Einar Ólafur (1937) Njála og Skógverjar. *Skírnir* 111, 15–45.

Sveinsson, Einar Ólafur (1943) *Á Njálsbúð. Bók um mikið listaverk.* Reykjavík: Hið íslenzka bókmenntafélag.

Sveinsson, Einar Ólafur (1953) *Studies in the Manuscript Tradition of Njálssaga* (Studia Islandica 13). Reykjavík: Leiftur hf; København: Ejnar Munksgaard.

Sveinsson, Einar Ólafur (ed.) (1954) *Brennu-Njáls saga* (Íslenzk fornrit 12). Reykjavík: Hið íslenzka fornritafélag.

Sveinsson, Einar Ólafur (1956) *Við uppspretturnar Greinasafn.* Reykjavík: Helgafell.

Sveinsson, Einar Ólafur (1971) *Njáls Saga: A Literary Masterpiece* (ed. and trans. Paul Schach). Lincoln: University of Nebraska Press.

Svensson, S.H.B. (1867) *Sagan af Njáli Þorgeirssyni ok sonum hans. Historia Njalis et filorum* (Textum scholis academicis subjiciendum 1). Lund: J. Gleerup.

Sæmundsson, Matthías Viðar (ed.) (1986) *Brennu-Njáls saga.* Reykjavík: Almenna bókafélagið.

Sømme, Sigmund (1951) Selskabet for Folkeoplysningens Fremme. In *Opplysningsarbeid i Norge gjennom hundre år* (pp. 7–15). Oslo: Arbeidernes Aktietrykkeri.

Sørensen, Arne (1942) *Dansk og nordisk samling.* København: Det tredje Standpunkts forlag.

Taniguchi, Yokio (trans.) (1979) [Njáls saga.] In *Aisurando Saga* (pp. 601–857). Tokyo: Shincho-Sha.

National Cyclopædia (1967) *The National Cyclopædia of American Biography.* Vol. 3, s.v. 'French, Allen'. Ann Arbor, Michigan: University Microfilms.

Thorsson, Örnólfur (ed.) (1991) *Brennu-Njáls saga.* Reykjavík: Mál og menning.

Tomasson, Richard F. (1975) The Literacy of the Icelanders. *Scandinavian Studies* 47 (1), 66–93.

Torfæus, Thormodus (1866) *Ancient History of Orkney, Caithness, & the North* (trans. Alexander Pope). Wick, Thurso, Kirkwall: Peter Reid, Miss Russell and W. M. Allen, William Reid.

Treece, Henry (1946) *How I See Apocalypse.* London: Lindsay Drumond.

Treece, Henry (1964) *The Burning of Njal.* New York: Criterion Books.

Turner, Frank M. (1981) *The Greek Heritage in Victorian Britain.* New Haven & London: Yale University Press.

Turville-Petre, E.O.G. (1957) Introduction. In George Webbe Dasent (trans.) *The Story of Burnt Njal* (Everyman's Library 558). London; New York: J.M. Dent; E.P. Dutton.

Tuuri, Annti, trans. (1996) *Poltetun Njállin Saaga*. Helsinki: Kustannusosakeyhtiö Otava.

Tveterås, Harald L. (1964) *Norske forfattere på dansk forlag 1850–1890. Den norske boghandels historie*. Vol. 2. Oslo: Norsk boghandler-medhjelper-forening.

Tymoczko, Maria (1990) Translation in Oral Tradition as a Touchstone for Translation Theory and Practice. In Susan Bassnett and André Lefevere (eds) *Translation, History and Culture* (pp. 46–55). London and New York: Pinter Publishers.

Umbra [Charles Clifford] (1863) *A Tour Twenty Years Ago*. London: F. Shobert.

Vigfússon, Guðbrandur (1878) Prolegomena. In Guðbrandur Vigfússon (trans.) *Sturlunga saga, including the Islendinga saga of lawman Sturla Thordson and other works*. Vol. 1 (pp. xvii–ccix). Oxford: Clarendon Press.

Vilhjálmsson, Sigurður (1948) Höfundur Njálu. *Tíminn* (29 May), 4 and 6.

Vísir (1941) Bækur á næstunni. *Vísir* (October 9), 2.

Wade, David (1989) *The Tree of Strife, a dramatisation of Njal's Saga*. An unpublished script.

Waller, S.E. (1874) *Six Weeks in the Saddle: A Painter's Journal in Iceland*. London: MacMillan and Co.

Wawn, Andrew (1987) *The Iceland Journal of Henry Holland 1810* (Hakluyt Society, Second series 168). London: Hakluyt Society.

Wawn, Andrew (1991) The Assistance of Icelanders to George Webbe Dasent. *Landsbókasafn Íslands. Árbók 1989. Nýr flokkur* 15, 73–92.

Wawn, Andrew (1992a) The Spirit of 1892: Sagas, Saga-steads and Victorian Philology. *Saga-Book* 24 (4), 213–52.

Wawn, Andrew (1992b) The Victorians and the Vikings: Sir George Webbe Dasent and *Jómsvíkinga saga*. In Genet Garlon (ed.) *Papers of the Ninth Biennial Conference of Teachers of Scandinavian Studies in Britain* (pp. 301–15). Norwich: The University of East Anglia.

Wawn, Andrew (ed.) (1994) *Northern Antiquity. The Post-Medieval Reception of Edda and Saga*. Middlesex: Hisarlik Press.

Weber, Leopold (1930) *Njal der Seher. Eine isländische Heldensage*. Stuttgart: K. Thienemann.

Wellek, René and Austin Warren (1977) *Theory of Literature* (third edition). San Diego, New York, London: Harcourt Brace Jovanovich, Publishers.

Wendt, Frantz (1978) *Besættelse og Atomtid 1939–1978*. In John Danstrup and Hal Koch (eds) *Danmarks Historie*. Vol. 14. Copenhagen: Politikens Forlag.

Wøller, Johan (1940) Dansk Nederlag og nordisk Fremtid. *Det tredje Standpunkt* 4 (2), 16–19.

Zaluska-Strömberg, Apolonia (trans.) (1968) *Saga o Njálu* (Seria dziel pisarzy skandynawskich). Poznan: Wydawnictwo Poznanskie.

Zernack, Julia (1994) *Geschichten aus Thule. Íslendingasögur in Übersetzungen deutscher Germanisten* (Berliner Beiträge zur Skandinavistik 3). Berlin: Freie Universität Berlin.

Zeyer, Julius (1919) V Soumraku bohu. In *Obnovené obrazy* (pp. 1–247). Praha: UNIE.

Þorkelsson, Jón (1886) Íslenzk kappakvæði. *Arkiv for nordisk filologi* 3, 366–84.

Þorkelsson, Jón (1889) Om håndskrifterne af Njála. In Konráð Gíslason and Eiríkur Jónsson (eds) *Njála, udg. efter gamle håndskrifter*. Vol. 2 (pp. 647–783). København: Commission i den Gyldendalske Boghandel.

Þorsteinsson, Björn and Bergsteinn Jónsson (1991) *Íslands saga til okkar daga.* Reykjavík: Sögufélagið.

Øyslebø, Olaf (1982) *Bjørnsons 'Bondefortellinger'. Kulturhistorie eller allmennmenneskelig diktning?* Oslo: Gyldendal Norsk Forlag.

Index